George Burnham

Burnham's new poultry book

A practical work on selecting, housing, and breeding domestic fowls

George Burnham

Burnham's new poultry book
A practical work on selecting, housing, and breeding domestic fowls

ISBN/EAN: 9783337146986

Printed in Europe, USA, Canada, Australia, Japan

Cover: Foto ©Lupo / pixelio.de

More available books at **www.hansebooks.com**

No. 1. BUFF OR PARTRIDGE COCHIN.

As bred by D. W. Herstine, G. H. Warner, I Van Winkle, J. M. Wade, G. M. Champney, J. Graves, E. J. Taylor, W. Simpson, Jr., etc.

No. 2. QUEEN VICTORIA'S ORIGINAL COCHINS.
Drawn in 1844, by Harrison Weir, London.

BURNHAM'S
NEW POULTRY BOOK.

A PRACTICAL WORK
ON SELECTING, HOUSING, AND BREEDING
DOMESTIC FOWLS.

By GEO. P. BURNHAM,

AUTHOR OF "NEW ENGLAND POULTRY BREEDER," THE "CHINA FOWL,"
"DISEASES OF POULTRY," "SECRETS IN FOWL BREEDING,"
THE "GAME FOWL," ETC., ETC.

ILLUSTRATED WITH DRAWINGS OF MODERN POPULAR VARIETIES,
PLANS OF POULTRY HOUSES, &c.

BOSTON:
LEE & SHEPARD, PUBLISHERS.

PREFACE TO THE PRESENT EDITION.

THE first edition of this work was published a few years ago, and met with such success that two more editions were soon called for, and have been exhausted. Many calls having been made for copies, the publishers now present this fourth edition to the public.

The increasing interest shown in every part of the country, in matters connected with the raising of domestic poultry, is a sufficient warrant for a new issue of a volume from the hands of the veteran author, whose knowledge and skill have been recognized for the last twenty-five years.

The contents will be found both entertaining and instructive. No man living is a more competent authority than Mr. Burnham; and his work will be equally useful to the novice, the amateur, and the experienced fowl-raiser.

It is safe to say, that, where there was one breeder of choice fowls a dozen years ago, they are now numbered by the score; and the American fanciers now have the finest specimens in the world from which to choose.

The aim of the author has been to present a record of actual experience, showing what he has accomplished in improving the modern stock of poultry.

The illustrations in this volume represent the best modern varieties; and it is believed that no poultry-book has been presented to the public in modern times at such a moderate price, so useful and so acceptable in all respects as this.

If the advice and the suggestions of the author are intelligently and steadily followed, the fowl-breeders of this country will be able to rear good poultry successfully and economically, and so secure both pleasure and profit.

BOSTON, April 2, 1877.

CONTENTS.

Chap.		Page
I.	General Introduction.	5
II.	On Eggs, and Hatching Chickens.	13
III.	Feeding and Rearing Young Broods.	23
IV.	Purely-bred Year-old Fowl, Upward.	34
V.	Poultry-Houses, and Accommodations.	51
VI.	Raising Poultry and Eggs for Market.	64
VII.	Illustrations of Poultry-Houses.	81
VIII.	Fowl-Houses, Coops, Chicken-Cages, Etc.	100
IX.	On Artificial Egg-Hatching.	121
X.	Patent Incubators, and Improvements.	128
XI.	Poultry Exhibitions, and Show-Fowls.	137
XII.	Varieties of Popular Fowls. The Brahma.	148
XIII.	The Original "Cochin-China."	169
XIV.	Old and New Partridge Cochins.	179
XV.	Modern Buff Cochins.	188
XVI.	The Houdans, Crevecœurs and La Fleche.	199
XVII.	The Dark Brahma Fowl.	207
XVIII.	The English Gray Dorking.	220
XIX.	The Game Fowl and its Uses.	227
XX.	Black Spanish and Gueldres.	245
XXI.	Dominique, Spangled Hamburg, Bolton Gray.	252
XXII.	Golden Sebright and other Bantams.	265
XXIII.	"Many Men have Many Minds."	271
XXIV.	The American Wild Turkey.	284
XXV.	Rearing the Domestic Turkey.	290
XXVI.	Wild, Bremen, Toulouse, and Native Geese.	301
XXVII.	The Aylesbury, Rouen, and Common Duck.	311
XXVIII.	What I know about Poultry and Fowl-Shows.	318
XXIX.	Twenty-five good Rules for Fowl-Breeders.	327
XXX.	Raising Fowls in Quantities, to Profit.	333

BURNHAM'S NEW POULTRY BOOK.

CHAPTER I.

GENERAL INTRODUCTION.

It has been aptly stated, by a modern practical author, that "the POULTRY INTEREST in the United States is a very important one;" and that "the introduction of *improved* Breeds or Varieties of Fowls, which insure greater size, finer quality, and increased productiveness in *eggs* or *flesh*, contributes just so much to the aggregate wealth of the country."

The truthfulness of this statement is beyond question. Yet the real value and importance of this easily managed and readily produced auxiliary to the augmentation of our national wealth, is not fully appreciated as yet; albeit much has been accomplished in the right direction, within the past twenty years, and, more signally, during the last decade, in America, towards the desirable object of producing in quantity as well as quality, the finest Domestic Poultry in the world.

The statistics, as shown by a late census report, set down the actual market value of poultry in the single State of New York, for example, at near three millions of dollars; which, at that period, exceeded the commercial value of *all* the swine in that State, equalled about one *half* the value of its sheep, the *entire* valuation of its neat *cattle*, and over four times the whole returned value of its *horses* and *mules*.

The amount expended for *eggs* alone, in the city of Boston in 1869, reached almost two millions of dollars. For poultry, near three millions. One large hotel in that city uses an average of one hundred dozen, daily, at the present time — or half a million eggs, annually. In New York city, a leading hotel proprietor informs me that in 1869 he used in his establishment one hundred and forty dozen, daily, during that year. Two hotels in Philadelphia exceed that average, at the present time. The cash value of eggs sent to London and Liverpool, from Dublin, alone, in 1866, aggregated one million four hundred and thirteen thousand pounds sterling — over seven millions of dollars, in gold! These are merely items in the vast aggregate — for actual consumption, at market prices — which contribute to swell the amount in *solid value* of poultry and eggs, to its enormous reality in this and other countries; a recent estimate placing their value in the United States alone, at $17,000,000!

The *Societe Industrielle* of Mulhouse, in the Department of the Haut Rhin, Alsace, publish a journal devoted to manufactures, and general scientific matters appertaining thereto. This Society has repeatedly offered, in behalf of the French Print manufacturers of that famed locality, large premiums for the discovery of a substitute for the albumen (or white) of *eggs* — of which substance they absorb immense quantities, in fixing the colors, in printing calicoes and muslin delaines.

To supply the large demand for this albumen — which, up to the present day, has no equal for the specific purpose mentioned, and for which as yet no substitute that equals it has been found — a vast number of hens' eggs are necessarily used, annually. In response to the liberal offer made through this journal, certain parties have produced a *kind* of albumen, made from the spawn of fish, and others from slaughter-house blood; neither of which have proved colorless, however, and consequently are not of the value of the original.

The requirements of the French print manufacturers therefore are such that they must have this albumen, to a given extent, and this demand has caused the establishment of large poultry-raising establishments, in the vicinity of Mulhouse, for the producing of eggs, from which this albumen is gathered; which fowl-houses are now carried on there under their style of management, with success and remunerative profit; and the demand, in every way, is ever increasing, for both eggs and poultry.

Everybody "loves eggs and chickens." Almost everybody eats eggs, in some form, more or less, daily. In the family economy, eggs enter largely into our food, our cakes, our confections; while for our custards, pies, omelets, and puddings — or fried, boiled, poached, or scrambled — everybody knows their intrinsic value in the household, in detail. Few families live without eggs, and most of us indulge largely in the beneficent luxury of both the producers, and this product of poultry. Thus, a moment's reflection will satisfy the incredulous of the truth contained in our early quoted assertion, that the poultry interest in the United States, is a highly important one; and we may add that it is so important and so valuable an interest, that it should continually be nursed and cultivated; with a care and zeal commensurate with its sterling merits.

We know that he who causes two blades of grass to grow where but one grew before, is a benefactor to his race; and he who may enhance the quality of our poultry, and increase its size and productiveness, in any way that shall result in *permanent* improvement, is equally a general benefactor to the people.

If an experience of thirty years in the rearing and management of poultry will afford one the means of informing himself as to the habits, characteristics, needs, and qualities of domestic fowls — the author of this "NEW POULTRY BOOK" may lay claim to having graduated; since it is more than thirty years ago, that he commenced, (in Roxbury, Mass.,) the breeding of poultry on a large scale.

The results of that long and varied experience will be found detailed in the following pages. The writer has, in his time, bred largely all the *varieties* of Domestic Fowls that have been popularly known in this country, and in England — from the diminutive Black, or Sebright Bantam, to the colossal Cochin, Brahma, or Shanghæ; and his experience has been such that he feels competent to the task of offering in plain language, such facts, deductions and directions, in reference to the selecting, housing, feeding, multiplying, and care of domestic poultry, as will — if carried out — assure to fanciers, breeders, or amateurs, both success and profit, as well as easy and healthful pastime, in the *modus operandi* herein proposed.

In the general making up of this book, however, the author has not relied upon himself, alone, for the facts and theories he now submits to the fanciers and admirers of that pleasant branch of rural economy — poultry-breeding. As will be seen in the following pages, due credit is given to the gentlemen who have contributed to the work; and who have furnished for this Poultry Book fine portraits and drawings of various kinds of popular domestic fowls; with plans of cages, coops, chicken-houses, etc.; all of which favors are duly acknowledged in the appropriate place.

It is believed that no work on this subject at present exists that is so simple in its details, so thoroughly practical in its suggestions, so complete in its general directions, or so *modern* in its bearings — as is this volume. It has been the author's aim to state directly and fairly what he knows from long-tried experiment, and to add to his own experience that of other reliable parties who aim to benefit the public through this humble means, in their laudable efforts to improve the poultry stock of this country, and naturally to remunerate themselves, sooner or later, for the outlay and care necessarily bestowed upon their several undertakings in this regard.

M. de Reaumer, member of the Royal Academy of Sciences, at Paris, more than a century ago issued a work entitled "The Art of Hatching and Bringing up Domestic Fowls of all kinds, at any time of the year." This volume bears a London imprint — being " printed for C. Davis, over against Gray's Inn Gate " — in 1750; and contains a large amount of valuable matter upon the subject now treated of, though that treatise refers more especially to the hatching and raising of chickens by means of artificial heat; a mode not adopted to any great extent, or with any marked degree of success, as yet, in this country. Mons. de Reaumer presented to the Academy his first paper on this interesting occupation, on St. Martin's Day, 1747, " when the public of that time seemed to have judged, as he had done, of the great advantages to be expected of *making a business* of chicken-raising ;" a business which he claims " requires several branches of knowledge, and a great many small experiments, the sum total of which constitutes the subject matter of *an art*," in his opinion; though M. de Reaumer candidly admits that " all that this art requires we should know, is so very plain, that it is as soon obtained as read."

At that remote day, to wit, one hundred and twenty-five years ago, this writer says that the " multiplying at pleasure and with the utmost ease, domestick birds, of which such a vast number is consumed, all over the world, cannot be overdone ;" and he avers that even at *that* time, the public " would be startled with the immense consumption made of them. By multiplying chickens and hens, we multiply the number of eggs. The procuring of corn and cattle in plenty," he adds, " has been a part of the views of the greatest ministers on earth ; nor is the procuring of a plenty of domestick fowls an object less worthy of their attention."

De Reaumer was right. And, though he published his " memoir " so long ago, the exact truth, as above quoted, is no less forcible to-day, that the propagation of *plenty* of domestic poultry is a desideratum. And, in our land, where the work may be so pleasantly and so profitably prosecuted (if undertaken and pursued rightfully, and judiciously) as it may be in any locality in this country, this object is pre-eminently worthy of the attention of all who enjoy the trivial facilities requisite to aid in accomplishing the acceptable results hinted at.

To enable those who have a taste for this pleasing employment to carry out their wishes, and to assist the amateur, the farmer, or the fancier, more readily to succeed in the raising of poultry—as well also as to inform such persons how and of whom they may procure the best breeding-stock, to begin with, and how they may manage either to become rivals among " fanciers," or successful competitors in the production of chickens and eggs for market, simply — is the design of this " NEW POULTRY-BOOK."

We shall give the true history of the large Asiatic fowls from our own personal knowledge and experience with that ever popular variety, and the reader will find, in the following pages that the writer freely accords credit where such credit is known to him to be due, to other gentlemen who have expended money, time and brains — as he has — in the purchase, rearing and experimenting with poultry, foreign and native.

It will be the aim in this volume, to state what seems desirable to be set down here, in succinct, plain language, uniformly; and it is confidently believed, that if the general hints and directions we offer are carefully followed out, that the novice in " the art " may easily raise *good* poultry and *plenty of it* — which may always be disposed of, at remunerating prices, as his reward in this agreeable kind of enterprise.

CHAPTER II.

ON EGGS AND HATCHING CHICKENS.

To begin at the foundation, we propose a brief chapter on eggs, and the hatching of chickens. And first — in selecting eggs for incubation, some care is necessary to ensure future success with them. The custom at the present time, is very general among beginners, to *purchase* eggs, for a sitting or two, from breeders, or dealers in the variety of fowls they prefer. This latter consideration is a matter of *fancy*, purely. Some incline to the medium-sized fowl — as the White Dorking, the Black Spanish, Leghorns, the Dominique, the Sicily, the Houdan, or the Guelderlands. Others favor the Cochins, Brahmas, Shanghæs, Crevecœur, La Fleche, or other large Asiatic or French birds. While a few prefer the Bolton Gray, the Hamburg, the Poland, or Game.

The transportation of eggs intended for hatching, to any great distance by express and railway carriage, has proved, in *my* experience, frequently injurious. I have forwarded thousands of dozens of eggs, in all directions, over this country — from Maine to Louisiana, and to the West — and I speak advisedly on this point, after thorough and persistent trial of every imaginable expedient in packing them, for the purpose — when I say that the vitality of eggs is endangered (more or less) by being transferred over long distances in the rough modes of conveyance we are obliged to forward them by.

A city editor has lately stated that " baggage-smashing, as a fine art, has reached a high state of perfection in this country, and the skill, ingenuity and perseverance exhibited by railway employes in reducing the strongest built trunk to a hash of wood, leather and iron, must be highly encouraging to the trunk makers. A heavily timbered, iron clad, armor-plated trunk will only stand a two days' trip, and the handling of two or three of these railroad wreckers before it is reduced to old junk." And in the case of the writer of the above, the contents of his stout trunk, " in fact the remains of everything of a perishable nature in it, attested the muscular energy and activity of the American baggage smasher," after a three days' trip. To the tender mercy of this unthinking, rough-an'-tumble fraternity, the party who furnishes eggs for incubation is obliged to entrust his parcels, and the resulting disappointment of the purchaser of these frail articles is so commonly known, almost in all directions, as to require little further comment here.

Still, breeders are compelled to undertake to furnish eggs for incubation in this way, and purchasers buy them, and accept the attendant risk. Probably it is the best way of disseminating choice stock, as yet known to us; and, since it is the *only* mode that can be made available, whereby the beginner who resides at a distance from the breeder of the particular fowls, or strain of blood he desires, can nowadays obtain eggs — the amateur must accept the situation, and get all the chickens he can out of his eggs thus transported.

In some cases, I am aware, both from my own experience in this matter, and that of other gentlemen, that eggs so sent from a long distance, *do well.* But I also know that both in forwarding and receiving eggs so conveyed, there is a percentage of average loss to the buyer, when in both instances I have known that the damaged eggs upon their receipt, were fresh and reliable upon shipment — to and fro.

But, as to the safety of transporting eggs, it is a point upon which the experience of breeders and dealers differs. Mr. Tegetmeier, the leading English modern writer on poultry, says, "The extreme care sometimes bestowed on eggs, intended for incubation, is quite unnecessary. The yolk is naturally so perfectly suspended, that injury cannot occur to it by any violence likely to be suffered by the egg, short of actual breakage. Eggs have been hatched in England, that were laid in America. The vibration and shaking to which they have been submitted on the voyage, not having injured the delicate germ." And we observe upon the circulars of many of our best breeders, the assurance that eggs *can* be shipped with safety to any distance, if properly packed. One dealer recommends the following simple, but very good method, for a transportation-box for eggs. He says " it should be made of thin (half-inch) stuff, with twelve squares or partings inside it, three inches in the clear, each way ; to be fifteen inches long, by twelve wide. This will afford room to bestow a dozen eggs, one to be placed on end, in *each* square by itself, in dry bran or screenings, with a thick layer of the same at the top and bottom ; the box to be at least eight inches in depth, inside. Fasten the top securely, and the eggs thus packed can *not* be broken, unless the box is smashed. The eggs in the box thus arranged, and entirely surrounded by the bran, will appear as follows — before filling up, and securing the top down." And this correspondent recommends that " only *one* dozen eggs be so packed in a box. If more are ordered, increase the number of boxes."

Like other fanciers, I am constantly applied to for eggs for hatching, the writers invariably proposing to " take the risk " of moving them. In such cases, I supply orders. Other breeders send their choice eggs in all directions, and it is of course understood that the buyer takes what risk there may be, in this perhaps absolutely necessary way of distributing eggs abroad, from choice stock.

The best mode I have ever yet known for *packing* eggs, to be thus transported, is a very simple one. First, wrap *each* egg separately in common soft brown paper; then place the eggs end-wise up, apart from each other, in coarse bran, or shorts; with a generous supply of the latter at top, bottom, and sides of the box. Eggs thus packed, upright, with the larger ends placed downwards, in *fine hay* cut very short, will bear transportation very well. If your express-man is not a confirmed " baggage smasher," and handles the box " with care," as should be indicated always upon the outside of the box, eggs *ought to* go through, with an approximation to safety from breaking, or having the life shaken out of them. I simply say, however, that, too often, they do not escape injury, *in transitu*; and 1 merely mention the fact, which is patent. I am lately informed that Mr. Van Winkle of Greenville, N. J. and one or two other breeders have invented a " safety-box " to ship eggs in; said to be a good contrivance.

Having procured your eggs, however, you will proceed to set them under your hen, or hens, which it is pre-supposed you have in readiness for the purpose, — and in choosing a sitter, I have found that a six-pound hen of any variety, is better than one that is heavier. Your large hens (if you have any) of the

Chinese varieties, for example, are too clumsy and heavy, usually. The Asiatic varieties are admirable sitters nevertheless, and there is no better hen-mother known than the Brahma or Cochin fowl. But they are awkward and innocently reckless, both with their eggs and towards newly-hatched chickens — easily breaking the former in their nests, and killing the latter, by trampling upon them, in their infancy.

So I advise that the setting hen, for choice, should be smaller, nimbler, and more careful — as the common barn-yarn fowl is, always. Let her be a short legged, compact-built, well feathered bird, of five or six pound's weight; and, out of nine to eleven eggs, you will get more living mature chickens, on the twenty-first day of her sitting, than with thirteen eggs under the heavy Shanghæ, or Brahma, which you imagine " can cover that number so much better " than the lesser-sized bird; and when the chicks break shell, the smaller fowl will not tramp them to death — before they can stand up, when freed.

Obtain your eggs for setting, (or supply them yourself,) from the newest laid ones, invariably. If they come from your own fowls, be careful, while they are accumulating, that you keep them dry, free from damp air, and from all unnecessary *motion in handling*, at any time. The internal fibres, air-bag, and yolk of an egg are a much more delicate conformation and substance than most persons imagine; and it is a very easy thing to injure the egg, for hatching, by roughly shaking, jarring it, or turning it over, carelessly. If, as you gather your eggs, daily, you stand them upon end in clean dry bran, leaving them thus till you want them for setting, you will find it advantageous.

Discard all over-sized, as well as undersized eggs for incubating. The monster-eggs frequently dropped by Chinese or Brahma fowls, are always double-yolked, and useless. The diminutive eggs, (laid at the end of the litter, usually,) are yolkless, or imperfect, and will not hatch. Select medium-sized roundish eggs, smooth-shelled; and never believe in the nonsense that some wise-acres would impose on you, as to the *sex* of eggs. The man doesn't live who can tell accurately from a look at the egg, whether it contains the germ of a cock or a pullet.

As a rule, you will not set a hen before the last of February, or middle of March — unless you chance to have a broody hen a few days earlier, and can set her under glass — in a hot-house, for instance. In any other case, the eggs will more than likely be chilled, upon a cold day, while the hen leaves them to feed — and thus your whole clutch is ruined. But supposing you set the hen when the weather favors, you place nine to eleven fresh eggs under her, in a box twelve or fourteen inches square and deep — forming the nest (slightly concave in the centre,) at the *bottom* of the box, with a thick sod, the grass side upward; upon which scatter a thin layer of fine fresh hay — and *let her alone*, from the hour you place her.

The nest should be in a moderately darkened situation, where the hen will not be disturbed, or intruded upon by any other fowl. If she is confined to restricted limits, so much the better, since a good setting hen does not care to roam away far from her nest. Let her food and fresh clean water be near at hand always, with a box of dry ashes, also, to 'roll' herself in, when she comes off to feed, and she will thus keep herself comparatively free from vermin; which oftentimes so annoys the sitter as to drive her from her nest before her time is out. The nearer you can approach in this process to what the fowl will do, naturally — if she " steals her nest " — the better success you will meet with, nine times in ten, remember.

There is no mystery or difficulty in hatching chickens with a good hen-mother. She should be left to attend to her business by herself, after you have thus provided her with eggs, nest, food, water and ash-box, and a quiet situation; and she *will* do this, if you do not disturb her. For conveniences of sitting-coops, nests, etc., the reader is referred to another chapter, hereafter.

The hen will sit three weeks. On the twenty-first day after she commences — if she has not been disturbed in the meantime — you may expect to hear the piping peep of the newly-hatched chicks, always *hoping* that you will get the same number that you furnished her the eggs for. If they were fresh and in order you may find as many. If you don't find but half or two-thirds this number, be satisfied with these, and try again.

A good plan in setting your hens, is, to set two or three the same day and hour. Then put all the chicks you get under one or two mothers, and take the odd one away. If the chicks are put under a strange mother within twenty-four hours after she hatches *her* eggs, she will adopt them ordinarily, without any trouble — and she will brood and rear a dozen or fourteen chicks as well as half a dozen.

On the twentieth day from the sitting, the chicken presents the following appearance before the breaking of the shell — as he lies, fully developed, in " his native element."

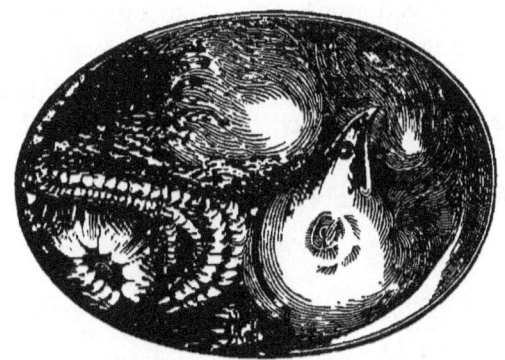

On the twenty-first day, he will burst the bonds that confine him, and come forth — if left to himself. Only in very exceptional cases should you interfere at the birth of the new comers. Some writers advise, if the shell is too thick, that the chick should be assisted to get out, on the twenty-first day, but recommend extreme caution, lest it be killed with kindness at this critical moment. Another author says, " if you attempt to release the chick from the shell, do it only by slow degrees, removing a fragment at a time, only once in twelve, or twenty hours."

As a general thing I recommend that you *let the struggling chick alone,* severely. The membrane which confines him, is so delicately threaded with blood-vessels, that the breaking of the shell, prematurely, and especially by an inexperienced hand, is almost certain to cause the young bird to bleed to death — even if released. Don't handle them; don't fuss with them. But let Nature and the hen-mother work, without your bungling aid, and all will go well at the hatching-time.

The tender solicitude exhibited by some amateurs, at the hatching time, is altogether gratuitous and unnecessary. Let your hen alone, and, if she is good for any thing, she will much better and more skillfully bring her little ones out of ordinary difficulty — than you and she together can — rely on it.

CHAPTER III.

FEEDING AND REARING YOUNG BROODS.

The chickens having now shown themselves, still let them alone for four-and-twenty hours, at the least. They do not want any thing to eat for one day after hatching. They should then be removed to a clean, fresh place, and the contents of the old nest should be destroyed, since after a hen has sat upon it three weeks, it will necessarily be occupied more or less with vermin, under the best of circumstances.

At first the chicks may be fed advantageously for a day or two, upon stale soaked bread, or a hard-boiled egg, broken up fine; and after the third day, for a week, on oatmeal or barley meal — allowing them to run with the hen, in the sunshine, if the weather is fine. But chickens are are very delicate, and sensitive to cold at this age — of any breed. So that care should be taken to have them sheltered from winds and rain till they are four or five weeks old. The season is then further advanced, (if they were hatched in March) and while the weather has become warmer, they have grown much stronger, too. After this time the hen will take care of them, if she have a good range, for some weeks, with the aid of a regular morning allowance of barley-meal, oatmeal, or other soft feed.

At from six weeks to three months old, the first down will drop from chickens of the Eastern varieties — as the Brahmas, Cochins, or Shanghæs; and most of their little plump bodies will oftentimes be, for weeks, bare of feathers. With other varieties, this does not usually occur. If they are not hatched *too* early in the spring, however, the weather will have become so comfortable that their growth is not retarded perceptibly in consequence of this natural fleecing.

If the breeder has the convenience for such an arrangement, he will find the advantage of having previously prepared a low-roofed lean-to, against the side of a tight board fence, or along the barn-side, facing the south or southeast, open at one or both ends, and slanting from a height of four feet, say, at the back, down to two feet in front — four or five feet wide. Chickens will run under such a shelter, which is ample to protect them from cold winds, rain storms, or the heat of the sun, at times. If the roof is battened, over the board-seams, it will be sufficiently tight too for the purpose; to be used, of course, only in spring and summer. In the very early season, a better arrangement, however, is, to cover such a roof with common hot-bed sashes, beneath which the young chickens will huddle, in raw weather, and

No. 3. TRIO OF LIGHT BRAHMAS. (after H. Weir.)
Presented to Queen Victoria, by G. P. Burnham. 25.

keep themselves very comfortable during the chilly and rainy days.

The hen-mother should be permitted to run with her brood until they are old enough to take care of themselves, ordinarily. A hen occupies from two and a half to three months, (sometimes three and a half months,) from the time when she commences to sit, to the day that she naturally quits her chickens. Thus, in the season when her eggs are most useful for reproduction, and at the time most generally favorable for laying — during which period she might lay thirty to forty eggs, at least — your *valuable* hen, if used for a sitter (instead of an ordinary fowl, as I recommend,) will have given you no eggs, as a rule; though some fowls, of the Chinese varieties, will begin to lay within a month after hatching a brood. Generally, however, this is the exception. And for this important reason, I also advise that you do not set your heavy hens; but " break them up," when broody, and bring them round to laying again, as soon as possible. To this particular point, I shall refer again, hereafter.

From the shell, allow your chickens all the *range* you can afford them. You will observe that they are constantly on the alert, if unconfined. They pick up — with the mother's aid — great quantities of *animal* food, insects, worms, etc; in the pasture, upon the ground, or on the lawn; and, until they come to be three or four months old, they do no harm, even in your garden. With ample range, fresh clear water, and shelter from cold rains and winds, young chickens will thrive, amazingly, with little other care.

Up to four or five months old, you will have found if you have a grass patch, or small pasture in which they can have run freely, (and if this be larger, all the better,) that your young chickens have needed very little attention beside what the hen-mother has given them, save the one regular feeding daily. They have been very easily kept — indeed! And this is because you have left them alone, carefully.

If you have no such conveniences as the grass-patch, or range mentioned, then you will be obliged, from the commencement, to resort to artificial feeding and care; which is far more troublesome, more expensive, and more uncertain, in results.

In such case, it is indispensable that you provide for your chicks such food and materials as most nearly approximate to the character of the other, and more natural mode, in rearing them. This can be done, of course — and is done, in thousands of instances, every year by fanciers.

But they should be supplied with green food — fresh pulled grass, lettuce or cabbage leaves chopped up, newly cut sods, occasionally, and plenty of broken mortar, oyster-shells, ground bone, etc.; and, two or three times a week, with animal meat, or scraps, with boiled potatoes, and cooked meal, alternately. And for general food, a mixture of oats, barley, and cracked corn, and rice. They should have a gravelled or earth floor to run upon — if confined, altogether; and in every case, the utmost care must be exercised in keeping them *cleanly*, and supplying them with plenty of fresh water. An ample box of ashes, with a pound or two of pulverized sulphur mixed through it, should stand where they can resort to it at all times; in which they will quickly learn to roll, and thus cleanse themselves from vermin. But *no* artificial means have as yet been discovered, by which chickens can so well, so healthily, or so easily be reared — as through the more natural mode of permitting them to enjoy a generous run, in their young days, out of doors, when the weather favors.

Specimen pullets of the Brahma, the Buff, or the Partridge Cochins have been known to commence laying at four and a half to five months old. Generally, however, they do not begin to lay till they are six or seven months old, and frequently older. I have found that this depends a good deal upon the time when the birds are hatched. For instance, early March chickens will ordinarily begin to lay in the fall. May chickens rarely lay until the following spring — the cold months of December and January being unfavorable to their development.

But, at five to six months old, the flocks should be separated. You will generally find among your broods a super-abundance of male chickens, in breeding the large varieties; at least, such has been my experience. These must be put into a coop or enclosure by themselves, and reared together, without interruption, to keep them from becoming quarrelsome and troublesome, until you can appropriately dispose of them. There should be no pullets in the same enclosure with these surplus male birds.

Your pullets may be kept separately, also, if convenient, until they mature. Then you should select those you intend to breed from, and put them with your *old* fowls, if you have any. If not, exchange one or two of your young cocks for a full year-old male, of different parentage, to proceed with; for, to obtain good chickens from your young pullets, you must avoid breeding them to young males of the same brood or age as themselves; and, in any event, a two year old *male* is better to breed to your young pullets.

Your first litters of eggs from these chicken-pullets will come in the fall, or winter. These you had better not set, if you could; but wait for their second litters, in early spring; to be set in February, or March, as before. The hatching will be better, the second chickens will come larger and stronger, and the time for carrying them through the next year will be better, than if you "force the season," and attempt to get chickens from the earlier laid, *first* litters, of your last year's pullets — however good such bird may be.

In reply to an old man in Michigan, who applied to the American Institute Farmer's Club for information about poultry raising, Warren Leland of the N. Y. Metropolitan Hotel answered as follows. The inquirer says " failing health and declining years make it necessary for me to give up the more laborious pursuits of life, but light exercise for mind and body is indispensable. Would the raising of poultry within 100 miles of a city market afford a profitable remuneration for the time and management required for the business ?

How much land, and what kind of soil, sandy, gravelly, or clay mixed, would be required for 100 fowls (hens and cocks)? should it be adjacent to a stream of water, or would a living spring do as well? What portion of the ground should be in trees, shrubs, and grass? How many could two aged persons care for, and what return might reasonably be expected from 100 fowls in chickens and eggs?"

Mr. Leland answers, "if this gentleman will come to my place, 25 miles north of New York, at Rye Station, I will show him how I manage my poultry yards. I have found that for every hundred fowls you must give up at least an acre. Rough land is as good as any. Hens naturally love the bush; and I lop young trees, but leave a shred by which they live a year or more. These form hiding places, and retreats for them. In such places they prefer to lay. I have great success, and it depends on three or four rules, by observing which I believe this old gentleman in Michigan can make a good living by raising hens and turkeys.

"I give my fowls great range. Eighteen acres belong to them exclusively. Then the broods have the range of another big lot, and the turkeys go half a mile or more from the house. The eighteen acres of poultry yard is rough land, and of little use for tillage. It has a pond in it and many rocks, and bushes, and weeds, and sandy places, and ash heaps, and lime, and bones, and grass, and a place which I plow up to give them worms.

"When the hen has commenced to sit, I take her

box, throw out the straw and earth, let it be out in the sun and rain a few days, and give it a good coat of whitewash on both sides. In winter, when it is very cold, I have an old stove in their house, and keep the warmth above freezing. There is also an open fireplace where I build a fire in cool wet days. They dry themselves, and when the fire goes out, there is a bed of ashes for them to wallow in. In Summer and Winter my hens have all the lime, ashes, and sand they want.

"Another reason why I have such luck is because my poultry yard receives all the scraps from the Metropolitan hotel. Egg making is no easy work, and hens will not do much of it without high feed. They need just what a man who works requires — wheat, bread, and meat. I believe in feeding it to hens."

Mr. Leland prefers the Brahmas, light and dark, and changes his roosters every spring — an excellent plan. *He* gets plenty of chickens and eggs, always.

When purchasing eggs originally, (from which you contemplate raising a brood or broods of chicks), urge it upon the party who furnishes you such eggs to begin with, that he forwards you the product of different families of fowls. This can conveniently be done, by the larger dealers, and there are plenty of honorable and reliable breeders, in this country — named in the succeeding pages of this volume — who will thus accommodate you. From such chickens you can proceed to breed, confidently, *without* the change of males, just suggested, if you prefer this mode; since the eggs are furnished you from fowls in no wise related, though an older cock than your pullets is preferable.

Many breeders make this a "point of honor" with their amateur patrons, for their own subsequent credit, when the buyer shall come to raise chickens from the stock thus sold by them. But if eggs cannot thus be had, unless the change in the male bird is made, *at the outset*, as I have proposed, the progeny will surely deteriorate; the next generation of chicks will come more or less uneven, weakly, imperfect, or deformed — as certainly as this vicious system of " in-and-in breeding " (among relations) is attempted. I insist upon this, because I know of what I am writing; and I have tried this experiment, thoroughly — to my cost — in the past five and twenty years of my poultry-breeding.

The French peasants have a novel mode of feasting their fowls, and at the same time of destroying the common grub-worm, with which in some districts, their land is literally " alive " in early spring, and of which pest I observed the farmer there thus rids himself. When the ploughing is being done, a large coop, or box is placed upon wheels, and filled with advanced chickens and fowls, forty, fifty, or a hundred in each; and this vehicle is taken to the newly ploughing field, and follows the open furrows. The fowls are let out of the perambulating coops as soon as the ground is turned over, for a given space, and they are quickly busy in gobbling up the myriads of grub-worms thrown to the surface by the plough — gorging themselves with these rare pickings, of which they seem inordinately fond.

The coop is moved on, as the birds advance behind the ploughmen, and the fowls feed constantly, all day long, in this way; devouring the fat grubs with intense gusto, and appearing never satisfied so long as there is a stray worm in sight. Thus the French *paysan* clears his grounds previous to planting, very effectually, from these destructive and pestiferous devourers of the rootlings of tender plants. These grubs breed in countless numbers in the fields of Normandy and Nivernais. At sunset, the fowls voluntarily re-enter the trundled coops, and are thus returned to their home-quarters, or are kept confined till next day, for a continuance of this duty, which appears to be rare enjoyment to them.

As to the general *feed* of fowls, however, I have often thought of the counsel of a noted patent-medicine vender, who, in his advice to patients venturing to take his nostrum, thus briefly alludes to the course of diet they should observe, meanwhile; "Eat the best you can get, and plenty of it." This simple recommendation is pertinent. I have found that poultry thrives equally well with humans, in this respect, and I both give to my own fowls, (and commend the rule to others,) "the best to be had, and plenty of it."

Variety in feed is desirable. In this corn-growing land of ours, that article seems the handiest and is certainly the heartiest, for fowls. But corn alone will soon sicken the healthiest fowl in the world. Barley, oats, screenings, cracked corn, rice, sun-flower seed, (easily grown) and whole wheat, mixed, for *dry* food; and scalded Indian meal-dough, bran-dough, boiled potatoes, and the scraps from your table, with green and animal food for fowls that are confined without a range, will keep them in a good healthy, prospering condition, usually.

I have practised feeding at regular intervals, and I have left dry food in the feed-boxes, continually, to which fowls had access, to eat of when they desired. The latter mode is less trouble. But the better plan is to give them a variety, changing the fare weekly — and let them have enough of the best, always.

CHAPTER IV.

PURELY BRED ONE YEAR OLD FOWLS, AND UPWARDS.

In our preceding chapters, we have submitted general directions as to selecting eggs, and the hatching, and raising of chickens. We will now look to the birds at from approaching a year old, and forwards, and offer our ideas in relation to breeding fowls, *purely*.

A young pullet will lay, in her first litter, ordinarily, fifteen to twenty eggs. Then she ceases, for a short time. Usually, she will not show signs of being "broody" (or desirous to sit,) until after laying the second litter. Some varieties of fowls do not incline to sit, at all; others but rarely; and others persistently; until you gratify this natural desire, or "break them up."

After laying the second or third litter, these last named — which include the Chinese varieties, notably — will stick to the nest, brood upon stones, crouch on *nothing*, and beat you out, unless you suffer them to have their way. As has been hinted, already, these heavy birds are not so good for setting, as fowls of lesser weight and size; and therefore they should be broken up, as well as for the other reason given, namely, that their eggs are too valuable to take them from duty for three months, in the best laying season of the year.

Fowls at about a year old, of this class, will make themselves most troublesome to you; and various stratagems are resorted to by the inexperienced, to prevent them from sitting, or to induce them to return to laying, instead. Most of these plans are cruel, or futile; but I have found that placing broody hens in an open bottomless pen, or coop, say four feet by six, and four feet high — constructed with a lean-to roof to shed the rain, slatted on all four sides with laths, or palings, and set upon the grass, or ground, *with nothing whatever inside it* but your broody hen, or hens — except the roost — will serve to cure them of this sitting fever quicker, with less trouble, and surer, than any mode I ever tried. If a vigorous young crower be put into the pen with her (or them) it is no drawback. But in such a coop she or they will go to roost, at night, and soon forget the broody inclination.

If she has no nest, no eggs in sight to sit on, no food or water, except what you place for her convenience *outside* of the coop, she will shortly get over her fever and go to laying again. But, shutting hens in darkened barrels, ducking them in cold water, or tying them out without shelter to "cool them off," is both brutal and inefficacious. If taken *in season*, when they first show symptoms of broodiness, and dealt with as I have suggested, you will have little trouble in bringing them round to laying again, in a few days, generally. If the eggs of such hens are not more than ordinarily valuable to you, at the time mentioned, then gratify this natural maternal instinct, by all means. But when eggs from "fancy" breeds of fowls cost (or will command) five to ten dollars a dozen, the feasibility of the plan proposed, on this point, I think will be apparent.

As to the capacity of a maturing hen to produce eggs, this quality differs in different breeds — some being more prolific than others. Accounts are published of the actual laying of two eggs in one day, by certain individual fowls of extraordinary breeds; and it is seriously stated by Richardson, a noted English writer upon Poultry, that the "Cochin China is a gigantic bird, very prolific, frequently laying two, and sometimes three eggs in a day." In support of this assertion, Mr. Richardson subsequently refers as his authority for this statement (which was called in question), to the "Rt. Hon. Mr. Shaw, Recorder of Dublin, to Mr. Waters, Her Majesty's poultry-keeper, and to J. Joseph Nolan, Esq., of Dublin." I think the author now quoted might have added to the list of his authorities for this statement, with slight research among the old-time doggerel writers, for I remember the couplet in the troubled peasant's song —

> "Some one has stole our speckled hen,
>   I wish they'd let her be;
> For oft she laid two eggs a day,
>   And Sundays she laid three!"

And I have no doubt, if there ever was one at all, that this was the original hen that "laid two eggs a day." I have lived to handle and experiment rather extensively with fowls in this country, during the past three decades, and, though I do not say that any of the above mentioned parties may not have known the fact stated, yet I must candidly add that *I* never saw the hen that laid two or three eggs in a day, as yet, and I am still in doubt on this point.

Purity of blood — as nearly as it can be attained — is very desirable. A vast deal has been written and said upon *this* point, and we have in this country at the present time, a great many strains of blood, imported from the yards and walks of known good breeders of poultry in England and France. When the chickens from the *product* of these strains (in the second and third descent) reach the age of from eight months to a year old, such young fowls will show for themselves, in feathers, form and features, how pure may have been the stock from which they originated!

At the age when it is advisable to put your fresh stock together, for breeding, care should be taken, (if you desire only to have pure descendants,) that *no* male bird, save one of the same breed with the pullets, shall *ever* have had access to them. The theory advanced by some writers, to the effect that it is necsssary to allow the male bird to consort with the female only for the time being, to insure due impregnation, and the subsequent production of the variety you may thus attempt to breed, is utterly fallacious. If the cock used is of the identical *variety* with the pullets, the changing of such individual male bird, from time to time, is an advantage. But to place light Brahma cocks in the same enclosure with Buff or Partridge Cochin pullets, for instance — *at all* — after the latter approach maturity, is fatal to the absolute purity of the *progeny* of such pullets, ever afterwards. I set this down as a certain *fact* — drawn from repeated experiment during my thirty years' experience in breeding. And at this very writing, I meet with the following absurd sentence in a communication to the N. Y. Bulletin, over the signature of a correspondent who usually writes well on other points, but who says, "I am convinced that there is *no harm in letting all varieties mix during the fall and winter*, and separating them a month before saving their eggs for setting."

This advice is certainly erroneous; for the sequence

I have noted follows, invariably, in the multiplying of *any* kind of live stock, and is never-failing. Let me illustrate this point.

Several years ago, a gentleman in Newfoundland sent me a large thorough-bred native bitch dog, which I bred for ten years. The first three years' litters of pups were bred from a fine male native Newfoundland, owned by a neighbor, and the progeny were so far uniformly perfect in color, long silky hair, form, and known characteristics of this notable race of dogs. The fourth year, I crossed her with a large Russian mastiff; and got a clutch of superior pups — with the curly hair, shorter nose, more upright ear, and the absence of the web-foot, etc., a very satisfactory *cross*, but no longer the "pure" Newfoundland. I bred that mother six years afterwards, consecutively, to the *original* Newfoundland male, belonging to my neighbor; and *never*, in a single instance, did this bitch bring a litter subsequently to the fourth year, *some* of which did not clearly show the marks, in feature, curly hair, short nose, small ear, or absence of the web — belonging to the *Russian* mastiff I had bred but once to her; and her *last* litter, born four years after that mastiff was dead, exhibited this taint more strikingly, than had any previous clutch of pups she ever gave birth to.

So it will follow with fowls; and through this careless way of allowing a male bird of a different race or variety — in color, or character — to consort with pullets, *at all*, come the imperfections so commonly met with, everywhere, among the fowls produced from what are deemed *pure* breeds and blood; in support of which principle, I offer another instance, in point. Twelve years ago, I purchased from a gentleman in Andover, Mass., a young imported Alderney bull, which I put upon my place in Melrose, and bred but once to a fine Durham heifer, in her third season, she having been previously bred to a full-blooded Durham. Her third calf was so strongly marked in color, and ultimately came to maturity so like the father, that she has since been mistaken scores of times for a full-blooded true Alderney cow, with the single exception that she was over-sized. The mother was never served by an Alderney bull, again — but for several years afterwards was bred only to the Durham. Yet her subsequent progeny, up to her death, two years ago, in *every* instance plainly showed either the fine muzzle, the deer-face, the fawn color, the delicate limb, the small ear, or the silky coat of the *Alderney*, to which she was bred but once in her life, as I know.

Thus with poultry. In scores of experimental cases, I have seen the effects of this contamination in form, color, and characteristics, when varieties of fowls have been permitted promiscuously to run together, and "mix during the fall and winter;" and, though there may not be "any *harm*" in such a course, yet if the breeder's purpose is to produce really pure bloods, he will find that which I have here recommended is true, to the letter — with fowls, as with any other kind of stock; and that the progeny of chickens, bred in the other careless way, will surely, in future generations, come more or less like the cattle of Jacob, of old — " ringed, streaked, or speckled."

Another instance. In 1854, I purchased on shipboard, at Central Wharf, Boston, six Broad-tailed (Australian) sheep — two bucks and four ewes. The peculiar characteristic of these animals is known to stockbreeders. Its tail is shaped like a flat thin pork-ham, depending from the small end; and, when cooked, this is said to be a very desirable edible — nicer and more succulent than so much tenderloin beef. In proportion to the body of this kind of sheep its caudal appendage is very large, and forms a marked and distinctive feature of this breed. I had three fine Cotswold ewes, which I imported from Canada at that time, on my place in Melrose, and I crossed them all with one of the Broad-tailed bucks. The lambs these ewes dropped next season, each came of good size and very like the Cotswold mother, with the exception that every one of them had the wide, thick, pear-shaped, heavy tail. I sold the six broad-tail sheep to a gentleman in Louisiana; and, a year afterwards I sent the three Cotswold ewes, with a fine heavy buck of *their* own breed, to Mr. F. Ducayet, of New Orleans. These three sheep were then with lamb, by this Cotswold buck. When the progeny were born, (upon Mr. D's place, at Bayou St. John,) two of the three lambs came with the broad tail, and the other resembled the Cotswold, more accurately. The gentleman to whom I sent these sheep wrote me subsequently, that " the young ones were of good size," but he " found two out of the three were *deformed*, having a monstrous bunch at the extremity of their tails! which he could not account for." (He never saw one of the broad-tail breed of sheep at all.) But this occurrence was one of interest to me, and I explained the matter to him — though at the time I had not had sufficient experience to suspect what so certainly followed. *He* bred these Cotswolds together, three years afterwards; and more than half his lambs came similarly "deformed," showing the broad flat tail of the other buck, to which they had never been bred but *once*, to my positive knowledge.

In an able article on the principles of breeding Domestic Animals, by S. L. Goodale, of Maine, that gentleman states that "a pure Aberdeenshire heifer, the property of a farmer in Forgue, was served with a pure Teeswater bull, by which she had a fine cross calf. The *following* season the same cow was served with a pure Aberdeenshire bull, but the product was in appearance a cross-bred calf, which at two years old *had long horns;* the parents were both hornless. A flock of ewes belonging to Dr. W. Wells, in the island of Grenada, were served by a ram procured for the purpose. The ewes were all white and woolly; the ram was quite different — of a chocolate color, and hairy like a goat. The progeny were of course crosses, but bore a strong resemblance to the male parent. The next season Dr. Wells obtained a ram of precisely the same breed as the ewes, to whom they were all bred, *but the progeny showed distinct marks of resemblance to the former ram*, in color, hair, &c. The same thing occurred on neighboring estates under like circumstances." Numerous other instances might be stated, if space would permit, and not a few might be given showing that the same rule holds in the *human* species, of which a single one will suffice here: " A young woman residing in Edinburg, and born of white parents, but whose mother previous to her marriage bore a mulatto child, by a negro servant, exhibits distinct traces of the negro. Dr. Simpson, whose patient at one time the young woman was, recollects being struck with the resemblance, and noticed particuly that the hair had the qualities characteristic of the negro."

Mr. James McGillivray, a well known Scotch Veterinary Surgeon, thus lately expresses his opinion in reference to this matter. He argues sensibly that " when *once* a pure animal of any breed, has been pregnant to an animal of a different breed, such pregnant animal *is a cross forever*, incapable of producing pure progeny of any breed." And Mr. McG. adds that " many agriculturalists are familiar to a degree that is annoying to them, with these facts, finding that after breeding crosses, their cows, though served with bulls of their own breed, *yield crosses still*, or rather mongrels ; that they were already impressed with the idea of contamination of blood, as the cause of the phenomenon ; and that the doctrine intuitively commended itself to their minds as soon as stated, etc." Many years ago there were in the Kennebec valley a few polled or hornless cattle. They were not particularly cherished, and gradually diminished in numbers. Mr. Payne Wingate shot the *last* animal of this breed, (a bull calf or a yearling,) mistaking it in the dark, for a bear. During thirty-five years subsequently, *all* the cattle upon his farm had horns; but, at the end of that time, one of his cows produced a calf, which grew up without horns, and Mr. Wingate said it was in all respects the exact image of *the first bull* of the breed ever brought there. And with a few more veritable illustrations, I will leave this interesting subject for those who deem it "no harm to allow their fowls of different breeds to run together, and mix, during the fall and winter," to consider and experiment with, at their leisure.

Some eighteen years ago, I imported from Mr. Nolan, of Dublin, and Mr. Baker of London, five or six different clutches of fine Madagascar (or Lop-eared) Rabbits. I built a house expressly for breeding these then popular pets in, and was highly successful with them, for some years — when I disposed of my whole stock, and gave up that trade. A member of my family had a trio of nice pure white common (upright-eared) rabbits, which had been kept on the place, and remained there some time after all the others left. The two females had been bred to a smut-faced Madagascar buck, two or three times, before I sold out. The three common white short-eared rabbits were then bred *together* two seasons, and threw more than a dozen litters, after I had not had a male Madagascar on my premises for many months; and through all that period of two years, neither of those two common white does — bred to the same white common buck, *only* — ever had a litter of young, some one or more of which did not possess the long lop-ear, or lop-ears, which is the distinguishing feature of the Madagascar breed. Upon these actual, personally tried experiments, I build the theory I am now explaining.

Mr. Darwin, an eminent English writer on cattle-breeding, says on this subject, "the reproductive system is highly susceptible to changes in the conditions of life; but *why*, (because this reproducing system is disturbed,) this or that part should vary more or less, we are profoundly ignorant. Yet, we can here and there catch a faint ray of light." And among these "faint rays" of light spoken of, is this important one, to wit — the clearly apparent influence of the male first having fruitful intercourse with the female, *upon her subsequent offspring by other males*. Attention was directed to this subject in England by the following circumstances, related by Sir Edward Home: A young chestnut mare, seven-eighths Arabian, belonging to the Earl of Morton, was covered in 1815 by a quagga, (a species of wild ass from Africa) and marked somewhat like a zebra. The mare was covered but *once* by the quagga, and gave birth to a hybrid, which had, as was expected, distinct marks of the quagga in the shape of its head, black bars on the legs, shoulders, &c. In 1817, 1818, and 1821, this same mare was covered by a fine black Arabian horse, and produced successively three colts; and although she had not seen the quagga since 1816, they *all* bore his curious and unequivocal markings.

Since the occurrence of this case, numerous others of a similar character have been observed. Mr. McGillivray says: "That in several foals in the royal stud at Hampton Court, got by the horse "Actæon," there were unmistakable marks of the horse "Colonel." The *dams* of these foals were bred from by "Colonel" the *previous* year. A colt, the property of the Earl of Sheffield, got by "Laurel," so resembled another horse named "Camel," that it was asserted at Newmarket that he must have been got by "Camel." It was ascertained, however, that the mother of the colt bore a foal the *previous* year by "Camel." Alexander Morrison, Esq., of Bognie, had a fine Clydesdale mare, which, in 1843, was served by a Spanish ass, and produced a mule. She *afterwards* had a colt by a full bred horse, which bore a very marked likeness to a mule, and seen at a distance, every one sets it down at once as a mule! His ears are nine inches long, his girth not quite six feet, and he stands above sixteen hands high. The hoofs are so long and narrow that there is a difficulty in shoeing them, and the tail is thin and scanty. He is a beast of indomitable energy, and highly prized by his owner."

We are now discussing purity of blood, and these paragraphs are intended for fanciers and breeders who are contenders for this very desirable attainment, and process. In another place (see chapter on "Raising Poultry and Eggs for *market*,") we speak fully of the advantages of *crossing* good breeds of fowls — for this latter purpose. At present, however, we are considering the best modes of producing and multiplying birds in their *purity*, as nearly as that laudable object may be attained.

I have mentioned the Chinese fowls, only, in this illustration; but it matters nothing as to the *variety* you desire to keep and raise — purely. A clutch of young Black Spanish, Dominique, or Dorking pullets, permitted to run indiscriminately at large with one or more male bird, of these different varieties, when the chickens are coming to be seven to ten months old, will be irretrievably contaminated, for the rest of their lives; and this course will render them useless for pure breeders — no matter what variety of male bird you subsequently, or exclusively, breed them to. And such pullets will never afterwards give you eggs from which you need expect thoroughly *pure* chickens. With a portion of the litters they produce, in some degree, or particular, will crop out this inevitable " cloven foot," sooner or later; and to this carelessness in breeding and intermixture, in other lands — in China, Calcutta, Spain, France, and England — whence we obtain what is deemed pure blood, (because it comes here, oftentimes, directly from those countries,) is attributable much of the disappointment we experience, when we come to see what this " pure " stock produces, with us.

" Like produces like," I am aware. But I am now writing about what I understand, pretty well. I do not heed the theories, or half-tried experiments of neophytes, in this matter of poultry-breeding. And I aver that it is not a possible thing either to obtain or to breed, and keep our poultry stock pure, unless this *rule of nature* is strictly observed, as I have now aimed clearly to set it down. Croakers may say this is reducing the matter to a fine point. And so it is — yet it is precisely so.

Your pullets, at eight to twelve months old, are in order to commence to breed from. A *two*-year old hen is in her prime, and will the second year, as a rule, give you larger eggs, though not more of them, than during the first year. Fowls lay their litters out — say from one and a half to two and a half dozen eggs at a time — then cease laying for a while, and begin with another litter. If you breed your pullets uniformly to a cock of their own kind, *from the outset*, you will naturally get evenly colored, and formed chickens, similar to the parent stock, unless the originals have been contaminated, as I have hinted at. But, once you cross your pullets with a male bird of any other distinct color or variety, I repeat it, you can never render such fowl available afterwards, as a *pure* breeder; no matter how you may try experiments with her.

A breeding-cock is better also at two-years old, than at one, even for your yearling pullets. But good birds of this age are not readily to be had, and so you must generally use the younger ones. If you have not permitted different kinds of fowls to run together (after your pullets had reached the age of five or six months,) you can place them with the cock that you desire to breed from, as mentioned in this chapter, and keep them thus, without change of the breed of the male; and the eggs from such fowls will afford you very satisfactory results, when you come to get chickens from them, in this second generation from your purchases.

No. 4. DARK BRAHMA COCK, (by H. Weir.)
One of the first trio sent to England by G. P. Bur. ham. 49.

The strong blood of the Asiatic species exhibits itself, continuously, when bred straight through — without mixture — from year to year; and in proof of this, we may point the reader to the "*Brahma*" fowl, (so called, at present, by universal consent,) which I have bred since 1849, '50. The light variety of this long favorite fowl — than which none better, will, in my judgment, ever be produced in this goodly world — are *to-day*, precisely, in a general way, what they were when I exhibited them at the Boston poultry-shows of 1850, '51, '52, '53, and afterwards.

The old Marsh stock of Shanghæs, now called "Partridge Cochins," (of which more hereafter,) have changed very little in the long years since 1849, when the importer originally got those magnificent birds direct from China, through a Missionary friend there, and bred them clean and pure in West Roxbury for years, subsequently, to the admiration of us long-ago fanciers of the "largest, and finest race of domestic fowl ever brought into America — " as they were then described; and of which identical stock I bred, and *sent to England*, in 1853 to 1857, hundreds of choice samples — from whose progeny, unquestionably come the beautiful birds which breeders in America are *now* receiving back again; these splendid specimens of "Partridge Cochins" that may be seen in the yards of many of our best fanciers, to-day!

There is no mistaking this variety, there is no mistaking the light Brahma variety. They are always alike, always the same, when bred clearly and purely.

So it is with other strains — as the purely bred Black Spanish, the Gueldres, the White Dorkings, the Leghorns, the Dominiques, and others. But where you find *any* of these birds that are up to the standard, themselves, and from which are bred chickens like them in all particulars, you will be sure to find that the breeders of them have never ventured to indulge in the pastime of "letting all varieties mix during the fall and winter," or crossing them for experiment's sake, even during the laying of a single litter of eggs; and such as these, *only*, can be relied on, to answer the hopes and desires of fanciers of PURE blooded fowls.

Your young breeding fowls should enjoy the range spoken of, if convenient. If you are compelled to restrict them to limited accommodations, however, then remember that they should be amply supplied with the greens, lime, gravel, fresh water, ash-box, and animal food already suggested. Without these — in confined quarters — your pullets will quickly drop soft-shelled eggs, (which are worthless for setting;) and *above all*, keep them as clear of the annoyance of vermin as possible.

And now, apologizing for this perhaps too lengthy chapter on purity of blood, — we will proceed to consider some of the conveniences requisite to keeping these breeding fowls in good condition.

CHAPTER V.

POULTRY HOUSES AND NEEDFUL ACCOMMODATIONS.

The fashion, dimensions, and proportions of fowl *houses*, pens, or coops, and the conveniences accorded to their poultry by different breeders and fanciers, are as varied as are the number of poultry-raisers in this country. Yet a good and sufficient domicil for these birds is, anywhere, a very simple affair, both in itself and its necessary appointments.

Gentlemen-fanciers, who possess ample means, and who are ambitious to see their aviary in keeping with other costly buildings upon their choice country estates, can spend a deal of money in constructing their henery, and in its ornamentation, inside and outside. But generally farmers and breeders do not care to indulge in this luxury, and are rightly content with what may be only needful and comely, for the comfort and convenience of their feathered stock.

QUEEN VICTORIA'S POULTRY HOUSE, WINDSOR CASTLE.

In England, many fine structures may be seen, which are devoted to the use of chickens and pigeons —one of which is the elegant poultry-house and aviary of her British Majesty, Queen Victoria, which the author had the pleasure of visiting a few years since, which is located in a quiet beautiful spot upon the "home farm" of this sovereign, on the margin of the great Park attached to Windsor Castle—a drawing of which we present on the opposite page.

For many years, as is well known, both Her Majesty the Queen, and the late Royal Consort, Prince Albert during his life, were ardent admirers of poultry, and munificent patrons of the pleasant pursuit of chicken-raising, which M. de Reaumer dignifies as an "art;" and it is also well known that the author of this volume had the honor of presenting to her Majesty the first mature Brahma fowls ever seen in England; in return for which the Queen kindly complimented Mr. Burnham by sending him a superb copy of her portrait, with a very agreeable letter, which will be found on page 152.

The Queen's Poultry House is a large half-gothic structure, with a central well-lighted apartment for viewing the fowls, and over this is an extensive dove-house. Its front and ends are for the most part glazed, and in the wings of the building are the sections or divisions for the convenience of the different varieties of domestic fowl; of which there are many very choice breeds kept.

In front is a broad lawn divided off with light wire

fencing, which affords space where the fowls and chicks may range to advantage. Inside of each division is a gravelled walk or patch, also. In addition to this main house are contiguous lesser buildings, yards and enclosures — dotted with food-houses, laying-sheds, etc. Her Majesty evinced a rare interest in this agreeable pastime, formerly; and, very much to her credit, as a woman, exhibited an affectionate zeal in this matter of every-day life, which is so truthfully portrayed by the poet :—

> "I love the neighborhood of man and beast;
> I would not place my stable out of sight.
> How grateful 'tis to wake, and hear the sound
> Of flapping wing and crow of Chanticleer,
> Long ere the morn that tells the dawn is near.
> Pleasant the path — by garden wall or fields —
> Where flocking birds, of various plume and chirp,
> Discordant, cluster round the leaning stack,
> From whence the thresher draws the rustling leaves!"

The nests in this extensive royal establishment are formed of dry *heather*, gathered from the fields, and are covered with twigs and branches of evergreen; so that the layers are quite in seclusion when upon their nests. A plan of these nests — for the convenience of laying and hatching — is given on opposite page; the style is both ornamental and useful, it will be found very inexpensive, and may readily be adopted to advantage in this country.

The nests are in ranges, about fourteen inches square, with the front running up eight inches from the flat bottom of the boarding. These can be built on or near the floor of the house, or at a higher elevation, as preferred.

LAYING AND HATCHING NESTS, IN THE QUEEN'S POULTRY-HOUSE.

Though this extensive and elegantly appointed establishment of royalty is very fine, the splendid poultry-house of Lord Penrhyn, at Winnington, England, in the County of Cheshire, is incomparably the most magnificent poultry-palace ever built.

This consists of a handsome, regular front, of about one hundred and fifty feet, " at each extremity of which is a neat pavilion, with a large, arched window. These pavilions are united to the centre of the design, by a colonade of cast-iron pillars, painted white, which support a cornice, and a slate roof, covering a paved walk, and a variety of different conveniences for the poultry, for keeping eggs, corn, and the like. The doors into these are all of lattice-work, also painted white, and the framing green. In the middle of the front, are four stone columns, and four pilasters, supporting, likewise, a cornice, and slate roof, under which is a beautiful mosaic iron gate; on one side of this gate is an elegant little parlor, beautifully papered and furnished; and at the other end of the colonade a very neat kitchen, kept scrupulously clean. The front is the diameter of a large semi-circular court behind, round which there is also a colonade and a great variety of conveniences for poultry. The court is paved, and a circular pond and pump are in the middle of it. The whole fronts towards a rich little paddock, in which the poultry have the liberty to walk about, between meals. At one o'clock a bell rings, and the gate in the centre is opened. The poultry being then mostly walking in the paddock, and knowing by the sound of the bell, that their feed is ready for them, fly and run from all quarters, and rush in at the gate, every one striving which can get in first. There are about six hundred fowls of different kinds kept in the place; and although so large a number, the semi-circular court is always very neat and clean. This poultry-house is of brick, except the pillars and cornices, the lintels and jambs of the doors and windows; but the bricks are not seen, being all covered with a fine kind of slate, from his lordship's estate in Wales. These slates are close-jointed, and fastened with screw-nails on small spars fixed in the brick; they are afterwards painted, and fine white sand thrown on, while the paint is wet, which gives the whole an appearance of the most beautiful freestone."

But such quarters for poultry, in *this* country, would scarcely pay! We have merely described these two fine establishments, briefly, to show how royalty and nobility care for their fowls' comfort, in England. With us, as we remarked at the opening of this chapter, the simplest and most economical arrangements for this purpose, having regard to the convenience and health of fowls, are all that is needed for their comfort and successful rearing.

Poultry-houses upon estates where the birds can have a good run, are only essential for the protection of your feathered stock, so that they may resort to them in cold, rainy, or windy weather — or be shielded therein during our seasons of snows and winter. If left to themselves, fowls will leave the cosiest of houses, during a portion of almost any day in the year — except when the snow lies too deep on the ground ; since they delight in the clear open air, and freedom from the restraint of all closed limits.

Consequently their houses should be so arranged as that they may enjoy both warmth and shelter, in the cold season. At other times, they will live abroad mostly, except when they are roosting, sitting or laying — if permitted to do so. For six or seven months in the year, therefore, (provided they have unlimited range) in a simple lean-to, shed, barn, or other out-building, where roots and nests can be accorded to them, they will be happy, thrifty, and healthy, ordinarily.

"But we want eggs in winter," exclaims everybody. Very well — you can have them by keeping your poultry warm and comfortable, during the cold weather. To do this you must have additional conveniences to a com mon lean-to, or shed. From May to November, generally speaking, in our Northern and middle States, this will suffice; after that, the fowls must be housed and cared for, or you get no eggs during the cold months that follow November.

The *floor* of the poultry-house should be dry, and of hard gravel, or earth. This should be cleansed daily, and kept clean. Inside, it should be whitewashed two or three times each season, to keep away, or help destroy the collecting vermin. The roof should be tight, as well as the walls, and good ventilation across and overhead is indispensable. Dampness, rain, melted snow leaking in, and cold winds, sicken or destroy more fowls than die from any other prime cause in our cold weather.

A window or flap upon each side of your poultry-house, for ventilation, is an excellent arrangement — to open and shut at pleasure. At night *one* of these should be closed to avoid the consequences of exposing your fowls to a draught of cold air, which is very injurious alike to fowl or human. In the winter season, these windows should be open only at intervals during the warmest part of the *day;* and always be closed tightly on winter nights.

The roost may be four feet high from the floor, for large, heavy fowls, and should be ascended to by means of a foot-wide board resting on either end of it, from the ground. Across this, horizontally, nail laths, the length of the width of the board, six or eight inches apart; by which your larger birds may readily ascend and descend from the roost. This simple arrangement will save many an injury to these clumsy fowls, first and last.

Let this roost be a single spruce pole, two inches thick, and directly underneath it, (say two feet wide) secure a boarding, upon which the droppings from the birds may fall in one place during the night. Clean this board often — thrice a week, at farthest; and save this manure by itself, in a clean barrel. It is better than the same quantity of the best guano for your garden, if you have one, and if not, the morocco-dresser nearest you will gladly pay you six to eight dollars a barrel for it.

Mr. Nutter, of North Bridgewater, Mass., has adopted a plan for saving and utilizing the droppings of his fowls, which is a good one. He arranges a shallow trough, of about the width we recommend, and the length of the roost, which he places underneath it, and cleans out frequently — to marked profit — he says. Mr. Nutter calculates that fowls are upon the roosts nearly two-thirds of the time, when kept in confinement, and the amount of manure he thus saves, from a couple dozen birds, (when mixed with loam, properly,) furnishes him with an excellent dressing for his goodsized garden, from which (after applying this compost) he has raised the finest vegetables in his neighborhood. In one corner of his fowl-house he keeps a heap of loam, or dry soil, handy, which he mixes with the droppings from time to time, as it is gathered from under the roosts; and he has found that the compost thus made in a season — even from his limited number of fowls — is not only super-excellent in quality, for his garden-dressing, but is quite generous in quantity. Prepared either in this manner, for the purpose indicated, or saved *clean,* to be sold to the tanners, your fowls' droppings are worth caring for; the more especially if you keep many of them.

The aspect of your poultry-house, lean-to, shed, or whatever building you may undertake to winter fowls in, should be towards the east and south. This gives them the early morning sun; and its front should accordingly be furnished with glass sashes — more or less — carried down to within a foot of the sill, if convenient, so that they can have the full benefit of this natural and cheerful heat, inside the house, through the glazing. Heating your fowl-house from a stove (as some persons do,) is absolutely pernicious, and of course altogether unnatural. In large establishments, where hot water or steam pipes could be run through the building, readily, such artificial heat might answer. But all this kind of thing, *I* have found to my cost, will produce more vermin than anything else; and I long since concluded that if the fowl-house is tight, the birds do better (with what sun-heat they can get, ordinarily) than through the other means, in winter.

The opposite plan is for a convenient double summer fowl-house, each half being provided with a roomy yard, in front. The whole area occupied, may be 75 by 40 feet, or less. The house has a plain board-battened roof 8 feet high front, 11 feet at rear; it is tight all round, except the slats in fronts; there is an entrance door to each part (front) and a hole for fowls to enter and leave the house (or shed) at each corner; yard and

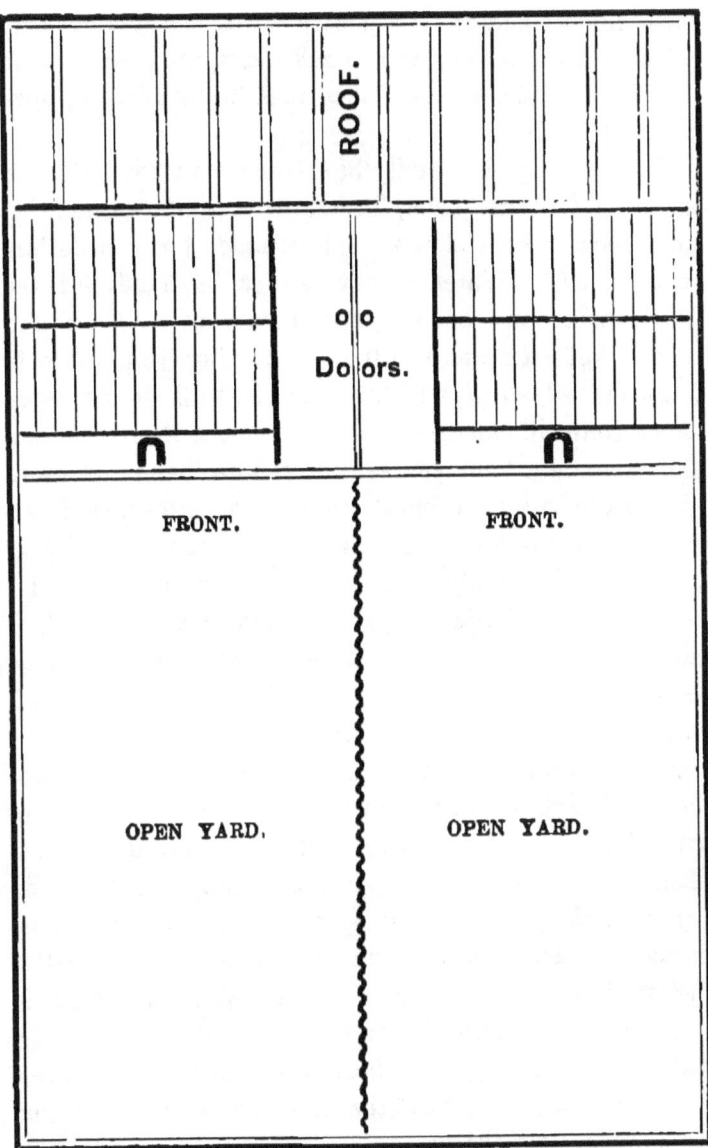

A CHEAP, DOUBLE BATTENED-ROOF SUMMER FOWL-HOUSE.

shed are divided in the centre by a continuous high closely-slatted fence; roosts and nests, etc., same as in plan p. 107; size of each shed part 20 by 15 feet; open yards 60 by 20 feet.

The slatting can easily be removed in the fall, and sashes put in its place, for winter use, if desirable, at small cost. Provision should be made for ventilation, at the sides. Water should always be handy for the fowls, inside any house — and plenty of it, fresh and pure. Not *snow*-water, either. Obliging your fowls to drink melted show, will take the flesh off your poultry faster than it can be put on, with the heartiest and most abundant food you can force into them. Remove the water-vessels, or empty them every night, in freezing weather — and replenish in the morning, daily; and you will quickly note the difference in the general health of your fowls, if you have only pursued the other careless mode hinted at. This recommendation may seem to be a trivial matter — but I have managed both ways. Perhaps the reader hasn't!

In the middle of the winter's days, ventilate your house, always — when snow, or sleet, or rain, will not drive into it. Fowls love fresh air; and, in confined places, diseases — roup, gapes, dysentery, vertigo, and vermin *will* generate, and spread amongst them, wondrously. Keep the poultry-house *clean*. Never scatter the feed about your floors. Keep your dry food in shallow boxes, where it can be seen, and got at, easily. Nail across the edges of these feed-boxes slats of laths, six inches apart, so that the birds can't stand in, and befoul or scatter the grain.

Give them light, fresh air when convenient, lime, scraps, the dry offal from your table, ashes to roll in, and fresh water — and they do well, even in confinement, if looked after, daily.

I have said that you can have eggs from your fowls, in winter time. This will depend, in a measure, of course, upon the age of your layers. Early spring pullets will begin to lay in the fall, and will continue right along, during the colder months, if you keep them warm, dry, and properly fed. *Old* hens do not lay much, in the cold season, usually. Indeed, my experience has taught me that a hen becomes " old," when she reaches her third or fourth year. *After* this period, she will scarcely pay for her keeping, for the eggs she lays. As a " show " bird, (barring the unsightly scales that will then accumulate upon her legs,) she may answer a purpose. But I have found that the China fowls " lay themselves out," by the time they come to be three years old; and many die, before reaching that age, or bag down, astern, so that they become worthless, in my estimation.

To have fresh eggs, in winter, then, you must depend upon your previous spring-hatched pullets; and they must be kept where they will be warm. They should also be well fed, and allowed animal food, chopped fine, with plenty of lime, and gravel, always. These articles largely furnish the materials for eggs and egg-shells, which the bird readily obtains, in the summer season, amidst its roamings. And this brings us to the subject of raising eggs and chickens in quantities, for market purposes, simply.

CHAPTER VI.

RAISING POULTRY AND EGGS FOR MARKET.

At the request of Hon. Isaac Newton, late Commissioner of the U. S. Department of Agriculture, at Washington, D. C., I prepared the paper on this subject, which appears in the official Report of that Department for the year 1862. I was absent in the army up to the fall of 1864, and did not see this article until a year after that Report was published. But it contains in a general way, my ideas upon the subject of raising poultry *in quantities*, as well as in reference to the producing of *eggs for market*, so accurately, that I give place to that paper, here, with such notes and explanations as my subsequent experience prompts, upon this important branch of the fowl-trade.

The communication alluded to, is illustrated from drawings of my own poultry-houses, upon the estate I then occupied in Melrose, Mass., and the principal building is still standing there. The illustrations in this and the next chapters are also copied from the Department Report, for '62, and are correct. I insert this article, entire; from which it will be seen, by comparing it with other parts of this "New Poultry Book," that I have not materially changed my opinions in reference to the general points therein treated of; though — during a visit to Europe, in the year 1867, I learned some facts connected with the details of this paper, which I have noted, in the appropriate place. This article appears under the title that heads this chapter, and is as follows: —

"A great deal has been written in the few past years on the subject of advantageously breeding, keeping, and fattening poultry, and producing eggs *for market*. Many suggestions and numerous theories have been presented to the public through the medium of books, and the press of our own and other countries upon this theme; and much of the information and advice thus promulgated has been of a visionary and impracticable character, though, at the same time, no inconsiderable amount of valuable information has thus been elicited from actual experiments made public, regarding this agreeable and now highly important pursuit in rural life.

It is the object of the present paper to present the results of a practical experience in this department, in a familiar manner, and to offer for the benefit of the farmer, the breeder, and the amateur, certain facts and hints acquired by the writer through a long experience with, and a careful observation of, the habits, wants, and characteristics of domestic fowls; and to point at the probable profits attainable by breeding poultry and raising eggs for ordinary *market* purposes.

The *common* fowls of the country are at this time, of course, in great excess of numbers over any and all of the "fancy" breeds of late introduced among us, from abroad. Yet it is a notable fact that, by means of the importations of foreign blood made within the last dozen years, and especially through the introduction of the large Chinese variety (*Gallus giganteus*) amongst our farmers and poulterers since 1850, the distinctive characteristics of this race of birds are now very widely disseminated among the domestic fowls of America; and it would be unusual at the present day to meet with the flock in our farm-yards and poultry-houses about the country, where the marked features of the Chinese race of fowl are not to a greater or less extent visible.

That the mixing of this foreign blood with that of our own native races of domestic birds has proved of great advantage, no one who has bred poultry extensively in the last twelve or fifteen years will deny; and whether we consider the item of increase in *size and weight*, at a given age, attainable with certainty through the crossing of stronger foreign blood upon our native breeds, or that of the well-decided advantage thus obtained in the enlargement and increase of weight and numbers of eggs obtained from the product of this crossing, the general gain by the process is most clearly in our favor. It is, therefore, but truthful to premise that the mixture of the Chinese blood with that of the common fowl of the country has proved of great benefit, and that the continuance of the practice will be found of corresponding advantage in raising poultry for the market, inasmuch as the product of the crossing matures much earlier than does the old native stock, thus giving, within a shorter period, more pounds of flesh in good season; while, for the producing of eggs, the half-bloods are known almost uniformly to commence laying at a much earlier age than the common fowl, thus affording us eggs abundantly at from four and a half to five and a half months old, and afterwards. For these reasons the writer fully agrees with a recent English author of reliability and experience, that the introduction of the new races of fowls in late years "has resulted unquestionably in diffusing over the country greatly improved breeds of this interesting and useful kind of live stock; that more judicious modes of treatment than were formerly practiced have been made known; and that our markets certainly will by this means henceforth be more fully supplied with both eggs and fowls of a vastly superior quality."

Within the writer's experience, if from this cross chickens are hatched in the months of February and early March, the male birds, properly cared for, will by July and August attain to a generous size for the table, and, if well fed during this period, they will average a dressed weight of five or six pounds each, or eleven pounds the pair, which, at the ordinary value of poultry in market in the months last named, will afford a very handsome profit upon their cost and keeping. At about the period when the cocks are thus killed off, the pullets of this cross and age will begin to lay almost uniformly, and will continue to furnish eggs during the entire winter, coming in for sitters na'urally in the months of February and March, when their litters have been exhausted.

As to stock for *breeding* purposes, a selection is best made from the short-legged China (Shanghæ) *male* birds, to be introduced to the common native female stock. From their chickens, *selected* birds only should be kept for future breeding, and the cross thus obtained are best *bred back* to the China male again, reserving from season to season only the short-limbed and well-shaped pullets from this crossing for subsequent use. In this way the better characteristics of the foreign blood are more uniformly retained, though it will be necessary constantly, as above recommended, each year to select the most promising fowls in shape, size, &c., for breeding purposes; for it is a well-known fact that all crosses deteriorate after the first one.

For obtaining the greatest amount of eggs, or for the production of the best average quantity of flesh, fowls should never be kept beyond the age of two years old. It is well-settled that during the first year of her life a well-fed hen will lay more eggs than ever afterwards. From the end of her second year she begins to fail as a breeder, and chickens usually raised from old hen's eggs are never so vigorous, so healthy, or otherwise so promising as are those hatched from the eggs of young birds; that is to say, those from one to two years of age.

Male birds are in their prime only down to the end of the second year, and should not be kept for propagation beyond that period of life. For ordinary breeding purposes a vigorous young male bird will serve advantageously twelve or fifteen hens, the former number being preferable as a rule. The males should be changed every season from one flock of females to another, and no male bird should be permitted to run with the same hens during more than a single season, under any circumstances.

For the producing of eggs only, no male bird is necessary to be kept with the laying hens; and during the season of moulting it will be found of advantage, decidedly, to separate the cocks from the pullets altogether. These hints are offered for the consideration of those who desire to breed fowls systematically and to the best advantage in moderate quantities. Where large numbers of birds are kept, it is not absolutely necessary that these recommendations should be altogether observed; but for the purposes of comparatively " good breeding," making no pretension to simply keeping up a purity of race, but rather for the every day purposes of the farmer, who is satisfied with fair profits, and who breeds for the ordinary market, the hints proposed will be found generally advantageous. Late competent authority affirms that for breeding upon a large scale " only the best of both sexes should be selected, and these not too near akin."

If it suits the fancy or object of the owner, his fowls may be of several breeds, without any risk of intermingling, the select breeding stocks being kept up by merely changing the cocks every second year, and not more than one cock to thirty hens need be kept for the general stock, as it is of no consequence whether all the eggs are impregnated or not. This has reference not to high breeding for the show rooms, but to the production only of poultry-meat and eggs. The cost of fowl-keeping first and last, if all the necessary food is purchased at ordinary market prices, will average not far from ten cents a head per month. With the run of the farm-yard, however, and only a moderate number of fowls, the cost is much less. In large numbers, say hundreds or thousands, the expense of keeping will reach the first-named estimate fully, if the birds are confined to limited quarters. This sum is fixed for the food dealt out only, the additional expense of care, and interest upon investments for cost of buildings and fixtures, land occupied, &c., is not included, and must depend, of course, upon the extent of the establishment, the taste and means of the poultry-keeper, &c.

Where the fowls are kept for profit, and especially when large numbers are present, attention should be directed to saving the feathers taken from them, (if dressed for market,) and also the manure from the houses — no inconsiderable item of value each year. Wilson, in his "British Farming," says that "where a hundred common fowl and a dozen geese or ducks are kept, the quantity and value of the manure produced by them (but little inferior to guano,) if kept by itself and secured from the weather, will surprise those who have not made trial of the plan." Where five hundred or a thousand fowls or more are kept, the importance of this item will be worth remembering.

In raising poultry, whether the object be to produce chickens for the market, or to obtain a supply of eggs, the first principle to be observed is absolute cleanliness in and around the houses they occupy. During the brief fattening process, if this plan be adopted at all, a range for the birds intended to be slaughtered is not necessary. On the contrary, for two or three weeks devoted to finally fattening fowls for the spit, the more quiet they remain in their confinement (always supposing them to be kept cleanly and free from vermin) the better. For the London and Paris markets, light even is excluded from the fattening coops during the few weeks devoted to putting the fowls in their best condition before killing. But this process is of doubtful utility, and the "cramming" method in vogue among so many breeders is generally deemed not only inhuman, but is undoubtedly not remunerative.

Fowls collected together in any number will get sick, and the query is often made, "How can they be cured?" If the fowl houses are kept thoroughly dry and clean, and the poultry free from vermin, there will be but little sickness among the chickens. When the case occurs, however, remove the bird that droops, at once, knock it on the head, and bury it beneath the roots of the grape-vines. This will be a profitable and effectual riddance of sick fowls. Robert Scott Burn, in his "Lessons of my Farm," very rightfully asserts that "the cure of disease in ordinary fowls is not worth attempting, and the best way — mercilessly, or rather mercifully — is to devote the sick bird to the hands of the executioner. A fowl under the slightest sickness, deteriorates so fast in condition that it is best to kill it at once, and thus put it out of misery, and avoid contamination to its neighbors. Far "better kill than attempt to cure." It costs more than it is worth, and where there are numbers to contend with, the cure of fowl sickness is exceedingly difficult and uncertain." Such is my own experience, and such is my invariable disposal of sick chickens.

For both laying and breeding fowls a range is a necessity to their comfort, health and profitableness. Without this convenience, to a greater or less extent — and the more liberal the range the better — it is futile to attempt to grow fowls to profit, and idle to expect them to produce eggs regularly. Good range, pure water, dry shelter, animal food, and entire freedom from filth, are all needful to promote high health and continuous prosperity in the poultry yard; but more or less range for laying fowls is the first essential to their well doing. To afford this desirable accommodation space is required; and where a considerable number of birds is kept upon a single farm, the room assigned to each lot should be as liberally accorded as possible, in order to prevent immediate sickness among the stock, for the crowding of a large number of fowls into single enclosures is certain to generate roup and other diseases.

No. 5. DARK BRAHMA HEN, (drawn by H. Weir.)
The first sent to England, by G. P. Burnham. 73.

Fowls must be colonized, in small numbers, to be bred profitably. This, in my experience, has proved a *sine qua non*. According to the " ancient laws of Wales," the intrinsic value of poultry in England one thousand years ago, was very insignificant. " The worth of a goose," affirms this authority, at that period, " was one legal penny ; of a gander, two legal pennies ; of a brood goose the value of her nest ; of each gosling half a penny, until it lays, and afterwards a legal penny; a hen was one penny in value ; a cock two hens in value ; every chicken was a sheaf of oats, or one farthing in value until it roosts, and after that a half penny, until it shall lay or crow." This value was made up in the good old times, and contrasts singularly with the nominal value of certain fowls in the year of grace 1854–'55, for example, when cocks and hens of the then favorite breeds of imported Chinese stock commanded readily in England, as well as in the United States, such almost fabulous sums as five, ten, and even twenty guineas each! But neither the penny valuation of a thousand years ago, or the nominal pounds sterling value of the fancy breeds of 1854 '55, are of material consequence in this article, and we allude to the fact simply by way of comparison.

Of a more practical character are the estimates which follow. The London Board of Trade officially returns, as the number of eggs imported into England from France and Belgium for five years inclusive up to 1857, a yearly average of 147,342,219. For four years inclusive succeeding this period, that is, from 1858 to 1861, the average number annually imported was 163,581,140. In the year 1843 the number was but 70,515,931. In 1851 the number was 115,526,236, the amount of import duty paid during that year being £25,700, or about $128,000. In 1861 there were imported 203,313,310 eggs. At eight cents per dozen (the average wholesale market price realized) the money value of this single article for the year 1861 reached $1,355,542. This was for eggs alone, imported into England and sold in ordinary market to first hands at wholesale prices, and had no reference, of course, to the large quantities raised by England upon her own soil, and consumed by her home population in the interior.

In the year 1856 the value of poultry imported into England was £221,400. The annual increase of importation since then, up to the year 1859, was about twenty-nine per centum. In 1861 the whole value of eggs and poultry imported into England reached the extraordinary cash value of £385,000 sterling, or nearly $1,800,000. This has reference to the reported value of marketed poultry only, and includes no estimates at all of the large quantities grown and used at home, or the heavy sums paid for stock imported by breeders. During the last year (1861 to 1862) this vast valuation is very considerably increased, as the statistics clearly show.

In the vicinity of all large cities and towns fresh eggs are always in request, at the most remunerative prices. Every tiller of the soil possesses, more or less, facilities for feeding poultry economically, and has also the space upon his land to make them comfortable and thrifty. But some time must be given to looking after them daily, and a degree of *care* is requisite to keep them in " good heart," and to render them of profit in the end. Our Shorthorns and Alderneys, our Suffolks and Chesters, our Southdowns and Cotswolds, all require care to keep them in fine condition. Why not, proportionately so with our poultry, which, having reference to the comparative cost and product, pays with certainty so much greater a percentage of profit, year by year ? In France, every farmer has his chicken yard, and the amount of poultry and eggs consumed by, and exported from, that country is enormous. Monsieur de Lavergne, for example, estimates that the poultry of Great Britain for this year (1861–'62) is valued, in round numbers, at twenty millions francs, ($4,000,000,) while the total value of the two products — poultry and eggs — in France, at the same period, reaches rising two hundred millions of francs, ($40,000,000.) This last estimated product leaves a large margin for exportation from France over and above the requirements for home consumption, which surplus is sent over to England. These figures, relating to the quantities of poultry and eggs used and raised in France and England, are quoted, briefly, to afford an idea of the importance of this branch of rural economy in other countries, and thus to suggest its magnitude in our own.

In Paris and London, as in the large American cities also, the demand for early chickens (for the table) is always large and equally steady. Prime chickens command from nine to twelve dollars the dozen in American markets during the season. In England they bring from twelve to fifteen dollars per dozen. English farmers and poulterers, even at this day, are considered far behind either the French or Belgians in this branch of domestic economy. If our American farmers would pay more attention to this subject, and so manage as to put upon the market their poultry in good condition *early* in the season, annually, (say in the months of May and June,) a more than commensurate profit would follow the slightly increased expenses, and extra trouble of the earlier rearings, inasmuch as matured chickens will command a considerably higher price in the months of May and June than during July and August.

The most economical and advantageous mode of producing poultry and eggs for market has long been a mooted question; but favorable results depend principally upon the facilities at hand for multiplying fowls most readily *in quantities*. That poultry is, and can be, raised to profit in large numbers, is no longer problematical, the opinion of many modern writers upon this subject to the contrary notwithstanding. For instance: Monsieur De Sora, of France, who is the most extensive breeder of poultry in the known world, has been eminently successful in this business. His market for chickens and eggs is Paris, where tens of thousands of his *poulets* are annually disposed of for consumption in that city. But Monsieur De Sora has no use for setting hens. He raises all his chickens by artificial incubation, that is, by steam heat. His establishment is immense, and a large amount of capital is at present employed in the prosecution of his vocation.* Yet he began with a few hundred dollars only a few years ago, and has progressed, until now he employs over a hundred hands constantly in the different departments of his colossal poultry house. Monsieur De Sora's product of eggs during the last year averaged almost 50,000 dozen *weekly*, which, with the sales made of his early chickens, yielded him $280,000 gross, in round numbers. His expenses, all told, were some $145,000, leaving him a profit of $135,000, for the year, or 675,000 francs. He feeds his stock upon animal flesh chopped up, varying the fare with vegetables and grains cooked. During the three months in the fall of the year he sends to the Paris market over one thousand dozen fattened capons, say from September to the end of November. His process of artificial incubation is being carried on continually, but the bulk of his chickens are produced during the late winter months. His net profits are now estimated at about fifty per centum

---

* This description of "Monsieur De Sora's" establishment, and the accompanying statistics above given of his poultry operations, were gathered from an article in a leading American agricultural journal; and though they savored of monstrous dimensions, at the time, it was not thought to be au improbable account; since it is known that very large poultry-establishments were then in existence, near Paris, which supplied that chicken-loving city with its myriads of *poulets*. But, when the author was in France, he sought for "Monsieur De Sora," and could find neither him, nor this great establishment described. Though the consumption of chickens and eggs in Paris is enormous, the demand is supplied by a great *number* of poultry-raisers, in the suburbs of the capital — or *was*, before the late war there — none of which, however, as far as I could learn, approximate to the colossal size indicated in this paragraph, describing De So a's establishment. — G. P. B.

upon his gross annual receipts of nearly three hundred thousand dollars! To our vision these immense figures appear very formidable, but De Sora's poultry establishment is an enormous concern. During the year 1858, he wintered 100,000 birds, and in 1860 over 112,000 of the ordinary varieties, discarding, as he does, the Chinese breeds in their purity, altogether. His plan of producing chickens is almost identical with that of the Egyptians, who, it is known, raise enormous quantities of fowls by artificial heat for market with constant. success. This mode is not convenient or feasible, however, in this country, as a rule. The above instance is quoted merely to show that fowls *can* be raised *in quantities* to advantage. With our farmers the plans of nature must be followed and adopted.

Eggs must be raised in the natural way with us, and chickens are best produced through the ordinary process which has been so long in vogue with us, to wit: the sitting of hens. A western journal estimated the value of eggs in the United States, in 1859, to be equivalent to one hundred and twenty-two millions of dollars, at eight cents per dozen. The New York Evening Post subsequently set down the value of eggs and poultry in the United States, in 1861, at the enormous sum of two hundred and sixty-five millions of dollars, reckoning at New York market rates for these products. The shipment of eggs from a single county in the State of Ohio, over the railroads eastward, in one month, was recently officially reported to be 115,200 dozen. From the State of Maine thousands of barrels of eggs are shipped monthly to the Boston and New York markets. These facts are cited as instances only. When we consider the immense numbers of eggs used in home consumption in every locality of the country, annually, and the vast quantities that are shipped from the interior to all other cities and large towns on the sea-coast, as well as the great supply of poultry that is daily furnished to the chief marts of the country, in addition to both the poultry and eggs which are consumed by all classes of Americans from their private domains, the calculations above noted are by no means unreasonable, though at first sight they appear almost fabulous.

In lesser establishments, such as seem to be sufficient for, and to satisfy the taste of the occupants of most farms in the country, where the raising of poultry is not made a speciality, the most indifferent accommodations are deemed ample for the comfort and welfare of the fowls ordinarily connected with the place. A simple lean-to, an out-building, a rickety shed attached to the barn side, the barn itself — without other provision — in the estimation of many farmers, is considered " well enough " for the use and convenience of the chickens. But where one or two hundred fowls can just as well be profitably kept in a thrifty condition as a dozen or two can be neglected and starved, it is well that every farmer should look at this item of live stock, and bear in mind that, with ordinary care, (considering the necessary investment of capital and the trouble of its keeping,) *no* live stock will return him anything like so generous a percentage upon his money as will his too often neglected poultry.

As a rule, the poultry-house or houses are better placed, all things considered, with the aspect facing towards the east and south, with high rear and side walls upon the north and west sides for the hatching coops, to ward off the cold winds and effects of storms, more especially in our northern and eastern States. Shelter and warmth, in bad weather, are as requisite to the continuous prosperity of poultry as are cleanliness and food. During the severe winters experienced in our northern latitude, domestic fowls will neither lay, nor be free from various diseases, if exposed to rough weather or the chilling winds."

FIG 1—A CHEAP AND GOOD POULTRY HOUSE.

CHAPTER VII.

ILLUSTRATIONS OF POULTRY-HOUSES AND COOPS.

"A cheap and good style of fowl-house may be constructed with a partial glass front and end, facing as above indicated, the sash running from just above the sill towards the peak, and upon the side towards the eaves, of any desired dimensions, upon the following plan:

Such a house has been in use for several years by the writer, and has been found to answer admirably for sitters, as for layers, with a slight change in the interior arrangements, from one season to another. The glass used may be of the very cheapest quality, "blistered" or "wavy" being as good as any; and the glazing may be such as serves for the ordinary greenhouse roofing, that is, lapped upon the edges, and done at moderate cost. This affords light and ample oppor-

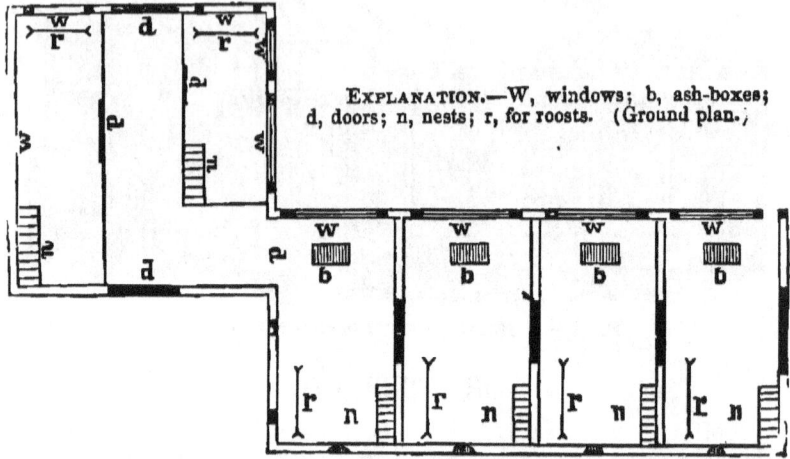

EXPLANATION.—W, windows; b, ash-boxes; d, doors; n, nests; r, for roosts. (Ground plan.)

tunity for warmth from the sun's rays continually, and has been found the most economical and comfortable of all styles of *winter* poultry house. The wing may be of any length. Clay-beaten floors beneath the roosting places are economical, easily cleaned, and afford slight attractions for vermin. Half round roosts of large sized spruce poles are the most comfortable, and these should be movable, to set upon cross-stilts not over two or three feet from the ground or floor. If these roosts are covered with strips of old woolen cloth, (tailor's list is best,) which, at nightfall, once a week, in warm weather, may be wet with spirits of turpentine or kerosene, the process will serve the double purpose of keeping the roosts free from vermin, and of freeing the bodies of the fowls from this same annoyance. Access to a gravelled walk or yard at the rear, in fine weather, is indispensible. A grass enclosure, if practicable, upon which fowls can range daily, is a desideratum in summer. In the rear of the above described house, was alloted half an acre for this purpose. In the absence of these two last mentioned almost *necessities* to the high health of domestic fowls, fresh gravel and sand, broken shells, &c., and green food of some kind, as cabbage leaves, ruta-baga tops, turnip leaves, grass, or the like, should frequently be thrown within their reach, which they will devour with avidity, and which will greatly tend to their continual improvement. Old mortar or oyster shells, broken up, are excellent for variety, if accessible.

The house already described (figures 1 and 2) may be used for laying hens during the fall and winter, and for sitters in early spring time. From such a house the chickens, when strong enough, may be transferred to the *open* or "summer" coops mentioned hereafter, and shown in figures 3, 4 and 5. It must not be forgotten that thorough ventilation of the poultry house is a *sine qua non*. Pure air, and plenty of it, when not freezing cold, is as desirable to fowls as to man. A dust-bath, formed of screened coal or wood ashes, is a luxury for fowls confined in limited accommodations. The premises described should always be kept as cleanly as possible, and at least, semi-annually whitewashed upon the inside. The water furnished poultry should be pure, and if a stream runs through the enclosure all the better; if not, fresh water should be supplied them regularly, and the vessels from which they drink should never be suffered to stand in the sun, at any season.

Fowls drink a great deal, daily. They should always have plenty of water — fresh, clean, and cool. From long experience and observation, the writer feels assured that no dumb creature better appreciates this provision for its health and comfort than does the domestic fowl.

In a recent address before the French Academie des Sciences at Paris, M. Genin declared that, after a careful study of three years upon the subject, and from repeated actual experiments, he could confidently state that the sex of eggs may be determined as follows: "Eggs containing the male germ can be distinguished by their elongated form, and a partially raised or ringed surface around the small end of the shell, while those containing the female germ are comparatively smooth, and more equally of a size at both ends." The writer has tried many experiments upon this theory, with but fair success. Though not invariable, this simple rule, in the selection of eggs for sitting, is comparatively safe. The remarks thus far submitted, have reference, in a general way, to the keeping of poultry upon an ordinary scale. With slight daily care and attention, as above hinted, any farmer can keep his hundred or two of fowls, which may readily be tended and provided for by the boys upon his estate, or even by the women of the household. From two hundred birds thus disposed he may obtain, annually, two thousand three hundred dozen of eggs, and, if inclined, at least fifteen hundred pounds of marketable chickens, before the close of August in each year. The products will pay him from four hundred and fifty to five hundred dollars *in money*, and leave him his original stock for the next year. His expenses will be not over two hundred to two hundred and fifty dollars, thus furnishing him with an equal sum of profit upon say two hundred fowls. Half this number will afford him half as much certain income, or nearly so. The cost of keeping fowls in such quantities as are alluded to, would not exceed sixty-five cents per head, if all their food is purchased and corn be rated at seventy cents the bushel. With the run of the farm, of course, the expense would be lessened. This leaves a handsome profit upon the investment.

The calculation here made as to returns in eggs, is set down at an annual yield of 140 eggs to each hen. This is fully up to the average, under the best care, and upon high feed. Some fowls will lay more than this number, but these are exceptions. From 120 to 140 eggs, yearly, is a generous supply, and I have never known any fowls except the Chinese, or the cross already described, that would accomplish more than this. The hen spoken of by some writers that "lays every day in the year" is a myth. By extra attention and care as to cleanliness and range in summer, with warm shelter and animal food in w'nter, fowls may be made to lay somewhat more liberally than is stated. But this forcing is done at too great a pecuniary cost, and also at the expense of their health, for they quickly become exhausted and worthless by the process. Hens will lay only a given number of eggs *annually*, and it is only by hatching your chickens early in the spring that they mature in season to lay during the succeeding fall and winter. The secret of having hens to *lay in winter* lies not (as asserted by some) so much in feeding them peculiarly, at that season, as in the simple fact of *hatching out the pullets in the right month of the year* to bring them to maturity in the fall.

As to the feed, variety is essential to the high condition and health of the birds. Fowls permitted to run at large, it will always be observed, are continually on the lookout for change in their diet. Insects, grasshoppers, worms, stray bits of animal and vegetable food, are devoured by them greedily at all times, and are sought for in every cranny and corner. Grains, bread crumbs, small bones, &c., are very grateful to them. So it is better to follow nature, in feeding them, as closely as possible.

For fattening fowls the best corn is the cheapest standard for food in this country. Boiled rice and potatoes and shorts or "middlings" of wheat are excellent. Small potatoes and broken or even "damaged" rice, which can usually be readily obtained in any large city, serve an admirable purpose, and will be found economical for every-day feeding. Occasional allowances of barley or oats, or both, are highly advantageous to laying fowls. Sunflower seeds, which can be so easily grown profusely along the entire range on both sides of all fences, without taking up room or causing any trouble save the original planting, are one of the very best alteratives and changes in diet that can be obtained, and fowls will devour these with a gusto, always. In the writer's judgment, fowls should never be stinted in food. As much as they will eat without waste, and of the best, is deemed the most economical in the end ; and this method will keep poultry always in good condition for the spit at brief notice, while laying fowls are thus continuously supplied with the material for affording the largest number of eggs regularly after they begin to lay. When the poultry is necessarily confined within enclosures, coarse meat, such as sheeps' plucks, liver, the harslets of swine, pounded bones, obtainable at the nearest slaughter-house at very trifling cost, should be given them as frequently as thrice a week. They will devour this food eagerly, and it supplies the place of that which they need and obtain when allowed to range at liberty. Where large quantities of fowls are kept, they must of necessity be confined in colonies, to comparatively limited quarters, and artificial high feeding becomes necessary, while some sort of animal food is requisite to keep them laying, and in good condition.

Male chickens intended for the market may be kept together advantageously in considerable numbers in the same coops, if brought up together from the outset. No pullets should ever be placed in these cages or yards. As fast as the birds reach the proper size and weight for killing, they should be disposed of. For this particular purpose, cock chickens are the most profitable, as they furnish more meat at a given age, and are of no account (in numbers) otherwise, after they attain to a size suitable for the table.

FIG. 3 — RANGE OF SUMMER OPEN CHICKEN HOUSES — FRONT.

These male birds should be well fed from the shell. They will generally pay a large profit upon the investment, and may be killed at from four to six months old.

The plan of a fowl house already given (see figures 1 and 2) is such as the writer had in use for some years, in size, proportions, and appointments. Below is the design of houses adopted by him also for many years for summer use only, in which large numbers of chickens are annually raised for the market, and which are built at trifling cost.

FIG. 4. — SUMMER OPEN CHICKEN HOUSES — REAR.

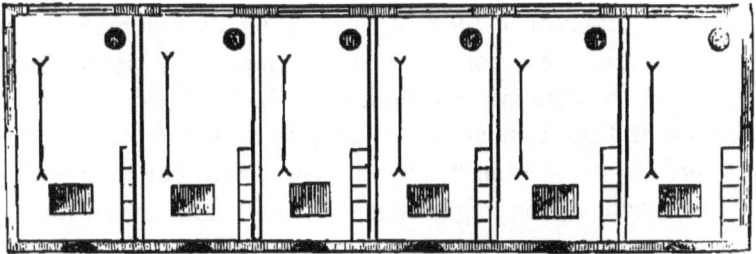

FIG. 5.—GROUND PLAN OF OPEN SUMMER CHICKEN COOPS.

Six of the compartments (or coops) are under one roof, and four different houses stand at the four angles of an oblong square of land half an acre in extent, thus:

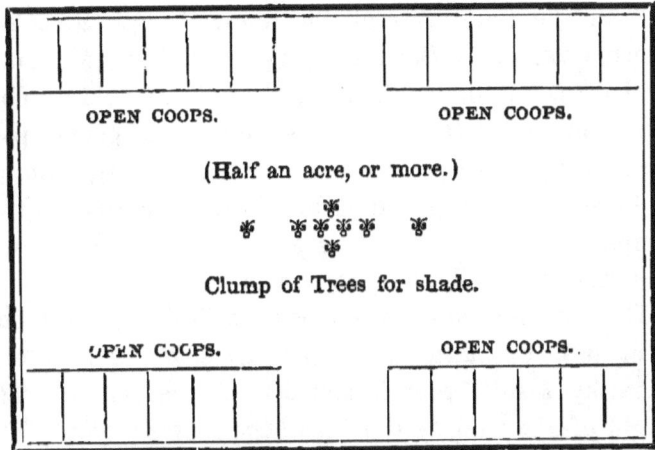

This arrangement colonizes the different lots of chickens, with the mothers, from March or April to June and forward, and separates each from interference with the others. The land might be subdivided into four lots, but the expense of fencing would be considerable, of course, and has not been found necessary upon the writer's system of management. In each of the six *coops* indicated, have been kept from early March or April, twenty-five or thirty chickens, with two or three hens each, the aggregate upon the half acre in the four *houses*, averaging during the summer 600 to 650 chickens, raised for and sold in market from June to August. A portion of the chickens, say one-fourth, are allowed to run into the whole lot (which is in grass) during three or four hours daily, when they are driven in and another fourth part are released for exercise.

One house is usually devoted to male birds, exclusively. In the fall, a few of the finest of both sexes are selected to add to the next year's breeding stock, and the balance, seven or eight months old, are sold for consumption, at thirteen to fourteen cents per pound, paying a profit of 40 per centum at least, on cost, interest on investment, keep and care. During the season, fine samples of birds for breeding purposes are sold in limited numbers, readily, at better rates even.

These open or summer coops described, are constructed of laths or paling-stuff upon all sides, and are protected by a shed roof, battened over the seams. The height of the front is eight feet, the rear six feet. The doors (to each subdivision) are also made of the same open or lattice-work, or palings, and each *division* is twelve feet by seven. The six divisions make each *house* about forty feet by twelve. This is cheaply built, but is ample for all the purposes of raising the chickens to marketable condition, from the time they leave the hatching-house with the hen-mothers, as described.

The floors of the houses should never be *boarded*. The earth is much better, cheaper and healthier. The roosts described are movable (being rested upon crotches) and may be set up in any portion of the coops where most convenient. If the floor is kept hard and dry, the sweepings from the cages may readily be saved and removed to the compost-heap, twice a week or oftener. In any of the northern States, even, such coops as the above (for summer months) are far preferable to close houses of any kind, for the rearing of chickens. The boarding of the roofs, and partially down the sides from the eaves to the lathing, (as shown in the engraving,) affords ample protection from the wet weather, and the young birds are thus early inured to the open air, and invariably do well with good feed and the daily run they have in the grass plat in front.

The winter laying and sitting house described below, (figures 7 and 8) may be also used for summer chicken-raising, if desired. The sashes in front can be taken out and lattice-work substituted; or the frames of the windows can be covered with two-inch mesh-wire screening, which is inexpensive and very durable. By this change the poultry-house is rendered cool and airy, which for the "heated term," would be found too close and warm, for summer use, with the glass windows. This house should be carefully cleansed in the spring, after the early chickens are removed to the open coops, which should be located, of course, on another part of the lot, and if in the whitewash-tub is thrown a pound or two of powdered sulphur, the wash will be greatly improved, so far as aiding to destroy any vermin present is concerned.

The lattice-coops will have already been cleansed, of course, for the reception of the young birds. The entire fixtures in these chicken-houses consist of a water-vessel for each, a feed-box, a low roost upon brackets, and a dust-box, two feet square for ashes. Into this latter it has been found a good plan to mix with the ashes a handful of powdered sulphur, occasionally, which helps to destroy vermin. In a few weeks from their entrance to these coops, the chickens will follow the mothers to the low roosts, and I have never found any difficulty in keeping two or three hens with their broods in each of these compartments. Beneath the eaves front and back, a board a foot wide forms a facia, beyond which (upon the lowest side) the roof overhangs about five inches, to carry off the rain. The whole arrangement is put together of rough boards and laths or fence-palings, and its cost is very moderate. I have had these in use, now, for twelve years, and have found them all that is needed for *summer* houses for market poultry.

Now, if six hundred chickens can be produced thus successfully upon a half-acre lot, no good reason naturally appears that *any* given number may not be similarly raised — for market purposes, be it remembered - and kept, advantageously, from the early hatching period suggested, through the summer months, while the weather will commonly permit of their being left comparatively *in the open air*. To attempt to *house* large numbers of fowls in close quarters during the severe winters at the north, is not recommended. Thus in order to raise chickens by hundreds or thousands, a great deal of space is necessary, as I have already aimed to show.

Now, when winter approaches, and the weather gets too cold for comfort, upon the plan suggested, all the previous spring and early summer chickens will from time to time have matured and been disposed of, and only the fowls for winter laying and the next spring sitting remain on hand. The accommodations of the previous year are now used for the convenience of these birds, say from October to February, and March, and the hatching of *their* broods, subsequently — their chickens, in turn being transferred, in due time, to the open cages described.

For the accommodation of the *layers*, and afterwards for the sitters in early spring-time, the plan on the following page is in use by the writer. (Fig. 7. and 8.) This house for sitters and layers, furnished with great simplicity, has been found ample for the purposes indicated. The building was erected ten years since, of rough No. 4 boards, set upright upon a two by four-inch joist frame-work, with four-inch corner-posts and centre-studs, and is battened upon the outside (over the seams) with three-inch paling-stuff. The roof was finished in the same manner, but shingling is better for this purpose. The corner-posts of the central portion of the building are sixteen feet high, the pitch is " one-third,"

FIGURES 7 AND 8.

GROUND PLAN AND ELEVATION.

and the dimensions of this part are seventeen by fifteen feet. The two wings (as shown in the elevation) are shed-roofed, falling back from the front, are twelve feet high, running down to seven and a half feet in rear, fifteen feet wide, and extend right and left from the outside of the central building, in each direction forty-five feet, making the whole house ninety-six feet long by fifteen feet in width, except the centre, which (for ornament in this instance) projects out two feet in front, as shown.

This house is surmounted by a cupola five feet square, with a vane, which adds to the comeliness of the premises, but need not be indulged in except to suit the taste of the builder. The central portion is *two* stories high, as is Fig. 1. The upper loft is floored over, and is useful for storing grains and vegetables, corn, &c., and can be turned to good account for cooking food for your fowls, if desired, or, by a proper contrivance, can be made the centre for a heating apparatus to add to the comfort of the birds (with pipes running right and left) during the coldest of weather. This loft is approached by a ladder from the rear, outside, through a door above the upper floor in the gable end. The building may be whitewashed upon the exterior, and made to look clean and respectable, or it can be clapboarded and painted to correspond with the residence or other farm buildings. To economize the cost it may be put up with boards and battenings simply, with the commonest glass sashes — tight, comfortable, and very serviceable, at moderate expense, and will last many years, if properly *framed*. The sashes are upon a line in front, and are glazed in the manner already indicated in plan, Fig. 1. In this house about fifty hens can be conveniently set at one time — say, in the ten apartments* five each — who will not interfere with each other if properly cared for, daily. During the late fall and winter months, this building will accommodate, in its ten divisions, over a hundred laying hens comfortably.

During the early spring, an average of a dozen eggs may be placed under your sitters, and, with good luck, four hundred chickens may be produced, and these from the earliest broods. These may be removed in due time to the "open houses," and another fifty hens may be placed upon the nests vacated by the first ones, who, with proper care, will bring out another four hundred chickens, more or less, say in six weeks after the earlier sittings. It will be understood that upon the removal of the first broods, the sitting boxes should be nicely cleansed before the second hens are placed upon the nests. By the time the second broods come off, it will be the last of March or the first of April.

All the young stock may be safely transferred to the open houses by the beginning of May, where they can thenceforward be fed and cared for as previously directed, and fitted, like their predecessors of the year before, for the summer and fall market. From the new stock the best samples of pullets are selected again, to

---

* The length of page in this Poultry Book is insufficient to show the *ten* compartments, so we show only *eight*. They are all alike, however.

add to the next year's breeding stock, as before; the old fowls (two years of age) are killed, the young cocks are all put in separate houses, to be used for the earliest maturing and largest chickens, and affairs go on during the fall, as during the season previous.

By adopting the plans thus laid down, with the buildings and appointments herein suggested, a thousand chickens can be readily and profitably raised for the summer market, annually, while ample conveniences are thus afforded, also, for at least one hundred laying hens during the winter months in the glazed house, (Figs 7 and 8.) If the desire be to raise *more*, increased space must be accorded to your fowls, and more buildings should be erected. It will not answer to increase the huddling of the birds under one roof. If the buildings are *smaller* even than those described, and more numerous, being scattered over acres, instead of confining the stock mentioned to half an acre, and to a building of the size given, it will be all the better for the general health of the birds, undoubtedly. Crowding fowls into too narrow a space, is one great cause of the fatalities attending the attempt to breed them.

Fresh air, light, cleanliness, varied fare, pure water, range, grass or occasional green and animal food, shelter from wet and raw winds, with plenty of gravel and ashes to roll themselves in, are all requisites to success. With these advantages and fair attention, provision being made for the warmth and comfort of the laying hens in *winter*, chickens can be raised for the table and for market in any quantities, and to highly satisfactory profit; and eggs in abundance may also be had, in any dry location within reasonable distance of the larger cities and towns of America, as has been proved through years of experience, and of successful experiments."

An infallible mode for preserving eggs fresh and in perfect condition through the year, is given in chapter XXIX. This plan is for saving eggs for consumption, or sale, only -- *not* for future hatching, of course. In July and August, eggs are worth a cent and a half each, on the average. This is the time to "lay them down" most economically. From Thanksgiving to Christmas, they bring three to four cents apiece. The gain to any family, by this simple and certain means, (or to the egg-seller,) is apparent. The cost of the process is but nominal.

The sale of poultry, dead or alive, in France, is conducted on an admirable and judicious plan; much better than is our system of marketing this article, in America. All the poultry is sold in Paris, at La Vallee, the metropolitan market, at auction, daily. The chief city agents, to whom the farmers consign their poultry, eggs and butter, are licensed by the authorities, who sell it at public vendue, at a certain hour, and forestalling is unknown there. The highest bidder gets the poultry, and the scene at these sales is a very interesting and active one. So in the smaller towns. At the ringing of a bell, the crates, boxes and baskets are first uncovered, and the bidding is very lively, for choice, the buyers taking their position outside the marketplace; and in a little time after the opening, thousands of eggs and thousands of chickens are knocked off to the highest offers, to be sent at once to London, Paris, &c., for consumption.

"PLYMOUTH ROCK" FOWL.

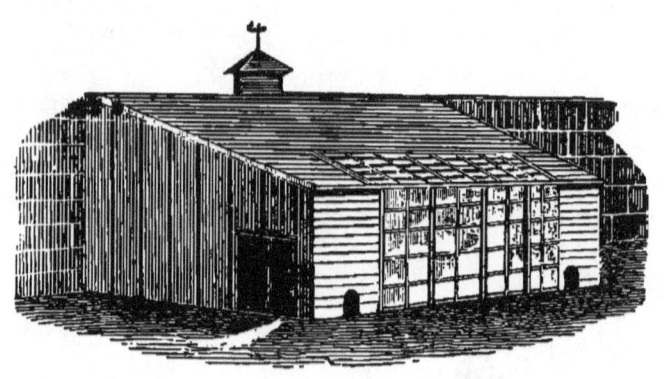

CHAPTER VIII.

MODERN FOWL-HOUSES, COOPS, CHICKEN-CAGES, ETC.

Having given in the last chapter economical plans of some of our own Fowl-houses, Summer-coops for chickens, etc., we will now offer other illustrations possessing merits, both exteriorly and interiorly; and the first is that of a very convenient well-fashioned one, ventilated at the top.

The above cut represents a very good and cheaply constructed Fowl-house, with glass sash-front, mostly facing the south and east. It is simple, yet ample to shelter a moderate number of chickens, in winter; and if it can be thrown up (with the right aspect) the back side against a high stone wall, or upon a barn side, out of the way, it can be built for a trifle. The door may be on either side, and fowls can enter or leave it from the front, as shown in the engraving. The sash may be run up, on the front of the roof, four to six feet; which lets in more sun and light. It can be divided by a slat partition, inside, and two varieties can thus be kept to advantage — letting the fowls out for a run alternately, a few hours, daily. The arrangement of the nests, roosts, etc., can be similar to other plans to be found in our pages; and the size of it may be 30ft, front, by 20 deep, to afford accommodation for a dozen to twenty fowls, in each side, amply — if care is taken to keep them cleanly, constantly. The height can be four to five feet front, run up back to ten or twelve feet, as convenient. This proportion of slant will serve to carry off the rains. The roof-sash should be laid on in the green-house form, in order that the water may run off free over the eaves. Here is a very nice arrangement for late winter and the spring season.

GLASS CHICKEN-HOUSE, GREEN-HOUSE PLAN.

The above is a plan for a half span glass-roofed

house, put up on my own premises some years ago, and of another of the same class in use by my next-door neighbor, for a cold grapery, originally; but serving admirably for the raising of young ea*ly* broods of chickens, in which they grow finely. My own is 60 by 16 feet, with a plank tan-packed double partition-wall on the north side. The top and other three sides are all glazed, in the usual green-house mode. The range of small lower sashes (beneath the front eaves) open at pleasure, for ventilation; the framework inside of the sashes being covered the whole length with coarse wire screening, to prevent the birds from getting out, when the windows are open. Entrance on the west end. For chickens hatched in March and April, this has proved a most excellent shelter, and they have come along during these cold months, and on through May, very rapidly — under the genial warmth that pervades the interior of this glass-house in sunny weather. It is more expensive than some others, but I have found it an excellent arrangement for the young chicks, during the early inclement New England weather. And for valuable fancy stock, nothing in the way of a spring fowl-house can excel it.

"Topknot," in the N. Y. Bulletin, says — one of his fowl houses, is built as follows. Size thirty feet long, by sixteen feet deep, posts eight feet high — boarded and battened. Roof pitching both ways and covered with cement and gravel. Three windows in front and rear, two feet high and six feet long, close up under the eaves, so as to give a good circulation of air above the fowls; sliding skylights in the roof in front, which together with the other windows have wire netting, and are kept open, except in the coldest of the weather. The floor is rat-proof, being made of cement grouting; one third of it is six inches higher than the rest, and kept clean to feed on. The low part has three inches of sand upon it, and over this the fowls roost. The perches are hung on hinges to the side of the building, and are raised up in the day time, and when let down for use at night, are 20 inches above the floor. It is very important for large fowls that the roosts should be large, so that they can sit comfortably on them and not injure their breast bones, and close to the floor, so that that they will not injure themselves in coming down. The building, which fronts southeast, and is lath-and-plastered, is divided in three rooms, with board partitions three feet high, and wire netting above. Large yards for each, with fence four feet high, which is sufficient for Asiatic fowls, also extra yards to change and give the grass a chance to grow. This will give the reader some idea of what the writer thinks a model Fowl house.

Among the best patterns of American poultry-houses, is that of Mr. John C. Wells, of Athens, Pa., though it is not a very large one. But for the ordinary fancier, or breeder of two or three varieties of fowl, it is ample. He describes it as 40 feet in length, 12 feet walls, and 10 1-2 feet to the roof-peak. It is of a light frame, ceiled outside, the roof boarded and shingled. It is divided into six compartments, five being devoted to

the fowls. The first compartment is for setting hens,
&c. These divisions are 9 by 10 feet, separated from
each other by a picket and slat fence. In each part
are five nests, a neat drinking fountain, boxes of ground
bone, gravel, ashes, etc., with a feed gutter, slatted
across to prevent the birds from fouling or wasting
their food.

Large windows of 30 lights of glass each, 8 by 10,
light up the interior, and afford the fowls plenty of sun;
and at the south end are other windows used for ventilation, &c. There are six outer yards, one for each
compartment, 80 feet by 10 feet. The premises are
painted outside, whitewashed inside, and the floor is of
gravel. Mr. Wells breeds the Dark and Light Brahmas,
Houdan, Black Spanish and White Dorkings. He has
some fine spring chickens, and his manner of raising
them proves very satisfactory. He has no gapes, nor
has his chickens been troubled by vermin. He sets his
hens in small kegs with the tops out, covered with wire
netting; a hole is cut in the side for the hen to go in
and out, and the inside is white-washed, or washed with
kerosene oil. (The latter is a very good plan.)

When he has a hen that is broody, he scalds the keg
with boiling water, to cleanse it, makes a nest with cut
hay or straw, and to keep the lice out he either places
tobacco leaves in the bottom of the keg, or wood ashes
and sulphur. When the chickens are hatched, he removes all pieces of shell and bad eggs from the nest,
and does not disturb them again for 24 hours, when he
feeds them with hard boiled eggs, crumbled. In about

two days he removes them from the nest and puts them in a coop with a wooden floor, covered with dry earth, and when they are two or three weeks old, they are taken from the hen, and put in charge of his "Artificial Mother," until they are old enough to roost, then they are placed in other quarters. (This artificial mother is A. M. Halsted's, of Rye, N. Y., we are informed,) and Mr. Wells says of it that "it works splendidly, and everybody is in ecstacies over it." (See page 132.)

In the rear of Mr. Wells' six yards is a very large grass plat, enclosed by a tight board fence, 9 feet high; and his fowls have access to this run, alternately, through small gates at the foot of the yards. Mr. W. has latterly found it necessary to sheathe his building, and has done so with felt and siding, which increases the warmth inside greatly, in cold weather. This building, complete, cost $600. But it could be built for less. We have one on a similar plan, of our own, described hereafter, glazed, whitened, battened, etc., 30 by 25, in three divisions, that cost less than $300, all told. Two hundred dollars ought to build and equip a very good fowl-house, large enough for summer and winter uses, with good yard-range accommodations outside, for all the purposes of an amateur who breeds only two or three varieties.

Here is another plan, copied from "Tucker's Annual of Rural Affairs," very good, and quite inexpensive. This is large enough to afford interior accommodations for thirty fowls, and is proposed to be built ten by sixteen feet. It is thought by another writer in the U. S.

Report quoted from, that fifty fowls would not overstock such a house, but he adds, at once, that "experience teaches us that it is unsafe to house in one apartment *more* than fifty fowls, at the same time, and even with that number, ventilation should always be free, during the coldest of weather." Ventilation should be good and ample, *always*, and thirty chickens would be enough to house within such limits as are described below, for this

NEAT AND CHEAP POULTRY-HOUSE.

Let the house face the east or southeast; and it would be an improvement to stud the building all round with three-inch studs, and to line it with inch matched stuff. It should be covered with sound, matched boards, and battened. The spaces between the studs should be filled in with dry tan; and it would add greatly to its warmth to make the roof double also, and fill as at the sides. The floor should be ten or twelve inches higher than the earth on the outside of the building, and the best material of which to make it is a mixture of sand and gravel, pounded down very firmly. Plant deciduous trees thickly about the house to keep it cool in summer. Perches for the Shanghæ and Dorking should not be over two or three feet high; for Spanish, about four feet; and for Games and Hamburgs, five feet high would not be too much.

FIG. 1.— GROUND PLAN. FIG. 2 — A CROSS SECTION.

These two last cuts above, show (1) the lower arrangements inside, with roosts, nest, &c.; and the other (2) the end elevation. The writer continues to commend what we have already advised — that every house should have its dry dust-bath box, lime, pounded oyster-shells, etc., and fresh pure water, daily. Here is a handy portable "tent-coop," for either a sitting hen, or hen and chickens, for the first month or two after hatching, and a slatted feeding gutter.

FEED-TROUGH AND TENT-COOP.

This coop is battened and made like the pitch-roof of a house or barn, 2 feet high, 4 feet square, simply; has *no* floor, but is held together at the two ends by a four-inch cross-strap of boarding; slatted in front so the hen cannot get out, and the chickens can; and may be moved about and set in a new place daily, if desirable. The feed-trough is a broad gutter, with two square ends to hold it upright, and slatted across (as before explained) to keep the fowls from scattering their food. Both these are handy, and easily made.

In this same Department Report for 1862, another writer furnishes a few plans of cheap poultry-houses which we give here, and which are, briefly, thus described.

A PRETTY FOWL HOUSE.

"Let it front to the south and east; build with nine feet posts a room eight by thirteen feet, on the ground. This will accommodate two dozen fowls — sufficient for one family's use, or for breeding any single 'fancy' variety. A dove-cot can be arranged in one end if desired, to which one gable window will afford sufficient light for *that* purpose. The nest-boxes may be placed over the feeding-boxes, two or three feet from the floor, as may be convenient." (*We* should recommend that the size be at least ten by fifteen feet, however, since it costs little more, and is much more roomy than the above.) "Lay a tight matched floor about six feet above the lower floor. The roosting-poles should be placed crosswise of the gable, and near the stairway, commencing at the bottom next the stairway, the first about eighteen inches distant and so on to the top. The loft should be cleaned daily, or have a daily sprinkling of dry black muck, or disintegrated burnt clay, or burnt plaster; the whole to be removed frequently, and carefully put into barrels or boxes under cover, for the future use of the farm or garden. A door should be made in the rear-side of the dove-box for its frequent cleaning. A trap-door may be made over the back end cf the entry, to be reached by a perpendicular round ladder, to get to the dove-box."

A very well contrived coop for a hen and chickens, was awarded a prize at the late N. Y. show, and the following account of it is given in the Poultry Bulletin. It is both simple and practical, and any one can readily make it on the farm.

This handy contrivance is made as follows. "The floors are two feet wide and four feet long, on half of which, is built a house two and a half feet high to the peak; half of the roof is on hinges, to facilitate the cleaning of the coop, a sliding door is in the back, and a small hole with wire netting on in the peak for ventilation. The other half of the floor has a glazed frame on it, twelve inches high at the house, and eight at the end; the sash hinged, through which the chickens may be fed, the sides have sliding doors, to be closed at night, which makes it rat proof. This makes a nice place for the chickens to run and feed in, during a storm, and in the mornings before the grass is dry." It may be made somewhat larger than this, to advantage, we should say. But the general *plan* is a very good one. And below is a simple ground-plan for a cheap hen house and yard for the use of one variety, say 30 to 50 fowls.

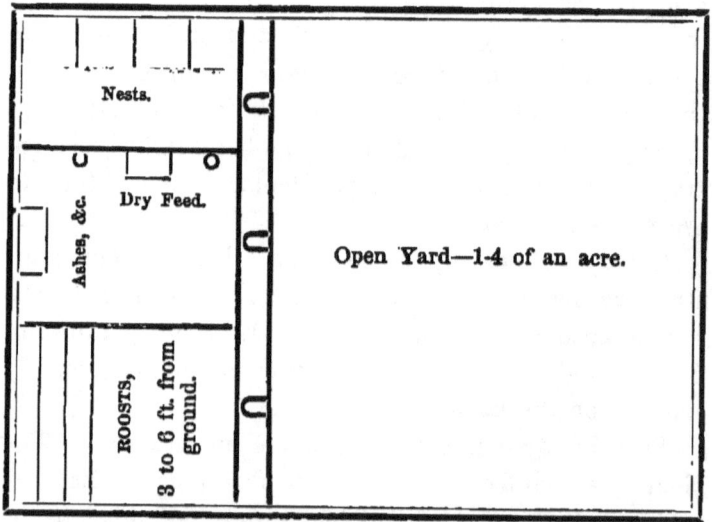

GROUND PLAN OF YARD AND FOWL HOUSE.

Let the aspect be to the south, or south-east, and make your three apartments by slat partitions, with doors to communicate, about 10 by 20 feet each — the central (feeding) one the largest perhaps. Fence the yard with palings four to six feet high, according to the kind of fowls you keep. Fit their roosts one above another, two feet apart, from three to six feet high. Keep your box of dry feed, ashes, etc., in the middle room. Place half a dozen nests in the end apartment; make these in boxes 12 to 14 inches square and deep. Have your open yard or run, a quarter of an acre if possible, or larger, if you have spare land. A half or quarter of this open space will answer, if kept clean. But fowls love range, and room to roam in. Light it from the front south side, with sash from the ground sill upward, to eaves. It may be a lean-to, or pitched roof, battened — 8 foot corner posts — fowl entrances from yard — main door outside at either end.

I still adhere to the opinion as expressed in my paper quoted from the Department Report, that " it will not answer to increase the huddling of birds under one roof," and that " crowding fowls into too narrow a space is one great cause of the fatalities attending this attempt to breed them." Yet I believe that if the general directions contained in this and the last chapters are followed out as therein proposed, large numbers of chickens and eggs can be so raised *for market purposes*, to advantage.

The fact will not be lost sight of here, that through the mode I have there suggested, the great *bulk* of the chickens so raised will be disposed of during the summer, to be eaten, at so much per pound, dead weight. Thus the stock brought up from spring to autumn will be out of the way. No such numbers of fowls could be *wintered* within the accommodations of the poultry-houses therein described, of course; and this is not the purpose of the recommendations quoted.

The plan, however, has worked within the limits described to advantage, and as is proposed in the closing paragraphs of the article mentioned, if more than say a thousand chickens are to be raised, increased space must be accorded, and more buildings must be put up. Instead of half an acre, scatter the houses over acres, and " colonize " the birds at a distance from each other's premises. In no other way can you succeed.

RAT-PROOF CORN-BIN.

Here is a plan for a cheap rat-proof corn or grain house, which may be set upon stone or cedar posts, eighteen inches above the ground; to be built to suit the needs or convenience of the poulterer, in which may be safely stored corn and grain out of the reach of vermin. A small ventilator at the top serves to keep the contents from heating or mould, when stored within it in large quantities. The shape of this bin is smallest at the bottom, where the sills rest on square pieces of plank, 15 inches wide and long, fastened to the tops of the projecting piles (of stone or wood) as shown in the drawing. From this narrower foundation, the bin widens out at each side, to the eaves. It may be built of rough boarding, running up and down, and battened, roof and all. A slatted window, or blind, in front over the door, improves its appearance. No steps are necessary, unless it is preferred to have a flight hung upon hinges, to turn up, when not in use, outside the door. With this arrangement, the poultry-keeper may have a convenient depository for his grain, where rats cannot trouble him.

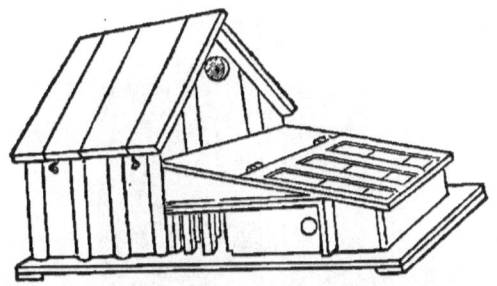

HEN AND CHICKENS' COOP. (Described on page 110.)

The "Patent Folding Coop," or Pen, is a very convenient and desirable invention, originated by G. E. Cleeton, of New Haven, Conn., intended for use in the Poultry Exhibition room, and which, for uniformity's sake, in our shows, we should say is just the thing for the purpose to which this seems admirably adapted. Fowls may be shown in this neat cage to good advan tage, as it is open at the top, front and back, and the judges can readily see and handle the fowls thus cooped. This cage of Mr. Cleeton's is not expensive, and *folds up* into a thin space, when not in use. It can thus be transported to and from a distance, easily. It is light, safe, strong, and pretty. Several premiums have been awarded this practical and useful coop, and it is certainly a very good and handy arrangement, as, during the journey, birds may be shipped in common boxes, and on arriving at their destination, the folding coops may be opened out, when the birds can be arranged for exhibition. The trouble and expense of sending a large number of ordinary coops has often deterred breeders from sending their birds to distant exhibitions.

COOP OPENED AND SET UP.

But we have now said enough of fowl-*houses.* The plans herein set down can be chosen from to suit the taste, means, and premises of the breeder or fancier, and he can expend twenty, fifty, or a thousand dollars on these structures, as he pleases. The most important point is to get the right aspect, and let into the house all the sun and light he can conveniently, in cold weather, especially if he attempts to hatch and raise chickens *early* in the season. The birds (of all larger breeds) that are successfully got out of their shells, and are subsequently best cared for *in the earliest months of the year*, are the ones that "loom up" in the succeeding fall and winter, for the shows; while pullets thus started, are sure to begin to lay much earlier than the later hatched ones, and usually prove the "all-winter-laying breed," we hear so much about.

But we must attentively follow *nature's* requirements, to breed poultry advantageously. Mr. R. H. Stoddard, of Hartford, writes correctly upon this point, when he avers, that "whenever we strive to make any animal live contrary to the habits its race has been for ages accustomed to, we find that nature, unwilling to be thwarted, revenges herself in some way. The *wild* hens, before they were taken from their native forests had pure air to breathe, the free breezes circulated through their leafy roosting apartment, and their range was covered only by the sky. For the reason why fowls in extremely *large* flocks refuse to lay freely, we must consult the conditions of nature. In the Indian jungles, the wild parent stock, like all allied species of fowls that live principally upon the ground, associate during the breeding season in small families, each having its male head, and appropriating an exclusive territory for a range. This being the law, as unalterable as that of the Medes and Persians, man must respect it. For three thousand years (perhaps six) men successfully kept domesticated fowls. They have succeeded by scattering *small* flocks in every village, thus unconsciously imitating the state of things in the jungles of India. Herded together in a multitude, the ancient instinct thwarted, the yields will not be nearly so great as they were in flocks of tens or twenties. Scores of illustrations in poultry-keeping might be given where nature resists infractions of her laws. It will not do to neglect any point, because it seems a small matter. No ordinance of nature is small."

The cause of the deficiency in the supply of poultry in the United States, it has been truly said, is found in the lack of careful, systematic enterprise among us. In certain locations, "fanciers" favor raising good birds, few in number, strictly for the show-rooms. Thousands of others pretend to "keep fowls," forgetting that with the right kind of systematic care, fowls may be made to keep them! Poultry-raising upon an *extensive* scale, is a business altogether different from all this. The demand in the markets of this country is ever increasing, for eggs and chickens, for absolute consumption. And we have endeavored to show (in the last two chapters) that this demand may be met, without limit, if the raising of poultry is conducted upon *system*.

But fowls should be attended to, like cattle, sheep, or other live stock — for they are more susceptible to diseases, and more delicate than the others. Many of the troubles incident to poultry may easily be prevented; for these come from ill management, or too often *no* management at all; and he who undertakes to raise poultry in quantities, by merely crowding hundreds of birds together within confined limits, will simply "have his labor for his pains," in the end.

At the same time, by colonizing his stock in convenient locations about the farm, or estate, each colony becomes a separate establishment, by itself; and the aggregate results will tell — however large the aggregate numbers may be.

Mr. E. C. Newton, of Batavia, Ill., has had but a few years' experience in poultry-breeding, but has been quite successful, and writes us in this wise, regarding his fowl-house and stock. He says: "Few people who have interested themselves in this pleasant business begun as *I* did. I was forced into the trade, because my neighbors' hens succeeded in scratching up my garden as fast as I could plant it! I purchased a few Black Spanish fowl, at first, and found they could not be beaten at laying eggs. My stock was out of birds imported from Scotland, and proved highly satisfactory, for one variety. I then remodelled my barn, and rendered it comfortable for my stock, and in the spring of '68, I bought a trio of the light Brahmas, from Massachusetts, with which breed I was greatly pleased. With care I raised 60 chickens, the first season. I then sent to Connecticut for eggs, and raised six fine Buff Cochins, a few Hamburgs, and Dominiques, Leghorns and Silver Polands. I kept only the Buff Cochins, however, until I heard of the dark Brahmas, and purchased my stock of these last at Philadelphia — adding to my flock of breeders some fine Houdans, from Taunton, Mass. Out of all these varieties, I raised 260 chickens, and in 1870 procured from New York a clutch of the Partridge Cochins — a splendid fowl — in my judgment.

I found my premises too contracted for my large and increasing fowl family, and then bought a thirty-acre farm near this city, moved on to it, and erected a spacious poultry-house 100 feet long, 12 to 20 feet in width, fronting south, well lighted and ventilated, and I am now located here, with what I consider a first class selected stock of five varieties, of which I send you illustrations, drawn from life, and which are considered all *good* birds. My poultry-house is after a plan of my own. It is divided into ten apartments, one for boxing and packing fowls, etc., and the other nine partitioned off for the fowls' convenience. The partitions are of wire-work, and you can stand at one end and look through the whole length of the building, inside. Outside I have ten large yards divided by a seven foot fence of pickets, and my doors are arranged with wire connections, so that I can raise or close them all at once, from one spot. In front of my building is a raised story, containing grain-bin, &c , and I have arranged spouts running down into the coops, or apartments, through which I can easily feed the grain.

I feed from troughs or hoppers, for I believe that it is natural for fowls to eat as often as they feel inclined, and they will not eat too much, or more than they want, if food is left constantly before them. For dry feed, I give as great a variety as I can conveniently, and add a dinner of soft food twice a week, which I season with pepper, salt and sulphur, occasionally. A box of broken bone, gravel, ashes, etc., is always at hand, with lime, and fresh clean water, daily. A few drops of tincture of iron, mixed with the water, I find excellent, and I think it a preventive of gapes. At any rate, I have no gapes or chicken-cholera among my birds, yet.

I sprinkle lime under the roosts, and clean out everything once a week, from the house-floors. As to a preference of breeds, I will only add that, in my experience, the Spanish are very valuable as layers, when only *eggs* are wanted. The Houdan is another excellent layer and good for the table — among the best. Of the four Asiatic varieties, I find little difference except in color; their habit is the same, generally. But I consider them far ahead of *all* others, for they lay well, reach good size, fatten easily, and will give you plenty of eggs, in the months when eggs are worth 50 to 75 cents the dozen, in market. This alone renders the Brahmas and Cochins highly valuable. I send you cuts of my fowls, and I have aimed to make them correct as possible, as likenesses of my fowls." (These drawings of Mr. Newton's fowls, very fairly executed, will be found in their appropriate places, in our pages.)

It has not escaped observation that many fowls have a penchant for eating the small feathers off their companions' necks and breasts, especially when they are in closely confined quarters, or in contracted poultry-houses. And this destructive disposition is particularly evinced among the black Spanish fowls, though other varieties indulge in this same pastime, upon opportunity. Very frequently this habit is noticeable with birds confined in cages, during exhibition days — to the great damage of their plumage, and the disgust of their owners.

Whenever a poultry-keeper discovers this inclination among his fowls, if he will saturate a bit of sponge in common kerosene oil, (or spirits of turpentine) and bathe the parts which the offending fowls thus peck, it will quickly put an end to the birds' desire for further taste of *that* kind of edible. It may be necessary to follow up this sponging, with the liquid named, for a day or two. But it is a certain *cure* for this annoying disposition on the part of grown fowls, who thus search for the blood-filled pin-feathers of their mates. But when they get a taste of the pungent spirits, they are done with this thing! Generous feeding of animal food at such times, is a great preventive to their looking after this kind of nourishment, which they tear from the skins of their neighbors, to the serious detriment of their submissive associates in the fowl-house.

WADE & HENRY'S STONE DRINKING FOUNTAIN.

No. 7. WHITE-FACED BLACK SPANISH.
As bred by Jos. M. Wade, C. H. Edmonds, A. M. Halsted, E. C. Newton, and Others.

CHAPTER IX.

ON ARTIFICIAL EGG-HATCHING.

To this subject I propose devoting some few pages, though the process is little understood in America, and less practised among us. For myself, I have not attempted to hatch chickens by artificial heat, except in an experimental way, and have never succeeded in it, satisfactorily. Yet it is done — in England, France, Holland, and Belgium — to advantage, at the present time; and in some countries it has long been practised to good profit, while the business of artificial hatching is being looked into somewhat in this country, latterly.

The Egyptians have for centuries hatched chickens in enormous numbers, by means of artificial heat, in ovens, in steam-heated casks, etc. But we have not yet reached this point in the advancement of "the art," and there are no poultry-raisers yet in this country who undertake thus to multiply domestic fowls, to any great extent.

Monsieur De Reaumur desired in his experiments, long years ago, " that some method might be found out for hatching chickens in a great quantity, at pleasure, that would not require heavy expense, that might be easily practised in the country by the simplest rustics, even, and which might form an agreeable amusement to other classes there; to all who take a pleasure in the variety of sights and operations the poultry-yard af fords; to those who delight in furnishing it in plenty with fowls of different species; to those who, if asked *why* the care thus taken should not be as reputable as that which we employ in cultivating plants, trees, and flowers, in a garden — would not hesitate upon their answer; to those, in short, who, being apt to think that this subject is ennobled by its utility, think also that animate beings — such as birds — may furnish more satisfactory observations to a philosophical mind, than those that merely vegetate." And he concludes that " the care of multiplying fowls would thus become an employment worthy of such naturalists as have in a superior degree the talent of observation, that of contriving experiments, and the constancy necessary to pursue them, to widely beneficial results."

Mr. G. K. Geyelin, of London, visited France a few years since, under the auspices of a large English Poultry Company, for the purpose of examining into the modes pursued there in multiplying fowls in great numbers; and in his subsequent report to his associates, he mentions having met with four different plans in vogue, in France, for artificial incubation: which, though said to answer well there, are yet (in his judgment) " far from being applicable to hatching in a commercial point of view. It matters indeed very little *what* system is adopted, provided the heat is maintained at an even temperature: to obtain this, various regulators have been invented, but none of which can as yet dispense with personal care. They all say that their regulators are perfect; if the temperature of the room can be kept at the same degree of heat during incubation, that then they can regulate the heat of the incubator, to any given degree. But as such conditions of a uniform temperature are impossible to maintain, (considering the variations in the temperature of the atmosphere) he considers artificial hatching too *expensive* for ordinary purposes, and only to be adopted at certain times of the year; and then only in establishments where the heat can be maintained at a uniform temperature, day and night, by personal care. He adds —

"At the *Jardin des Plantes*, in Paris, the manager of the poultry department, M. Vallee, employs an apparatus of his own invention, which he has patented, and for which he has obtained prizes at two exhibitions. The principle consists of water, heated by means of a lamp, as a medium for hatching; the temperature is regulated by admitting more or less cold air by means of a valve opened or closed by a mercury float.

"At the *Jardin d'Acclimatization* two systems of artificial incubation are in use, and although both are on the hot-water principle, yet they differ materially; the one is heated by means of a lamp and the temperature regulated by a valve admitting more or less cold air, which is effected by a piston acted upon by the expansion or condensation of air under different temperatures; the other consists merely of a zinc box covered with non-conducting materials. This apparatus requires neither lamp, regulator, or thermometer, the hot water is renewed every twelve hours, and it is said to answer admirably. The eggs are placed in a drawer underneath the water tank, but I cannot help thinking that with an atmospheric temperature at or below freezing-point, it would be very difficult to prevent the rapid cooling of the water.

"The last system of artificial hatching is that shown me by M. Manoury, at Mouy. It consists of an ordinary wine cask lined on the inside with plaster of Paris. In this cask several trays with eggs are suspended, and the top of the cask is provided with a certain number of vent-holes for admitting air, which is regulated by means of vent-pegs: the cask is surrounded to the top with a thickness of about four feet of horse manure. Though I am assured that this principle answers well, I entertain serious doubts about it, for the same reasons as before stated."

In this connection, we may say that in our own experiments in artificial incubation, we made use of the "*eccaleobion*" patented in 1850 by a Norfolk County mechanic; which proved alike a very simple, and an unsuccessful affair, in our hands. This contrivance consisted of two large cylindrical tin vessels, one of which was so constructed as to set inside the other, leaving a space of about three fourths of an inch around the entire circumference and base of the smaller vessel. This space was filled with common whale *oil,* and this liquid was heated, from the flame of a triple-tubed spirit lamp, (attached underneath the bottom of the outside vessel,) to the requisite temperature, 100° to 103° Farenheit. Into the inner compartment, upon racks inserted for the purpose, we placed (at a time) three or four times, from a hundred to a gross of fresh laid eggs, lighted the lamp, covered the top, and set them to hatching. In a few instances, we found live healthy chickens, at the expiration of twenty-one days from the sitting. But the number of chicks obtained was so trifling, in comparison to the quantity of eggs otherwise used up in the process, and the constant vigilance found to be necessary to keep the temperature of the heated oil just right — night and day — was such that we abandoned the object sought, through *that* process, in disgust.

More successful, however, has proved the newly invented apparatus of Americans for artificial chicken-hatching, which have been improved, and latterly perfected by Messrs Jacob and Henry Graves of North Market street, Boston. These " improved incubators," have now been in operation under the inventor's supervision at the place named, over a year, I think — and I have seen a good many nice chickens hatched out with this contrivance. It has also been successfully in use in Pennsylvania, during the last year. The patentee describes this invention in the next chapter, and it may be seen in operation at his place, where he informs us it has worked very satisfactorily, thus far. It has been patented.

By the Egyptian method of hatching eggs, in ovens, the estimate is made that over a hundred millions of chickens are hatched out, annually. But the difficulty *after* incubation, is the rearing of the chicks. An English author on this subject says that "being in London, I was driven to Cheswick by a friend, to visit Mr. Cantelo's " hydro-incubator," and it astonished me, to see at an inclement season, chickens of all ages, from those just emerging from the shell to that of being ready for the table, each in perfect health, and in such rude health as I had never seen. There had been reared, in one building, at one time, over 1300; all to be disposed of, from the London poulterers' shelves, and still not equal to the demand. The advantages of this mode are that they have no hen-mother to drag them through the wet ditches, or to trample them to death, and they have no hens or larger chickens to peck at them; they have their artificial mother, kept up to the temperature of the natural mother; and it is beyond conception, how they will adhere to the warmth of this mother, prepared for them, and run in under the woolen cloth, as if it was natural to them. Each age has its separate compartment, with an opportunity, in fine weather, of passing out to a grass-plot; and you will see them enjoying themselves in the open air, and, when at all chilled, returning to the artificial mother, and making themselves perfectly comfortable.

"The hatching apparatus is a table, the upper part of which is kept up to 106 degrees, and is padded with Indian rubber; the eggs are placed in a tray, with perforated bottom, and laid on a woolen cloth, and raised, to come in contact with the rubber, which sinks and covers the eggs as much as the natural mother is supposed to do; thus nature is represented as nearly as possible. After incubation, the artificial mother consists of a number of heated pipes, about an inch and a quarter in diameter, and about the same distance apart; beneath these pipes is a sliding-board, which is always at such a height as to allow the backs of the chickens to touch the pipes, and is gradually lowered as they increase in size. This board is removed and cleaned every day, or replaced by another, which had served the day before, and had been cleaned and aired during the twenty-four hours preceding; above the pipes (about an inch) is another board, similar to that below, from which descends a curtain in front of the mother; this board serves the double purpose of economizing the warmth, and preventing the chickens from dirtying each other,— and the young chickens having been once placed beneath this mother, will only leave it to eat, drink, and exercise, and return to it, of their own accord. The patentee, Mr. Cantelo, has had equal success in rearing turkeys, pea, and guinea fowl; and, although I have seen ducks in all quarters of Great Britain, I have never seen, in one lot, so fine a collection as those produced by the Hydro-Incubator. Having, on my journey, visited the great aviary of the Earl of Derby, I there found the Incubator in its perfect working state, and was informed by his lordship's intelligent curator, that it was most valuable for hatching out the eggs of foreign birds."

GRAVES' IMPROVED INCUBATOR.

CHAPTER X.

PATENT INCUBATORS AND IMPROVEMENTS.

The inventor of the above raised during the year 1870 several fowls, hatched out in this machine, and he says of it—" It is a well known fact that all Incubators hitherto brought before the public have failed to accomplish the work desired; the reason of this being a lack of uniformity of incubating heat. We claim in our improvement, a uniformity of incubating heat; which we obtain by the expansion and contraction of spirits and mercury, acting on floats which are attached to levers; these being so constructed, that when the spirits and mercury expand, it lifts the levers, thereby diminishing the blaze of the lamp, and also opening valves connected with the egg-drawer, whereby the hot air escapes. The heat necessary for hatching chickens is from 95° to 105°; but from 100° to 103° is the desired heat. Our machine is so constructed, that when the mercury reaches 100°, the lights on the lamps begin to diminish. Should the heat continue to increase in the egg-drawer, and the mercury rise to 103°, the light is shut off, so that there is no heat from the lamps. Should the heat in the egg-drawer go above 103°, the valves connected with the egg-drawer are opened, and the hot air passes off, thereby cooling the egg-drawer; and as the heat diminishes the valves close, and the light is let on to the lamps. Should the temperature in the egg-drawer go below 100° the blaze increases, on the lamps, thereby bringing the temperature back to the desired point. It will be seen at once that we have a self-regulating machine. This is what has been sought for for many years, and without which *no* incubator is successful." These gentlemen have also what appears to be a very good artificial mother which they sell to accompany their Incubator, for the brooding of the newly-hatched chicks, and which is heated and the temperature guaged the same as in their Incubator, so that any desired heat can be maintained. With these artificial mothers and incubators are forwarded full directions for putting the machines into working order.

The Incubator of A. M. Halsted, of Rye, N. Y., is another American invention, the proprietor of which states that it is the result of years of study and careful experiment. Every year brought some improvement. Success attended the working of his machine, and with the first one, even, imperfect as it then was, three-fourths of the eggs placed in it were successfully hatched. Until the aparatus was simplified, however, it was deemed prudent not to place it in the hands of

HALSTED'S INCUBATOR.

those who had not made artificial incubation *a study*. The inventor considers his machine so simple, that persons of ordinary intelligence can manage it, and the owner claims several points of superiority over other incubators, for this invention. Experiments have proved in the hands of several poulterers who testify to its utility, that it promised to be one of the most reliable artificial egg-hatchers yet brought to the notice of the public.

The Artificial Mother accompanying Mr. Halsted's Incubator is a very good one, and has been made, after many experiments, to answer its purposes admirably. John C. Welles, of Athens, Pa., H. B. Todd, Mott Haven, N. Y., J. H. Fry, of New Brighton, and others have tried, and very highly commend it. We insert cuts illustrating both these inventions, but the article explaining them did not reach us in time for insertion. We are indebted to this inventor for the most sensible and lucid paper on this subject we have yet seen, and regret that our work was so far advanced, upon its receipt, that we cannot publish it, entire.

Mr. Halsted has satisfied himself, however, from long and patient experience, it appears, that artificial hatching cannot be rendered satisfactorily successful with *any* invention as yet matured, except the machine be in the hands of those who *understand*, and are disposed to *study* the process, faithfully. He adds — "*I* can, with care and attention, hatch 75 out of 100 eggs, in my Incubator. But I will not *warrant* that another person can hatch a single one, with *mine* or any *other* Incubator; since one day's mismanagement, while in process, proves fatal. The difficulty is that "directions" *cannot* be followed by the inexperienced. It is like commencing a new language; and when the novice comes to apply terms, the result proves unintelligible, and confusion follows. The absolute regulation of temperature is an exceedingly difficult matter to compass; and long-tried experiments have proved, to *my* satisfaction, that we have not yet, in this country, reached even the rudiments of artificial incubation, with any show of certainty. I *know* (because I have proved it individually) that artificial hatching *can* be accomplished. But that it ever will become a frequent or common method, I doubt. While therefore, I frankly state that — alone, and by itself — the incubator is a failure, comparatively, still as an *aid*, I deem it invaluable, in finishing what the hens begin, as thus: after allowing your hen to sit 10 days upon the eggs, remove them to the Incubator, and set another clutch under her. She will continue to cover three or four settings. You can *complete her work* in the machine; and your chicks will come out strong, healthy, free from vermin, and none are trodden to death. *Then* comes in the usefulness of the "Artificial Mother," which requires little care, and

HALSTED'S "ARTIFICIAL MOTHER."

no study to manage. After five years' trial, I repeat it, I would never be without *this* machine, if I could procure or make one. My success has been constant and perfect, and I thus raise one-fourth more chicks. A mother such as I use costs but $10. The size above represented is 20 inches wide, 42 inches long, and 15 in greatest height. This will hover and raise 50 chickens, and will last for years. Others have tried it successfully, and I recommend it, from personal knowledge of its utility. But whoever attempts to use an *Incubator*, to any extent, as a means of hatching chickens, *from the outset*, must first inform himself, thoroughly, by patient study and care, as to the details of its rightful management — to make its use successful." As Mr. Halsted is himself an inventor of one of these machines, this opinion is certainly a candid and valuable one.

The "*hydro*-incubator" of Mr. Cantello, of Chiswick, has attained to some degree of popularity in past years in England, but it has been found by experience in all countries, save Egypt, (where the warm climate aids them in their oven-hatching process) that it is the *raising* of the chickens after hatching, that becomes troublesome. They need the natural mother's care, and the "artificial mothers" don't answer — thus far — though that of Mr. Halsted, and Mr. Graves, portrayed above, seems to our view to be the best we have ever seen.

The inventors of Cantello's hatching machine claim that only twelve to thirty per centum of the chicks hatched by this invention, can be brought up. A one-tray Cantello's machine, they say, will produce on an average seventy-five birds to the hatch — eighteen times in a year—or 1,350 fowls, A two-tray incubator will give 2,700 a year, and so on. But no provision is proposed except through the artificial mother, (which in their case is often a failure,) to bring up the chicks. And in this respect we incline to the opinion that artificial hatching by any means in our cold uncertain climate, cannot be rendered successful to any extent.

Mr. Graves and Mr. Halsted are very confident however, with *their* inventions, and they *have* already raised and matured a good many chickens. If they can make their Incubators work, regularly, and if *these* "artificial mothers" prove reliable — they have accomplished an important thing indeed, for the poultry interest in America.

How readily these machines, or any other for artificial incubation, may be adopted by poultry-raisers in the United States, remains problematical; but upon a moderate scale, as is indicated in the articles furnished us by the inventors, the contrivances both of Mr. Graves and Mr. Halsted certainly promise well, and are much the best of any " incubators '' which have had their birth in " Yankee invention," and have died for lack of patronage among us in the past twenty years.

The Report of Mr. Geyelin, from which we have quoted the four modes of artificial hatching adopted in France, gives a further account of the "*live* hatching machine" used in several places, there — which process has been also adopted with success by a few breeders in the West, and in Pennsylvania within the past five years. This is but the *natural* way of hatching — *turkeys* being used instead of hens. Mr. Geyelin says upon this point that this

"Natural hatching differs from what I ever saw before, and in some parts of France forms a special trade carried on by persons called *Couveurs*, or Hatchers. They hatch for farmers at all times of the year at so much per egg, or purchase the eggs in the market and sell the chickens as soon as hatched, from threepence to sixpence each, according to the season of the year. This system may aptly be called a living hatching machine; and in my opinion it is the very best and cheapest way of hatching, as will be seen by the following description:—

The hatching room is kept dark, and at an even temperature in summer and winter. In this room a number of boxes two feet long, a foot wide, and a foot six-inches deep, are ranged along the walls. These boxes are covered in with lattice or wire work, and serve for *turkeys* to hatch any kind of eggs. Similar boxes, but of smaller dimensions, are provided for broody fowls. The bed of the boxes is formed of heather, straw, hay, or cocoa-fibres, and the number of eggs given each turkey to hatch is two dozen.

At any time of the year, turkeys, whether broody or not, are *taught* to hatch, in the following manner: Some addled eggs are emptied, then filled with plaster of Paris, and placed in a nest; after which a turkey is fetched from the yard, placed on the eggs, and covered over with lattice. For the first forty-eight hours, she will endeavor to get out of her confinement; but soon becomes reconciled to it, and then fresh eggs are substituted for the plaster of Paris ones; they will then continue to hatch without intermission, *from three to six months*, and even longer; the chickens being withdrawn as soon as hatched, and fresh eggs substituted. After the third day the eggs are examined, and the clear ones are withdrawn, and sold in market. These turkeys are taken from the nests once a day and fed — the nests cleared of excrement, and thus they are kept busy for months. After a time they cease to feed of themselves, and are necessarily 'crammed' with food and water."

The writer visited several different places in France, where this turkey-sitting process was largely carried on

— in one place (that of Mr. Auche, at Gambois,) noting sixty turkeys there thus occupied. Often a hundred are so employed on a single place. These birds seem to be so fond of this sitting process, that instances are reported where they sit constantly for five or six months, the chickens as they come being taken away, and raised under " artificial mothers," or glass, subsequently. The sitters are said to grow fat too, during this long period, and are very steady in their work, after commencing — appearing rather to like the ease of this monotonous occupation.

The setting of turkeys upon hens' eggs, may undoubtedly be rendered largely profitable, in producing chickens for early marketing, from the facts above quoted, since double the number of eggs can be placed under each bird, at a sitting. This is so much gained, in point of time ; and if the chicks thus hatched are looked after with care, from their birth, a majority of them can easily be brought up to marketable size and condition — of the ordinary varieties of barn-yard fowls. For the multiplying of fancy stock and good breeders, however, the hen-mother is the only sure thing to begin and end with, in our confirmed judgment.

A MODEL (MALE) SHOW BIRD.

CHAPTER XI.

POULTRY EXHIBITIONS AND SHOW-FOWLS.

To the eye of the initiated, the above spirited engraving will at once suggest the copy of a capital portrait of a perfect Cochin or Shanghæ cock, at from a year and a half to two years old, in fine plumage and high condition. The general form is that of a fine Dark Brahma, but its color better represents the Buff or Partridge Cochin bird. We consider this a very faithful likeness, however, of a first-class male representative of the Chinese race, and an admirable model of a crower for the Show-pen; executed for us by Bricher and Conant, in their best style.

The original establishment of Poultry Societies, for the amusement of enthusiastic breeders, the improvement of the domestic feathered race, and for the Exhibition of, and competition in, the various strains and varieties of Fowls bred by fanciers, amateurs, and dealers, dates back some years, in England — where premiums were first awarded to those who contributed what were deemed by the judges to be the best representatives of the different kinds of birds thus bred, from year to year. In this country, Fowl Shows are of a more recent date — the first one of any magnitude having occurred in Boston, Mass., about twenty-one years ago; which was inaugurated at the Public Garden by the author of this Book, in conjunction with Dr. J. C. Bennett, Rev. Mr. Marsh, Col. Jaques, Dr. Eben Wight, Mr. Alden, H. L. Devereaux, Capt. H. H. Williams — and a few other gentlemen, which proved a great success. The first Poultry Society in America was then formed, and other similar associations sprang up subsequently, in New York, Rhode Island, Connecticut, &c. Latterly, the New York State Society has taken the lead, in this direction, in this country.

In Massachusetts, the New England Poultry Club, centering at Worcester, has been in successful operation a few years, and in the spring of 1871 another new society was formed at Boston, by a number of eastern breeders and fanciers, who thought the 'hub' the most appropriate place for their exhibitions; from the fact that it is the Capitol of the State and is more convenient for the shows of the association — all the Massachusetts and New England railways entering and verging from that city. The gentlemen connected with this enterprise are well known among the lovers of good poultry, and several of them have not only bred fowls carefully, but for a good while ; and no doubt they will so conduct the affairs of the "Massachusetts Poultry Association" as to cause it to aid in the furtherance of the important objects generally contemplated and proposed by these excellent societies. When properly and rightfully managed, these can be made the media of wide-spread good, and are conducive to *real* improvement in the character and production of poultry. The advantages of such associations are too often turned to the especial account of individuals, or cliques, however — it is to be regretted; an error in management which we trust may not creep into the conduct of the newly organized 'Massachusetts Poultry Association;' and a reasonable guarantee against which mistake is afforded at the outset in this Society, in the selection of its officers — Messrs. Philander Williams, W. J. Underwood, E. C. Comey, Henry F. Felch, C. Carroll Loring, Geo. B. Durfee, John B. Moore, J. N. Cady, E. L.

Rice, Nath'l. Foster, John P. Buzzell, Jacob Graves, Col. Geo. A. Meacham, Mark Pitman, C. E. Tuttle, C L. Copeland — and other enthusiastic breeders, gentlemen of integrity and good standing in the business community. This society was inaugurated under highly favorable auspices.

The production of specimens of different kinds of Fowls merely to compete for prizes at our Poultry Exhibitions, now-a-days, will scarcely remunerate the fancier for the requisite outlay for stock, the subsequent necessary care that must be given such birds, and the attendant expense that inevitably occurs first and last, in bringing the birds to the Show-room in the best condition and most acceptable shape, to compete for offered premiums. The benefits derivable from these exhibitions, nevertheless, which are realized by such breeders, seem to be satisfactory, since through this means from time to time they may be successful in carrying away the prizes; and the notoriety thus obtained, ensures the fortunate premium-takers abundance of orders *for this same stock*, subsequently.

Now it is scarcely to be expected, (and every one, upon a moment's reflection, can see the force of this assertion,) that *any* breeder of poultry can deliver to order, at call, precisely such birds as are thus given the preference at these exhibitions, unless he disposes of the identical individual specimens to which are accorded these premiums. And this result is not attained, ordinarily, except at enormous figures; since the successful competitor uniformly " puts his *best* foot foremost," in this sort of thing, and naturally, too; and he must rob himself, to accommodate a patron, in complying with the other's ambitious wishes. The same *stock*, of course, can be purchased, and occasionally, this turns out equal to the prize specimens. But, as a rule, amateurs can scarcely obtain in this "same stock," exactly such fowls as bear off the palm at the shows.

The "Poultry Bulletin," a well conducted monthly publication, under the auspices of the N. Y. State Society, has spoken repeatedly and fairly upon this point, and in a late issue upon the subject of raising "fancy" Poultry, with a view to its *paying*, merely, the editor says, aptly — "half our fanciers do not care whether it *pays* or not, and the care, study and expenses of journeys undertaken for the sake of the birds, if added to their cost, would demonstrate that poultry keeping, to the real fancier, is anything but a paying business in nine cases out of ten." And he adds that "the *raising of poultry, or any kind of fancy stock to be successful, must be conducted with a sensitive love for the kind of stock bred, and a fellowship with others of similar tastes.* Breeding fancy poultry, etc., to *sell*, will not do. Money may be made by it, for a few years, but reputation, never. After a fancier once establishes the reputation of his strains of blood, from careful breeding and good success in winning prizes, he can get very remunerative prices, for all the *good* stock he has to spare." And *this* result is the leading object to be attained in owning or breeding specimens 'up to the standard' for the prize-pens. Indirectly, this specialty contributes largely to the general welfare and improvement of Poultry, of course; but it is attended, as the Bulletin suggests, with heavy outlay, care, study and labor, to compete successfully, and is usually accomplished by the few "fanciers who do not care whether it pays, or not."

While, therefore, the good effected in its way by this means cannot be denied, it ought not be, nevertheless, either the province of the general breeder, or his purpose, to aim *only* at producing show-birds. Few of these premium fowls are duplicated, as we all know, by this time. And if a fortunate strain of blood be gained possession of, it should be bred clean and purely, and followed up — without admixture with other varieties — for results that will tell *at large*, in the end. In support of this theory, or principle, we have only to point to the unrivalled success of the well-bred Brahmas, the Shanghæs, Games, Dorkings, or Black Spanish Fowls, for examples. These birds have always been in demand, from the outset, and they will continue to be sought after for general use, in our judgment, long after the present producers of these unexceptional true varieties pass beyond the pale of poultry-breeders!

The emulation incited through the establishment of these poultry associations and their annual or semi-annual exhibitions, is altogether commendable, however, in the main. They bring together the best stock in the neighborhood for comparison side by side, and the society-principle keeps the breeders in friendly communication with each other (or ought to do so) whereby they may readily compare notes, and excel their neighbors, if possible, from year to year. The prices maintained at these shows for good fowls, are kept up to paying limits, and those who originally spend their money time and brains upon this kind of undertaking, are thus enabled to obtain remunerative returns for their investments and labors toward improving the general poultry stock of the country ; since successful contributors are now required to bring the quality of their birds up to a high mark — to win.

The breeding of good stock is in consequence reduced to a very fine point, with some fanciers among us. I have noticed the recent published accounts of one elaborate raiser of Brahmas, who has elevated it to the " pedigree " system — Mr. J. K. Felch, of Natick, Mass. His birds have been very successful in the show-room, and are noted for good size, color and truthfulness, generally. This nicety in the genealogy of poultry may answer to amuse the enthusiastic fancier who indulges in its observance, and it may prove sufficiently interesting to him to pursue its ramifications, and attend to the records it involves. But its utility is, in our humble judgment altogether equivocal, in a general way. Still, for original breeding-stock, such birds as the Brothers Felch produce and offer " with a pedigree," may be most desirable to certain purchasers. For ourselves, however, we agree with the editor of the Bulletin, that " the fowls must stand or fall upon their individual merits, when they come into the ring ;" and though this furnishing of a pedigree for *poultry* (which no one cares to dispute or to inquire into,) may serve the purpose of such ticketed stock, it is of no mortal use, certainly, to the general purchaser. The fowl bought is either a good or an indifferent one ; and a paper record of his ancestry makes him no better, no worse, surely. Yet this hobby of Messrs. Felch has proved no disadvantage to them — naturally ; and their laudable aim appears to be to breed steadily quite up to the required standard. In an earlier chapter on the subject of purely-bred stock, we refer to the manner of " Topknot," who permits " all varieties of fowls to run together in the fall and winter," promiscuously. Such breeders as Messrs. Felch, for example, we opine, would hardly run this sort of risk, and then undertake from succeeding hatchings of eggs of their stock, to furnish pedigrees very confidently !

In reference to the " standard of excellence " established in England in late years, and followed generally in this country latterly, much discussion has eventuated ; and in the fall and winter of 1870–71, certain leading poulterers connected with the New York State Society conceived that a revision and refining of this scale of points in fowls was advisable, to be adopted as the future required *American* standard, exclusively. A convention was called, but it was subsequently announced authoritatively that parties had made so many protests against adopting the standard, as revised by the Poultry Convention, on the ground of incorrectness in descriptions, the committee appointed to revise the same have determined not to take the responsibility of putting it to press, and propose another convention in May, 1871.

No. 8. GROUP OF ENGLISH GRAY DORKINGS.
D. W. Herstine, Philadelphia, Pa., 145.

It seems that the wide difference of opinion current as to the merits and demerits of certain nice points in color, conformation and other characteristics of the leading breeds of poultry is so apparent, and so much can be said on both sides, as to straight-combs, pea-combs, and straw-colored saddles in Brahmas, for instance, and fifth-toe or no fifth-toe in Houdans, muffs or no muffs on other *pure* varieties, etc., etc., that no definite agreement can be arrived at, among the *savans* in the chicken trade, upon this interesting subject. For ourself, we think this matter of 'standard' is brought down to a pretty fine point already, on this side of the Atlantic. And without designing hereby to criticise the ideas or opinions of any individual, anywhere — we cannot but respectfully suggest that the refining process, in this direction may be "run into the ground." easily, and would suggest that to our view it is very well, as it is.

For the reasons given, however, we are of opinion that Poultry Societies and their public shows are beneficial; albeit there has heretofore existed abuses in connection with both, that have not been creditable to those who have controlled these affairs simply for their own aggrandizement, or for the benefit of the selected few who enjoy the privileges of certain rings. A sensible "old farmer" at Ambleside, N. Y., in a late communication, indicates that in the Empire State, an extraordinary degree of interest has latterly been evinced through the influence of the New York Poultry Society, upon the subject of improving the character of the common fowls around him. He says: "Through the efforts of the New York State Poultry Society, many farmers not only in this, but other States, have already been aroused to the importance of improving their poultry, and have secured thorough bred males to cross with their own fowls, have also built houses and yards for their poultry and small coops for their hens and chickens, and have shut chicks up at night, and kept them from the rats and out of the wet grass. Those who have done this have been agreeably surprised at the result; their fowls, (ever from the first cross) are increased in size at least one third. The pullets are better layers of larger eggs, and in place of raising thirty per cent. of their chicks, they now raise seventy per cent. I see there are many new Poultry Societies forming in different states, and that the people are awakening to the importance of the benefits that will arise from the improvement of poultry. At the third exhibition of your Society, held in December last, I was much gratified to see the great improvement made by professional breeders of thorough-bred poultry. They there had turkeys weighing 37 lbs. each, geese 27 lbs., ducks 10 lbs., and fowls 10 to 12 lbs.

"It may be far in the future, but I believe the time is coming when every farmer will have his comfortable poultry house, and his choice poultry, and will look upon them as one of the blessings that God has given him to be taken care of and improved. When this time comes, the farmers' poultry and eggs will be of better quality, and will average more than twice their present weight, and be cheaper than any other food. The benefits of caponizing will then be better known and practiced by all, as there is as much difference between the flesh of a capon and cock, as there is between steer beef and bull beef. If the merchants and gentlemen of wealth, who now think poultry of so little consequence as to be unworthy of their notice (unless it is cooked) would look upon it in the light it deserves, and encourage and aid the Poultry Societies, then the good work would progress, and the results would soon be manifest."

We may all join in the expressed hope of this common-sense " old farmer " that such results may soon be brought about, generally. It is the influence that these societies exert upon the *mass* of poultry-raisers, that is of vastly more importance to the universal good, rather than whatever benefit may accrue to the few individuals who go in for the ' highest premiums,' with one or two or half-a-dozen fancy specimens, which " can't be beat," nor duplicated either! And so while we will do all that in us lies to promote the growth, advancement and success of the poultry Societies, and their shows, let us not forget that the true aim of such institutions should be not merely to improve fowl stock for the fancier and amateur, but to disseminate among the farmers of the land this improved stock — at reasonable rates ; and so contribute to the benefit of the community at large, as well as to the national wealth of our country.

LIGHT BRAHMAS.

CHAPTER XII.

VARIETIES OF POPULAR FOWLS.

Thus far we have endeavored to point out in concise and plain language, the better general course to be followed in the selection of eggs, hatching chickens, feeding and rearing the young birds, breeding older fowls, furnishing poultry houses, raising poultry and eggs for market, and briefly regarding the production of poultry through artificial incubation. We proceed to consider the qualities and merits of the different *varieties* of popular fowls at present sought after, and now bred in the United States.

As will be seen in the pages which follow, we are

under obligations to American breeders, in different parts of the country, for many of the tasteful and reliable illustrations which adorn our Poultry Book, with accompanying descriptions and valuable hints from these contributors, as to the character and qualities of the beautiful portraits furnished us. In one word — these gentlemen individually will please accept our acknowledgments, here, for their favors; which are appreciated by the author, and we are confident will be quite as well valued by the readers of this volume.

We commence our consideration of the merits and qualities of popular modern poultry, with what we consider the *leading* race, or variety, in this country — as it is, and has been for many years, also, in England — to wit, the *Chinese*, or *Asiatic* Fowl; and at the head of this list, we unhesitatingly place the justly famous "BRAHMAS," a variety that has enjoyed an unexampled popularity, for twenty years. We call them by this name, now, because this has become established by universal consent and usage. Yet, as the fact is well known, my own fowls of this splendid variety, were the first ever brought to public notice, both in this country and in England. Originally, I called them "Gray Shanghæs," for the simple reason that they were *gray* in color, and most of my first pure stock came direct from *Shanghæ*. Subsequently, other specimens turned up, and certain breeders then ambitious of notoriety, through mystification, trumped up the name of "Brahma Poutra" for this superb variety This title was found difficult of pronunciation, however, and it came to be changed, in various ways, directly. Different poultry societies and different dealers spelled it Bramerpooter, Brahmapootra, Burrampouter, Burampootra, Bramapoota, Brahmapootra, Bramah, and in a dozen other ways — and finally we have it conveniently reduced to "*Brahma.*" Let it stand! It is a good fowl, and not a bad name. We are content.

The true Brahma fowl is clearly of Chinese origin. The tasteful cut at the head of this chapter, represents a pair of E. C. Newton's stock. All the characteristics of this magnificent bird, like the "Buff," or "Partridge" or "White" Shanghæs which have reached us in the past twenty years, are identical, save in color alone. *No* specimen of either of these varieties (now called "Cochins") has been shewn ever to have seen Cochin China, or "the Brahma-putra, a River, that discharges its waters into the Bay of Bengal," as one late writer has stated it.

This is entirely immaterial, however. They came from the East, "and were first seen in New York," says this same author, "in 1850." Now the record shows that in 1849, '50, I purchased from 'Asa Rugg' (Dr. Kerr) of Philadelphia, for twenty-five dollars — at that time deemed a very remarkable figure for two chickens — a pair of large gray fowls, which then were called "Chittagongs." They were feathered legged, plumage clear white and black, like the Brahmas, and were undoubtedly the same variety of Chinese birds we now have here. Shortly after this, I procured from on board a ship direct from Sharghæ, half a dozen other gray fowls, which were enormous in size, but fanciers said " too white " at the time. I bred them all together a while, and then I sold the two original grays, and they were bred by Dr. Bennett, in Plymouth, Mass., with his *buff* Shanghæs. The first progeny came white and black, and had a slight top-knot, some of them; but were considered very handsome and uniform fowls. The owner placed them in the second Boston Fowl Show, then called them " Burampooters ;" they took a prize, while *my* gray fowls also took another, as " Gray Shanghæs ;" and, from that beginning, sprung the stock that was for years afterwards known the world over as " Gray Shanghæs," *or* " Brahmapootras." Mr. Cornish, or Mr. Hatch, had fowls of this stock (similar, in every particular) at this same show, I think. But all were fine, and we all succeeded subsequently, very satisfactorily with our fine ' Gray ' or ' Brahma ' fowls and their progeny.

Cut No 3 is a good representation by H. Weir, of a cock and hens, of the light Brahma fowls I had the honor to send to Her Majesty the Queen of Great Britain ; of which this stock are the exact counterparts, in great size, perfection of color, superior laying qualities, and all the desirable properties of good poultry. The London Illustrated News, in noticing the arrival of the Queen's poultry in England, said " they are a very choice consignment, and the largest domestic birds known, at the time of their shipment by Mr. Burnham from America, these weighing over twenty-two pounds the pair !" The following acknowledgment of these Brahmas, is

From Hon. Col. Phipps, H. B. M. Secretary.

WINDSOR CASTLE, ENG., 1853.

DEAR SIR:—

The cage of gray Shanghæ fowls intended as a present from you to her Majesty the Queen, has this day been received from Mr. Mitchell, of the Zoological gardens, and they have been highly admired by her Majesty. I have received Her Majesty's commands to assure Mr. Burnham of her appreciation of his attention, and to add that it affords another addition to the many marks of good will from citizens of the United States, which the Queen has received, and to which Her Majesty attaches so high a value.

I have the honor to be

Your ob't and humble servant,

C. B. PHIPPS.

A few weeks afterwards, the author received another letter, accompanying a beautiful portrait of the Queen, and referring to this cage of Brahmas (through her Majesty' Secretary of the Privy Purse, Hon. Col. Phipps,) as follows:—

BUCKINGHAM PALACE, MARCH 15, 1853.

Geo. P. Burnham Esq. Melrose, U. S. A.

DEAR SIR:—I have received the commands of her Majesty the Queen to assure you of her Majesty's high appreciation of the kind motives which prompted you to forward for her acceptance the magnificent Chinese Fowls which have been so much admired at her Majesty's aviary at Windsor. Her Majesty accepts, with great pleasure, such a mark of respect and regard, from a citizen of the United States.

I have, by her Majesty's command, shipped in the "George Karl," to your address, a case containing a

portrait of her Majesty ; of which the Queen has directed me to request your acceptance.
I have the honor to be,
Sir, your ob't and humble servant,
C. B. PHIPPS.

This extraordinary stock has bred for years with marked fidelity — in color, size, form and other characteristics, and thousands of superb samples have been sent by me all over the United States, and to England, Canada, France, Bavaria, Lisbon, Cuba, &c., where they have uniformly given the highest satisfaction. They are as fine this year and last, as ever — and will be found altogether unexceptionable.

I could add largely to these commendatory letters, by printing several received from those to whom this strain of fine poultry has been forwarded latterly from my yards; but I will conclude the opinions on my Light Brahmas, with the following communication, acknowledging the receipt of three cages of this variety, which I shipped south in April, 1871.

From Hon. R. B. Bullock, Governor of Georgia.
ATLANTA, GA., APRIL 8, 1871.
DEAR SIR. — The three cages of Brahmas you sent me, arrived safely this day, in fine order. They appear in good condition, are very handsome birds, and I am highly pleased with them. One coop I send to my plantation, one lot I retain in town, the third is for a neighbor. I shall most cheerfully recommend your fowls and establishment to my friends, and am
Yours truly,
RUFUS B. BULLOCK.
G. P. BURNHAM, ESQ.

On pages 156 and 157, I give admirably executed portraits of a cockerel and pullet, of well-bred Light Brahmas, about ten months old. The *feathering* of this pair of young fowls is very perfect, and those who appreciate this nicety of plumage, will find on examination of these two pictures, that they represent the color and markings required by the "standard of excellence" established in this country and in England — quite accurately delineated, though the *form* of both is not of course fully developed, at the age presented in these two cuts. The qualifications required by the 'standard' referred to, are, for the Light Brahma *Cock* — head white; neck white, with distinct black stripes down the centre of hackle feathers; breast, body and thighs, white; back and shoulder-coverts, white; primaries, black; legs, bright yellow, fringed to the middle toe with white feathers, or slightly tinged with black. *Hen*, white — similar in details; neck to be distinctly striped on the hackle feathers with black; breast and back, white; thighs and fluff, clear white; legs yellow, well feathered to toes — like the cock.

The pair of fowls delineated on these two pages are very correctly drawn, and will serve the nice fancier for a good model to imitate — if he desires to breed up to the standard.

On the history of the *original* Brahmas, Mr. W. B. Tegetmeier F. Z. S., in his London "Poultry Book," a magnificent and altogether reliable work, says "There is not a particle of evidence to show that they came from India. The banks of the Brahmapootra have long been in possession of the British, at least the lower part of the course of this River, and *no such fowls were ever seen in that locality.* In fact, the Brahmas originated *not* in India, but in America. The light Brahmas undoubtedly were identical with those Gray birds that in the first importation came from Shanghæ, and public attention was first called to them in consequence of an acute American fancier, Mr. George P. Burnham, presenting a consignment to Her Majesty; and these birds were subsequently exhibited by His Royal Highness, the late Prince Albert, at the London and other Shows, as "Brahmas." * * * These light Brahmas, with pure white or cream-colored bodies, and elegantly pencilled hackles, were in great favor; they were universally admired for their beauty, and esteemed for their good qualities, when suddenly a *new* variety sprang upon the scene. A pair of birds were shown at Birmingham, which were sold for 100 guineas. These were dark in color, and different in general character; *they were the first Dark* Brahmas seen in this country. These birds were subsequently figured in the "London Field," having been drawn by Mr. Harrison Weir."*

On this subject of the Brahma fowl, Mr. Saunders, the author to whom I just now briefly referred, in his work on "Domestic Poultry," speaking of Mr. Baily of London, the eminent breeder, says that Mr. B. informs him that "he has imported and bred the Brahmas

---

* Portraits of these origina Dark Brahmas, (which Mr. Burnham sent to Mr. Baily of London,) thus accurately described by Mr. Tegetmeier, taken from Mr. Weir's picture, will be found among the tinted illustrations in oui book.

LIGHT BRAHMA COCKEREL, TEN MONTHS OLD.

LIGHT BRAHMA PULLET, TEN MONTHS OLD.

for two years; and that they differ in many points from the Cochins, with which they are sought to be identified." This information from Mr. Baily must certainly have been given this author a long time ago, inasmuch as *I* sent out to London a cage of Brahmas, which were exhibited at the Birmingham, Eng., Show, in 1853, " one pair of which, from Mr. Burnham of the United States, the property of Mr. Baily, of Mount street, shown among the extra stock, were purchased from him by Mr. Taylor, of Shephord's Bush, at one hundred guineas — " says the record; and in the month of September, 1870, (last year) I received a letter from Mr. Baily, in which he writes me, among other matters, thus : " I *continue* to breed from the progeny, the old type of " Brahmas " you sent me, as you may have observed, from the fine birds I have sent to Mr. P. Williams, and others, in the United States." Now Mr. Baily has been breeding these fowls steadily for fifteen or sixteen years. And the fine Brahmas he has thus *returned* to the United States, (bred out of my stock, with others,) have taken first prizes, *repeatedly*, as their parents did, before them, at the principal shows in America, in the last four years — Mr. P. Williams' splendid samples frequently bearing off the palm, latterly, as among the best.

Mr. Mark Pitman, of Salem, who has enjoyed a large acquaintance with these fowls, and who with Mr. J. Graves of Reading, Mass., has a splendid stock, in a communication to the N. Y. Bulletin, thus states what *he* knows of the Brahma's origin; which coincides, in the main, with the facts I have always claimed, from the beginning. Mr. Pitman says "the Dark and Light Brahmas as originally bred, have both nearly the same origin, and *are the product of the union of the Buff Cochin hens with the Grey Chittagong cock.* They were not imported, but bred first in this country." And upon this point, I first stated years ago, (in another work of mine on Poultry) the following facts, which the editor of the Bulletin kindly quotes from that book, in a previous number of his paper. "The variety of fowl itself was the Grey Chittagong, the *first* samples of which I obtained from ' Asa Rugg '(Dr. Kerr) of Philadelphia, in 1850. But my friend the Doctor (Bennett) wanted to put forth something that would take better than his " Plymouth Rocks," and so he consulted me as to a name for a brace of *gray* fowls I saw in his yard. I always objected to the multiplying of titles; but he insisted, and finally entered them at our Fitchburg Depot show (in 1851) as " Burrampooters " all the way from India.

"Those three fowls were bred from Asa Rugg's Gray Chittagong cock, with a yellow Shanghæ hen in Plymouth, Mass. They were then " Burrampooters." Subsequently these fowls came to be called " Burampootras " ' Burram Putras " " Brama-pooters," " Brahmas," etc."

" An ambitious sea-captain arrived at New York from Shanghæ, bringing with him about a hundred China fowls, of all colors, grades and proportions. Out of this lot I selected a few *gray* birds, that were very large, and (consequently) "very fine," of course. I bred these with other gray stock I had, at once, and soon had a fine lot of birds to dispose of, to which I gave what I have always deemed their only true and appropriate title (as they came from Shanghæ,) to wit, *Gray Shanghæs,*" and to these corroborative facts I shall briefly refer again, in these pages. I never claimed aught but *this*: that my Gray Shanghæs, or Brahmas were the *first* bred in Massachusetts, and the first (of both Light and Dark) that were sent to England, from America. As to *where* I procured my stock from time to time, subsequently, (and I bought a good many fowls, I remember, in those days!) it is surely not of the smallest consequence, now. Mr. Pitman continues, as follows : — "Mr. G. P. Burnham, who surprised not only the Royal family of Queen Victoria, but all the breeders of fowls in England, by his present of an elegant lot of Light Brahmas to her Majesty, saw in the Darks still greater remuneration, and eagerly purchased, disposing of them, at what might even now be termed fabulous prices. This variety at once took the lead of all others, even of the long esteemed Dorking. From this importation, many of the large breeders of England and Ireland were supplied; but wishing to improve them if possible in size and color, those old sagacious breeders *crossed the hens with the black-breasted Dorking*, the only bird which would give the qualities desired; and this progeny was bred back again with the Dark Brahma cocks sent from this country; so that now we are receiving from Great Britain, not the original Darks, but the improved. A gentleman who visited those old establishments a few years after the first birds

A PRACTICAL TREATISE ON DOMESTIC FOWLS. 161

were sent from the United States,* was in time to detect this cross, which undoubtedly was intended to be kept secret; and at once observed the change in size, the black breast, and actually saw the fifth toe."

DARK BRAHMA HEN.   G. P. BURNHAM'S STOCK.

*I presume that Mr. Pitman intends here to intimate by the words "first birds sent from the United States" of this variety, that they were mine; though the language is rather ambiguous.

As to " purchasing " Grays, after a time, I did so very generously — from among the birds I had sold as chickens, or which were raised from eggs I supplied to scores of fanciers in this country, when the demand for the Brahmas was at its best. And I had to *pay* for these purchases, roundly, too!

On this subject of the Brahmas, Mr. Tegetmeier says that Mr. Burnham sent into England, the *first* Brahmas ever seen there. And Dr. Wm. Custe Gwynne says, in this same work, page 177, " a circumstance which confirms me in my view as to the identity of these birds (the Brahmas) with the *Shanghæ* breed, is the fact that the fowls previously presented to Her Majesty, by Mr. Burnham under the name of ' Gray Shanghæs,' *are admitted by Dr. Bennett,* (the author of the name ' Brahma poutra,') *to be precisely similar to his own.*"

This is true also. Dr. Bennett originated the name of " Brahma poutra ; " *he* bred my first pair of old gray fowls, when I got the second lot ; and *he* says that my Brahmas, (or Gray Shanghæs) and his Brahmas, " are precisely similar." . . . Thus much for this *name*. And in the other poultry work to which I have alluded (Mr. Saunders',) under the head of " Cochin-China Fowl," (which, by the way, is illustrated with a fine picture of heavily-feathered-legged Shanghæs,) it is stated that " the *Cochins* were first possessed by Queen Victoria," &c. So they were. But the " Cochin-China " fowls first possessed by her British Majesty, were no more like the *present* birds called " Cochins," or like this illustration in his work, than they were like the Malay, or

Game fowl — nor half so much; for *they* were tall, gawky, smooth-legged birds, as every one knows, who ever saw the originals; and the exact history of which we give in the next chapter.

Referring to the remarkable hardiness and general useful qualities of the Brahmas, the Editor of the Canadian Poultry Chronicle strongly recommends this breed to farmers, for a stock fowl — since they have been tried in that cold country, thoroughly. The writer in the above named Canada paper says, " much has been written about which breed is most profitable for the *farmer* to keep, and it will not be denied that there are some breeds possessed of such general characteristics for usefulness, as to render them *more* suitable and *better* adapted to the farmer and general breeder than others. That which combines within itself large size, good laying and flesh-forming qualities, and hardihood, requiring the least amount of care and attention either in chickenhood or maturity, will at once be admitted to be the *most* suitable fowl for the farmer. He wants not only a good supply of eggs during the year, but also meat for his table, or for the market. It is useful, not ornamental fowls he requires; although if both are combined in the same breed, it becomes a still greater favorite. We have no hesitation, then, in saying that the Brahma fowl possesses *all* these qualities, and many others beside; and that of all the recognized breeds of fowls, this is the best adapted and most suitable to the farmer.

" It is not our intention to draw distinctions between the respective breeds of fowls, nor to seek to elevate the

LIGHT BRAHMAS. BURNHAM'S IMPORTED STOCK.

one to the disadvantage of the other, but merely to show wherein the Brahma is the *most* suitable fowl of all others for the farmer to keep. The great size of the Brahma, at once renders it an object of attention. In this respect it surpasses all other breeds. Hens in their second year with moderate care, will weigh from 8 lbs. to 10 lbs., and cockerels from 13 lbs. to 14 lbs. each. The quality of the meat is also good; when tolerably fed it will be found almost, and very often quite equal to the Dorking. There is probably a little less meat on the breast; but this is compensated by the extra quantity of that on the thighs; indeed, many people think the leg of a Brahma cockerel one of the best parts of the bird. If the object of the farmer is simply to produce chickens for the table or market, then a cross between the Brahma and a Dorking cock will produce truly magnificent fowls; the largest, perhaps, that have ever been reared. Chickens thus bred, have at the age of six months, attained the weight of 18 lbs. the couple, and over — no mean matter for the farmer's consideration.

"As a laying fowl, the Brahma is, in our opinion, equal to any other breed. There is no doubt that the propensity to sit interferes considerably with the production of eggs. Notwithstanding this, the fecundity of the hens and pullets is very great. Brahma pullets will lay with great regularity at six to seven months old, and usually sit within two months after. They may thus be made exceedingly useful, where a regular supply of *early* birds for the market is desired. Indeed, no breed so eminently possesses the regularity and certainty in the time of incubation, without carrying it to a troublesome excess. It is also remarked that the hen in her second year lays much longer than the pullets, and in this respect makes the fowl as a layer, far superior to nearly any other.

"After the second year the tendency to incubate becomes greater, and increases with age. We would, therefore, recommend that hens, after the third year should be got rid of; nor indeed is there any necessity to keep them any longer, as pullets can always be had to supply their places. In connection with the production of eggs, we may mention another cross with the Brahma well worthy the attention of the farmer, that is, between a Brahma hen and a Spanish cock. This cross produces a fowl which for average fecundity surpasses any and every fowl we know.

"Altogether, then, we consider that the Brahma possesses a greater amount of usefulness and value than *any other* pure breed, and is also capable in an eminent degree, of communicating its good qualities to other fowls by crossing; and for this reason we strongly recommend it to the farmer as a stock fowl."

The Light Brahmas are so widely known, at this time, and good stock has become so generally distributed over this country, that we need only refer those who desire to purchase, to almost any dealer, for these fowls. But, in the west, Mr. E. C. Newton breeds them finely, and G. W. Felter, in Ohio. Wade and Henry, Phil'a., and I. M. Harvey, Chicago, Ill., C. N. Palmer, Gallipolis, Ohio. In New York State, J. Y. Bicknell,

& Co., E. J. Taylor, Waterloo, D. L. Stage & Co., Schenectady, C. A. Mayers, Auburn, D. C. Noxon, Beekman, A. Nelson and others at Buffalo, Isaac Van Winkle, Greenville, N. J. In Connecticut, all the breeders have choice light Brahmas, as well as in Massachusetts and Rhode Island. I. K. Felch, Natick, E. C. Comey, Quincy, Philander Williams of Taunton have

LIGHT BRAHMA HEN. WADE AND HENRY'S STOCK.

very choice stock of this breed. Mr. Saunders, on Staten Island has a superior strain, also. Ezra B. Dibble, of New Haven, is among the foremost Connecticut breeders of light Brahmas, and his prize stock, with which he took first premium at the last State Show, there, were pronounced as fine samples of this favorite race as ever were seen in that region; where this fowl is bred — as a rule — to great perfection. Mr. D. is a very careful breeder, and is satisfied only with being at the head of the list, in the line of specialties to which he now devotes himself — the finest Chinese varieties, principally.

G. P. Burnham of Melrose, and C. H. Edmonds of same place, think they have as good samples of this breed as can be found. Also, G. H. Champney, Taunton, C. Carroll Loring, Boston, and J. C. Ives, Salem. They keep and breed only from the best samples — uniformly. Portraits of this strain — of the same blood as that sent by Mr. Burnham to her Majesty Queen Victoria, may be found in this volume, see illustrations.

No. 9. TRIO OF BLACK-BREASTED RED GAMES.

As bred by E. J. Taylor, Bestor & Colt, George A. Meacham, I. Van Winkle, P. W. Hudson, D. L. Stage, etc. 169.

LOPKES "COCHIN."   QUEEN'S "COCHIN."

CHAPTER XIII.

THE ORIGINAL "COCHIN CHINA."

We place the above two drawings in juxtaposition, for convenient comparison by our readers, and we present a description of this much talked-of variety with pleasant recollections, since it fell to our lot to introduce the famous Queen's Stock of 'Cochin Chinas' into the United States, as is very well known. In view of the fact that the name of the author of this "New Poultry Book" is inseparably connected with the original of this variety also, which came through his importation into America, we feel competent to describe them, accurately. This *name* has been variously used among us, for twenty-two years past, but within a few years it has come to be generally accepted simply as "Cochin."

In Tegetmeier's celebrated modern "Poultry Book," in reply to the oft-repeated query "Are Cochin China and Shanghæ Fowls the *same?*" he answers " we have always entertained the opinion that they *are;* as we have invariably found that fowls imported from China," (of any colored plumage, dark or light,) "came from Shanghæ, or its vicinity." And thus this able authority upon the subject of poultry concludes that "Cochin China is a name altogether misapplied" to the Shanghæ fowl.

This accomplished author is unquestionably reasonable in his opinion, and he adds, forcibly, that "this conclusion amounts to conviction; since Mr. Robert Fortune, who has passed so many years in various parts of China, says "the man who first gave these fowls" (the Shanghæs) "the name of *Cochin China,* has much to answer for! *I* firmly believe that these two are one and the *same.* What grounds," asks Mr. Fortune, pertinently, "has any one for supposing these fowl ever saw Cochin China? It is a breed very little known in the southerly parts of China, and the Southern Chinese were as much struck with the size of this breed, as we were." Mr. Fortune adds that the *Shanghæ* breed are more common around that port and vicinity than elsewhere, though he has seen them all over that part of the country; "while the Southern breeds have long been known, but there is nothing marked in *their* character." And we may here appropriately add to this, briefly, our own experience with the Simon-pure, renowned, much lauded, *original* Queen Victoria Cochin Chinas, which as everybody knows we first imported into the United States.

In the previous chapter, appears the Queen's letter in reference to my *Brahma* fowls. In addition to this flattering compliment from Royalty, I give place to the following pleasant communications I received previously, from distinguished Americans to whom I forwarded samples of my early "Cochin" China fowls. These gentlemen were supposed to be good judges of live stock, and the author deems their opinions sufficiently disinterested as well as valuable, to reproduce them in this volume—even at this late day. And I publish the letters which follow, simply because I desire to show that twenty years ago samples of my original imported *Cochins* went into the hands of such well known gentlemen; who, in addition to their other vast store of knowledge, knew what good poultry was, and who appreciated these fine birds, which were bred from the Queen's stock.

From Gov. George N. Briggs.

MY DEAR SIR:— The cage of *Cochin-China* chickens you were kind enough to send, reached me in safety; and I am much obliged to you for this favor.

They are, beyond comparison, the finest domestic fowls I have seen, and I shall breed them with such care that I hope to be able to give you a good account of them in the future.

They are very much liked by all who have seen them, and you will please accept my thanks for your attention.

I am, respectfully, yours,
GEO. N. BRIGGS.

PITTSFIELD, MASS., 1851.

From Hon. Henry Clay.

Geo. P. Burnham. Esq.

My dear Sir. — I duly received your obliging letter, informing me that you had sent by the Express of Messrs. Adams & Co., a cage containing four fowls for me, and I postponed acknowledging it until the fate of the fowls should be ascertained. I have now the satisfaction to advise you that they all reached here safely.

They have been greatly admired, not only for their enormous size, but for their fine proportions and beautiful plumage. I thank you, my dear sir, most cordially, for this very acceptable present. It has been my aim for many years, to collect at this place the best improved breeds of the horse, the cow, the sheep, swine and the ass — though the last, not the least valuable, in this mule raising State.

To my stock on hand your splendid *Cochin-China* fowls will be a congenial and valuable addition; and, if we succeed with them, I will take care not to monopolize the benefit of them. I am greatly obliged to you, and,

With high respect, I am
Your ob't servant,

Ashland, 1851.   H. Clay.

From Hon. Daniel Webster.

Geo. P. Burnham, Esq.

Dear Sir. — The coop of chickens arrived safely, and are noble specimens of the Chinese fowl. You will rarely meet with samples apparently so well bred, and they will do any one credit. I thank you for the consignment, and consider them a most valuable addition to my stock of poultry. Accept my best wishes, and believe me, dear sir,   Yours, very truly,

Daniel Webster.

Marshfield, 1851.

Late in 1848, I sent out an order to England for half a dozen of these fowls; for *I* was unfortunately then one of "the men frantic after Cochin Chinas," and was the first American who imported any of the Queen's noted Cochins into this country, by a year or two, at the least. In 1849, I learned the following facts, namely:

Three of the Queen's famous Cochin China stock, which had so stirred up the people in England, had been exhibited, and had taken the gold medal prize at the Royal Dublin Show, and were then presented by Her Majesty to Lord Heytesbury, the Lord Lieutenant of Ireland. His Lordship had placed these fine birds in the hands of J. Joseph Nolan, Esq., of Bachelor's Walk, Dublin, to breed. I sent to Mr. Nolan, who exhibited the *first* pure bred Cochins in England, and from him direct I obtained two cocks and four pullets. One cock and two pullets were very good birds, the other three were indifferent. They were dark partridge-colored females, and red and brown males. I bred these first (and a second lot, which I procured some time afterwards, direct from Canton) and their progeny, for years subsequently, adopted the name of "Royal Cochins" for them, and realized very handsomely upon them. They turned out finely (the progeny, I mean,) they were extraordinary layers, quite uniform in dark partridge-colored plumage, and took prizes again and again at the fairs, both of my own raising, and those raised from my stock by others; but they *always* came full black-eyed, always showed the darkish colored limb, and always (never failing!) came with entirely *smooth* legs! This was the "Queen's Cochin China," which I procured direct from Mr. Nolan, who bred her Majesty's stock, which I subsequently bred in Roxbury and Melrose for years and years; and which is illustrated in this late "Domestic Poultry Book," with a pair of short, handsome, heavily feathered-legged Shanghæ birds, and denominated "Cochin-China."

Now we hear of the " Buff" Cochins, the " Partridge " Cochins, the " White " Cochins, etc., and the poultry-show Committees award premiums for birds thus named. This is all right enough, since everybody agrees to it. This *Cochin* is a good name, too. Let it pass. I do not object to this change, or the improvement. But I state *facts*. I have imported and bred these Chinese-Shanghæ-Brahma-Cochins for over a score of years; and I may be permitted to claim that I know something about " originals," I think.

Having stated thus much in a general though somewhat personal way, we will now take up the character of this extraordinary race of Chinese fowls as we find them to-day; and, adopting the name given one strain by Dr. Bennett, and the other as improved by the fiat of the Poultry Societies in England and America, point out their many excellences and intrinsic merits — content with the fact that the Eastern fowl is the best in the world, all things considered, and that

"The ROSE by any other *name*, will smell as sweet."

In order, however, that the readers of my " NEW POULTRY BOOK " may judge for themselves how nearly like to either the " Brahmas," or the *present* so-called " Cochins," were the *original* Cochins, of Queen Victoria's famous stock, I have caused to be taken from a copy of the London Illustrated News, the picture of those fowls, drawn from life by the celebrated Harrison Weir, in 1844, when Her Majesty's Cochin fowls were first presented to admiring poultry fanciers. By reference to the illustration of the Queen's Fowls, (see cut No. 2,) and a comparison of this altogether reliable engraving with *any* other illustrations in this work, or any late authority upon this subject, it will at once be seen that there is no similarity whatever between these two plainly distinct varieties — to wit, the original " Cochins," and the present so named " Cochins."

Yet our picture No. 2, is a good and veritable likeness of the Queen's Cochin stock, and is a faithful representation of *my* Cochins, already described in this chapter, which came from Her Majesty's fowls through Mr. J. J. Nolan, to me, in 1849. Let the reader compare the two; and then say for himself if the Queen's tall, long-bodied, smooth-legged, large-tailed China fowls of 1844 *were* Cochins, how appropriately the fowls of 1860 and 1870 are *named* " Cochins! " So much for *this* misnomer.

Of this much lauded fowl Mr. Dixon, says : " Whether the breed now under consideration did really come from Cochin China or not, is probably known only to the party who imported them, if to him. But they have been cultivated in this country previously to their introduction to general notice as the most conspicuous ornaments of the Royal poultry-yard. A gentleman living in Monmouthshire, informs me that, nearly thirty years ago, a friend sent him a cock and hen of the true ' Java breed.' The cock was so fine, large and handsome, that he was immediately made ' Cock of the walk.' The present stock on the farm, which I have seen, are entirely descendants, and are true Cochin fowl; so that in this case, Java and Cochin, are synonymous. The first parents of this lot came direct from India. The legs vary from a flesh-color to an orange-color, and are not so long as in the Malay; the eggs are buff-colored, of large size, and blunt at both ends; the chickens progress rapidly in size, but feather slowly."

Another writer describes the Cochin cock as having a large, upright, single, deeply indented comb, very much resembling that of the black Spanish, and when in high condition, of quite as brilliant a scarlet; like him also, he has a very large ear-lobe or ear-cheek. This is not an indispensable, if even a required qualification; it is, however, to be preferred, for beauty at least, if not as a mark of pure breed. The wattles are large, wide, and pendant. The legs are of a flesh-color; some specimens have them yellow, *which is objectionable.* The feathers on the breast and sides are of a light chestnut-brown, large and well defined, giving a scaly or imbricated appearance to those parts. The hackle of the neck is of a bright yellowish-brown; the lower feathers being tipped with dark brown, so as to give a spotted appearance to the neck. The tail feathers are black, and darkly iridescent; back, scarlet orange; back hackle, yellow orange. It is, in short, altogether a flame-colored bird."

C. N. Bement, in his "American Poulterers' Companion," published by Messrs. Harper, states that Mr. G. P. Burnham, of Boston, communicates the following in reference to two importations of Cochin fowl by him.

He says, "I obtained two lots of these fowls — one batch of six, from J. J. Nolan, of Dublin, and the other direct from Canton. The prevailing color of my birds is yellow, or yellowish-brown pullets, and yellow and red, or yellow, red and brown cocks. They have not deviated from this range of color except in two or three broods out of the dark Canton cock. The chicks come even in size and plumage; and down to the third generation they have bred exactly the same; this is a very satisfactory result, in my estimation. I have never yet seen a black, a gray, a white, or a speckled chick from this stock.

"For all purposes of a *really good* domestic fowl, whether I speak of productiveness, easy keeping, laying qualities, size, disposition, beauty of form and plumage, or hardiness (in this climate), after a careful comparative trial, I deem the Cochin *the best*. And to my fancy they have no equals among the varieties now known in America."*

There is not the slightest objection, at this time, to the acceptance of the title accorded to these fowls we are now receiving from England and Ireland, and which are being so splendidly bred by Messrs. Hicks, of Roslyn, L. I. Mr. VanWinkle of Greenville, N. J., D. L. Stage, Schenectady, N. Y., E. J. Taylor, Waterloo, Philander Williams of Taunton, Col. Meachem, of Somerville, J. Graves of Reading, Mass., Mr. Herstine of Philadelphia, E. C. Morton of Batavia, Ill., J. M. Wade of Philadelphia, G. W. Felter, Batavia, Ohio, and

---
*This quoted opinion of mine was given before I had so thoroughly tested the *Brahmas*, as I subsequently had the opportunity to do.—G. P. B.

scores of other importers and breeders — and now called 'Cochin,' under the sanction of the poultry societies.

But we have given an exact history of the *original* Queen's Cochins, in this chapter, (so far as it is known) and we also give an illustration of those birds, drawn from life by the best fowl-artist in Europe, Harrison Wier. These were smooth-legged birds, and bore no more similitude to those that are *called* Cochins, to-day, than they did to any other large fowl that can be named. Still, they came from the East, and were undoubtedly really Oriental birds. Possibly *they* first started " from Luckipoor, up the Brama-pootra; a river that discharges its waters into the Bay of Bengal;" for their origin is certainly very obscure, yet. Of two things, however, we feel well assured: first, that they are magnificent birds — and secondly, that the *Cochin* came originally from " up the Brama-pootra river," as certainly as ever the *Brahma* fowl did!

CHAPTER XIV.

OLD AND NEW PARTRIDGE COCHINS.

The first strictly Partridge-colored Chinese fowls I ever saw, to wit, in the year 1849, were in the possession of the Rev. Mr. Marsh, of West Roxbury, Mass. This gentleman was a retired clergyman, and had passed the best part of his middle age, I think, as a Missionary, in China, and returned home well worn in the service. He either brought this superb clutch of Oriental birds with him, or they were sent to him by a brother Missionary, direct from Shanghæ. And they were really unexceptionable in beauty, great size, uniformity of plumage, and all the characteristics of a *good*, and at that period, very desirable fowl.

The descendants of this clutch of genuine "Shanghæs," imported direct from one of the celestial ports, and known to be *pure*, (if such a thing existed,) from Mr. Marsh's breeding in 1850, down to a brood of this stock which I met with in Norfolk County last season, (1870) were strikingly uniform, throughout; and the hundreds of fanciers who have in the past two decades had and bred this noble strain of blood, would readily recognize *these* birds, wherever they should see them.

I bred hundreds upon hundreds of this particular strain of stock, and I sent out to England in 1852, '3, and '4, a great number of what was then known specifically as the "*Marsh* Shanghæs," as did other gentlemen here, who then bred both the Brahmas and the Shanghæs, largely.

Within the last two or three years, this old Marsh stock — in no wise changed, in no wise improved, in no wise different in any one particular of form, size, color, or characteristics, is coming back to us! The beautiful "*Partridge* Cochins," as they are now called, which have been imported from England into the United States, are identical with the Marsh stock. But they are a noble fowl. There are none better, standing above ground to-day, as representatives of this favorite race.

It may be that English breeders have, in the past ten years, got out from China, direct, fresh blood of this variety, to intermix with those sent them so generously from America, more than a dozen years ago. But these we get here now are so strikingly similar, in every point of excellence, that those who have made themselves acquainted with the Marsh stock of Shanghæs, at once recognize these birds as akin to that long-time noted strain of *real* Chinese poultry.

The Partridge Cochins, owned and bred by E. C. Newton, of Batavia, Ill., portraits of a pair of which, appear at the head of this chapter, are very superior specimens (though the cut is not so large as some others sent us) and there are perhaps few that equal these birds, (none excel them) for size, accuracy in points, and perfection in plumage, on this side the Atlantic.

Cut No. 1, frontispiece, represents one of the splendid Partridge Cochins which have carried away first prizes at our late Poultry shows, deservedly. They are bred fully up to the mark, and these samples, of which the likeness furnished is very perfect, certainly are not only elegant birds, but are at once recognizable by breeders in New England especially.

This variety of the now Cochin race will *average* in weight, as heavy as the best; and if cleanly bred, will exhibit the partridge feathering as uniformly in a hundred chickens, as will the Light Brahmas show *their* peculiar caste of plumage. And very beautiful feathering it is, too — clear-cut red, black and gold. Their form is all that can be desired, in this class of fowl — compact, well-rounded, full-breasted, short-legged and not over heavily-limbed, well-feathered to the toes, small gamey head, upright single comb, medium sized wattles, short tails and fluffy flanks and sterns —

on the pullets — altogether as handsome a Chinese fowl as is bred in the world.

They are good layers, the chickens are hardy, and easily reared, they come to maturity early, and are described by Mr. Newton, as being in habit and size very much like the Buff Cochins, except being more compact. The color of the cock is as follows: neck hackle, and saddle feathers are of a rich bright red, with a black stripe down the centre of each feather; back and wing-bow dark rich red, with a greenish black bar across the wing; the breast, under part of body and thighs, black; tail glossy black. Color of hen is light brown, with each feather penciled with dark brown; neck same as in cock; legs of both — dusky yellow. The Partridge Cochin will ever be one of the most popular breeds of fowls we have, or can have, if taken all in all upon their genuine merits, alone, and we speak of this fowl thus at length because we know it well, and have always deemed it one of the choicest breeds of China blood that ever came into America. Messrs. Van Winkle and E. J. Taylor, Waterloo, N. Y., Wm. Simpson, Jr., West Farms, N. Y., C. Brinton, Jr., Chadsford, Pa., and others. have had a constant demand for chickens and eggs, from the imported stock of this variety, which at present command the highest prices generally of any of the fancy breeds of Chinese fowls in this country. The reader is referred to the fine portraits given of these Partridge Cochins, see our frontispiece, and page 184.

I have casually alluded to this variety as one of the "fancy" breeds. But I fully agree with Mr. Anster

Bonn, a name well known in poultry annals, that "in spite of their high price, etc., I do believe these Cochins to be the best fowls for the poor man, or the farmer, considering them not as fancy, but as productive stock. I have eaten a great number of Cochins, and find them without exception, by far the finest-flavored, best birds for the table, which we have ever bought, bred, or eaten." As this authoritative opinion coincides so accurately with my own experience, I cheerfully add that Mr. Bonn does not thus overstate the real value of the Cochins, for general utility.

Mr. Van Winkle, of Greenville, N. J., whose Partridge Cochins are noted, and whose beautiful illustrations published in the "Hearth and Home" last season faithfully depict to the life his specimens of this choice bird, has perhaps expended more money for selected fowl, (which he has imported from England in late years) than any fancier in America; and he has been ambitious to obtain prize birds for breeding from abroad — without regard to their cost — that should be the very choicest in the world. And in reproducing this stock here, he has evinced the highly commendable and persistent aim to breed only the best of its kind for dissemination over the United States; "hoping," as he expresses himself, "to see as much interest taken in this country in the breeding of fine fowls as in England, and a better class of table fowls sold in our markets. It can be done. The demand for first-class fowls increases every year. It costs no more to keep GOOD than it does to keep *poor* fowls."

PARTRIDGE COCHINS. Imported by D. W. Kerstine, Philadelphia.

And Mr. Van Winkle is right in this. "It can be done." It is now being done. In this blessed year of our Lord 1871, the demand for good poultry, in every direction, was never so great in the United States; and American breeders have never before shown, either in their yards or at the State Exhibitions of New York, Connecticut, Pennsylvania, or Massachusetts and elsewhere, so fine a display, in enormous numbers, of magnificently bred poultry, as has been raised in the twelvemonth preceding this year of grace.

It is noticeable that the Partridge Cochins imported by Mr. Van Winkle, and some other gentlemen, from England and Ireland — of late years — are bred "to the feather" more accurately than those of any particolored bird we have ever had in this country, except the light Brahmas. The pencilling upon the body-plumage of the hens, particularly, is exquisitely perfect and precise in the best samples, when sent even from different yards in England. This shows how skillfully the thing is managed abroad. The requirements of the standard of the Societies there are such that, to compete successfully, these strains must be brought to the show-rooms bred to a very nice point.

But, as we have said, the blood of this variety is very strong, and we have seen so many hundreds of the old Marsh stock that have been bred from the original, purely, down to the tenth generation, all of which come so true to their illustrious parentage, in form, color, markings, size, and characteristics, that we have no doubt these we are now getting, in America, similarly bred, in the hands of the experienced parties who have secured this favorite stock, will continue to produce their like, continually. And none of the large Chinese fowls can be found to excel them.

D. L. Stage & Co. of Schenectady, N. Y. have not created so much stir in the chicken-breeding world as some of their competitors, but they breed good fowls, and sell a great many of them. The Dark Brahmas bred by this firm are from Boyle's Irish stock, the Cameron, and the Fry importations. (See cut page 215.) Their Partridge Cochins are magnificent birds from C. O. Pool's importation — well marked, and of mammoth proportions. Their Buff Cochins are of the celebrated Cooper strain, a trio of the original of which sold in N. Y. in 1870, at the round figure of $315. They have also the Leavitt Stock, very fine. Their Dominique are superior, from the establishment of Hon. John Wentworth, of Chicago. And their other varieties are of the first class. We do not hesitate to commend this unostentatious concern to the attention of those who want good poultry, as we believe them both competent breeders, and reliable in answering orders — uniformly. Messrs. Stage & Co. inform us that their orders this season are largely in excess of those of previous years, and they are breeding very extensively this year, to supply this increasing demand for their excellent stock.

Messrs. Wade & Henry, of Philadelphia, contribute a few illustrations to our present volume, which depict their fowls — of which they have an extensive and fine collection. They inform us that their Dark Brahmas are from imported and prize stock, and we have seen a few samples from their establishment, that are very large and well plumed. Their Light Brahmas are out of the best to be had in America, and are equal to the average of this well known breed. They keep for sale, and feed it to great advantage (they assure us) to their own poultry, "broken fresh bone," crushed into the size of whole wheat, of which fowls are very fond ; and of the beneficial results of which, in the feeding of domestic birds, there can be no question. They have a fine strain of the Hamburg Fowls, both Gold and Silver Spangled, which are highly prized for their beauty of form and plumage. They furnish both fowls and eggs of all the popular varieties, and do a very large business, in this line. Their admirable "stone drinking fountain" for the hen-house, is illustrated and referred to in another place. They deal in all the ordinary requirements and fixtures for the fowl-house and poultry-yard, and among their stock it is said they possess the largest and finest variety of *pigeons* in Pennsylvania. Of the Partridge Cochins, Messrs. Wade and Henry have secured some fine specimens of prize stock, and of them and the Buff, they make a specialty, the present season, they inform us.

CHAPTER XV.

MODERN BUFF COCHINS.

I have placed at the head of the list of China Fowls, the ever beautiful Light *Brahmas*, because after a long trial with them, under all kinds of treatment — good and indifferent — this right royal variety of Shanghaes have proved thoroughly unexceptionable; and for size, weight, comeliness, plumage, and truthfulness to their originals — they cannot be rivalled, in my judgment.

But the *Buff Cochin* of the present day, as it is produced by Isaac Van Winkle, S. A. Bassett, Thos. Gould, Jacob Graves, M. Pitman, J. Y. Bicknell & Co., Wm. Simpson, Jr., E. C. Newton. Benj. Hicks, D. W. Herstine, G. W. Felter, D. L. Stage, E. M. Wade, and others in this country — and Messrs. Sturgeon, Potts, Cooper, Baily, Punchard, Belden and others in England — ranks among the very highest in estimation, with many breeders, and perhaps most deservedly, for its peculiarly rich beauty of *plume;* while it possesses all the other desirable qualities of size, form, etc., in an eminent degree, as a chief and noble representative of the much lauded and often greatly abused Shanghæ, or China fowl. The superb specimens seen among us of late years, are certainly very attractive birds. And the portraits given of these fowls in this work are very fine.

The two next illustrations in our book, are portraits of a pair of the superb trio of Buffs which took premium at the late New York Society's show, and are the property of Mr. D. W. Herstine, of Philadelphia. These fowls are very large and are superior specimens of imported stock. We are informed by Mr. H. that they have also taken first prizes at several other exhibitions in Pennsylvania. The proportions of this pair are colossal.

One of the most remarkable single specimens of the *Buff* Cochin ever produced, probably, was that of Mr. Sturgeon, in England — as portrayed in Tegetmeier's work. The owner called this splendid fowl "the Queen;" and she was quite up to the highest standard of excellence, in every desirable point. From her and others of a similarly first-class character, great numbers have descended since her time, and the first premium birds of this variety at the N. Y. State Society's Show, in 1870, were well up to the mark, in comparison; as all who saw those extraordinary samples will at once admit.

The American Agriculturist, whose proprietors offered an extra premium for *this* variety also at that exhibition, says, " the Buff Cochins are a very attractive breed, from their immense *size*, their beautiful and very uniform *buff plumage*, their profusion of *feathers* and *fluff;* and they are useful as winter layers, as good mothers and nurses, and for their quick growth. The eggs are of fair medium size; the flesh not of the best quality when old, but very good when eaten as young chickens, and especially good as broilers of six or eight weeks old, if they have grown with sufficient rapidity. The winning group of nine specimens were exhibited by Isaac Van Winkle, Esq., of Greenville, N. J."

E. C. Newton of Batavia, Ill., whose modest cut of the Buffs is at the end of this chapter, writes that they " are one of the largest and most popular breed of Poultry in the country at the present time. They are of a beautiful golden buff color. Their legs are a yellowish orange and well feathered; single comb and black tail. They are hardy birds, and being well feathered, stand our northern winters without extra care; good market and table fowls—always in good order and easily fatted; great winter layers, good sitters and mothers. They bear confinement well, and a four feet fence will amply limit them."

The color of the Buff Cochin is more of a golden hue, than simply *buff*. The under shade upon the downy or fluffy portions of their plumage, is paler, but to look at when in their best feather, they are of a rich luminous yellow shade—sometimes aptly called "lemon colored." This hue is usually *even*, all over the bodies of the hens, and none of the China fowls exhibit the soft, downy fluff so remarkably as do these. Upon the flanks and stern this peculiarity is very fully developed, and gives the female a rich, contented, comfortable appearance, that is seen in none others of the race. In the cock of this variety, portions of his plumage are red, or darker, as the wings, neck-hackles, etc., but the yellow color prevails in both.

In England, for years, the Buff Cochin has been a favorite, and except when the Brahmas have been put into the exhibitions in competition for the prizes (simply "for the best Shanghæs," without regard to color) it has been with the Buffs that the leading premiums have been, for the most part, carried off. "The extreme neatness of their appearance," says Tegetmeier, "more particularly of the hens, the uniformity in all the groups, and the quality of the specimens shown, have combined to justify the awards of judges, and to secure for the Buffs the preference of amateurs, generally. And in addition to this, the breeding birds shown have been brought to equal 'n weight those of *any* other variety."

A very desirable recommendation to the Buff Cochin, is, that the fowl be strictly uniform in color, to answer the requirements of the present aimed-for standard; and the nine fowls exhibited by Mr. Van Winkle were quite up, in this particular. As to size, those I have seen for the past two years, here, as well as hundreds I saw in England, are fully equal, on the average, to the largest and heaviest Brahmas I ever met with, anywhere. This is another strong recommendation in their favor. Americans will never get over their fancy — as a rule — to possess the *biggest* fowls to be had. The great *size* of the Shanghæs has always been the leading characteristic which the Yankee breeder most admires; and no matter how perfect the Brahma, the Buff, the White, or the Partridge Cochin may be, in other respects, if he or she do not stand well up in the world, and bring down the steel-yard by his or her generous weight, as well, nobody wants *such* a Chinese fowl!

The Buff Cochins will do this. They are very large, weighty, elegant birds, and the portraits we give of Mr. E. C. Newton's, and those on pages 194, 195, give the reader a very fair idea of this magnificent variety, which is much sought after this year: than which no domestic fowls that move (and I do not now forget my fine light *Brahmas*) ever yet made a more satisfactorily beautiful appearance, on sward, in yard, or walk.

A clutch of well-bred Yellow or Buff Cochins, upon a bright green lawn, for instance, in the sunshine of a clear June day, is a goodly sight to see, if we are a judge of golden beauty, or have an eye for color. In England I saw hundreds of these magnificent groups,

No. 10. DOMINIQUE COCK AND HEN 193

and the favorite color for Cochins, there, is now the Buff, as a general thing. All the breeders have turned their attention, more or less, in this direction, within a few years, and some superb samples of this variety have been produced, first and last.

Among the importations that have been made to this country, the gentlemen whose names I have mentioned in the early part of this chapter have succeeded in getting out (at round figures) many superior breeding birds of this class; and it is very clear, from the active demand that is current for them and their eggs this year, that the Buffs will become a favorite color with us, ere long. You can scarcely do better, than with this fowl. They are not yet plentiful, latterly, among us, and *good* samples are held at high prices, yet. But they breed rapidly, and the matter of price will quickly regulate itself.

The following drawing is taken to represent the magnificent Buff Cochin prize-cock of D. W. Herstine, of Philadelphia — and the hen upon the next page is a portrait of another of the trio of first premium birds of this variety, at the last New York Exhibition (1870.) But these pictures, though they give the general contour of these splendid fowls, do not do Mr. Herstine's stock justice, in our opinion. We give place to the illustrations, however, and with the assurance to those who want really choice fowls, of this strain, that if procured of Mr. H. out of *this* blood, they will get finer birds than these cuts represent; though the pictures are very fair, in their way.

BUFF COCHIN COCK.

A PRACTICAL TREATISE ON DOMESTIC FOWLS. 195

BUFF COCHIN HEN.

A breeder in Norfolk County informed me, in March, that he had sold all the Buff Cochin *eggs* he dared to contract to deliver this spring, at ten dollars a dozen, from a superior clutch of near twenty Buff fowls he shewed me. And very fine ones they were, too. He has no Buff fowls to sell, and good ones can only be had at higher prices than those at which almost any variety of 'fancy' fowls are selling, this year. But they may now be had of the New York, Connecticut, Pennsylvania and western breeders, in this country, as is indicated in connection with the superior illustrations contributed to this volume; and, generally speaking, these gentlemen may be relied on, in their representations.

Every mother is prone to think her favorite bantling the prettiest and best in the world; and chicken-dealers who become attached to any specialty in their way, incline similarly to the belief that *their* Fowls are the most economical, the most beautiful, the most desirable to buy, or to breed. If this commendable difference of opinion did not exist, to stimulate competition, and keep up a laudable regard for the various fine breeds of Poultry we have to choose from, there would be little interest felt in the fowl-trade, to be sure!

And so we speak of this magnificent *Buff* Cochin with some earnestness, because we deem it, in every particular, a rare variety, in its beautiful perfection. For the present, in consequence of its noted superior qualities, this fowl will be taken up by fanciers, mostly. But there is no good reason why it should not be bought and bred and multiplied, by every farmer and poor cotter in the country, as *one* of his varieties of poultry stock, since — whether he desires to reproduce

YEAR OLD BUFF OR YELLOW SHANGHÆS.

it for sale to amateurs and small breeders, or for the better and higher and more useful purpose of contributing to the general improvement of the feathered stock of the country, or even for market uses only — this fowl possesses all the qualities needed, to fulfil his highest expectations.

For a *cross* upon the ordinary native fowl of the interior, the Buff Cochin may be considered as good as the best of the Chinese race. The blood is strong, the size ample, the laying qualities excellent, and no fowl is more hardy than are these. To mix with the barn-yard Poultry (where pure breeding is not sought for) the farmer who has *not* tried the experiment we now hint at, will surely find it in his account at the year's end, if he introduces a few of these noble birds among his common poultry.

CHAPTER XVI.

THE HOUDAN, CREVECŒUR, AND LA'FLECHE.

These are the notable FRENCH FOWLS, which have been imported into England largely, in the last half dozen years, and since the close of the American war into the United States, by fanciers, in considerable numbers. The high-sounding names of these birds — to wit, *Crevecœur, Houdan,* and *La Fleche,* gave them a sudden popularity in England, and they came as quickly into favor in this country, when their merits had been briefly made known, after their introduction among us.

When the author was in France (1867) he met with myriads of these fowls, scattered over the country, and the novelty of their facial appearance, with the horned comb, the white cheek, the towering crest, together with the superb metalic *color*, and the famous strut of some of them, arrested his attention, while he was looking about among the poultry in that country; and he thought these lively birds, as seen " upon their native heath," were altogether 'French-y,' when he first met with them.

But although the writer went largely through the country villages where poultry-raising is carried on, he found no enthusiasm among the French people, over their French fowls. None whatever! I met with no Frenchman who knew (or cared) anything about " pure " Houdans, La Fleche, or Crevecœur—though they dwelt in these three poultry-districts, and had bred these fowls all their lives. And very few natives can be found there who take any extraordinary interest in fowl-breeding, except for marketing, or in raising eggs for the albumen they can extract therefrom, and always find a ready profit upon, for the print-manufacturers' use.

I saw large numbers of these " French " fowls, about which so much has been written and said in late years in England and America, in the north and western Departments of France, as well as around Mulhouse, in the east. At Rouen, (where one sees ducks that *are* ducks, by the way,) about Rheims, at Villelaie, near Paris, at Houdan, in La'fleche and Crevecœur districts,

Dreux, Nogent, etc., I met with large numbers of these horned, shining black or flecked, active, pretty birds — which the owners would gladly sell at four to five francs each, in gold — for the best of them. But they have gone over to England, been well bred, and have sold at almost fabulous prices, in the past five years, there, as in this country as well.

They are claimed to be first-class layers, generally, disinclined to sit, their flesh is white and tempting for table use, and they are not an expensive fowl to keep. They are a showy, handsome bird, not a large breed — averaging (in France) less than the Black Spanish, which they strongly resemble, save in the peculiar formation of comb, muff, and head-tufts — and have found many admirers in England and America both — though I really could see nothing in them, abroad, that would tempt me to bring a cage of them home, at a cost of less than a dollar apiece ; as I might have done, and had my choice of specimens among thousands.

Still, there be many who fancy them ; and, as I have already remarked, they are being nicely bred, both here and in Great Britian ; where I looked for, but found only a few isolated trios, and these for the most part at the poultry bazaars about London and Liverpool. Probably there are more fine *French* fowls of the three varieties named herein, now in the United States, than there are in England ; and I am informed by several gentlemen who breed them, that the demand for both chickens and eggs of *this* present popular modern breed increases, largely, season after season, among us.

Prominent among the fine specimens of French birds in America, are those of Messrs. G. H. Warner, of New York Mills, Isaac Van Winkle, of Greenville, N. J., J. P. Buzzell, Clinton, Mass., Geo. Smith, Holliston, Mass., G. W. Bradley, Hamden, Conn., Hamilton and Kirkham, New York, Geo. A. Deitz, Chambersburg, Pa., E. C. Newton, Batavia, Ill., D. L. Stage and Co., Schenectady, N. Y., Henry Howland, Chicago, Ill., G. W. Felter, Batavia, Ohio — and others, with whom I am unacquainted. But there are many who are breeding this stock carefully, and who think very highly of it, thus far.

In reference to these French Fowls, of which this gentleman breeds the three varieties — Houdans, Crevecœurs, and La Fleche — Mr. Van Winkle of Greenville, N. J., expresses a very favorable opinion. He has a superb stock of these fowls, and avers that " the *Houdans* are one of the most valuable breeds of poultry introduced into this country for many years — exhibiting unusual fertility, maturing early, very hardy, both as adults and chicks, their bodies being large and compact. flesh white, etc.," and this fancier speaks from experience, after faithful trial with them.

Of the *Crevecœurs*, Mr. Van W. remarks that "in giving my opinion from experience on the merits of this variety of French fowl, since I have kept them, (and I have closely studied their points), I find them to be large birds, good layers of unusual numbers of large eggs in autumn, when most other birds are in moult — of a greenish metallic black, in color, having heavy crests that give them a remarkably handsome and original appearance, while they are very tender to eat, and most excellent to cross with other fowls." The beautiful engraving on page 199 will give the reader a good idea of Mr. Warner's and Van Winkle's Houdans.

In reference to the third variety, *La Fleche*, this breeder declares it to be "the finest domestic fowl known in France — where it has long been deservedly the favorite among both breeders and epicures; very large, handsome birds, of upright stately carriage, jet black in plumage. The comb is unlike that of any other fowl, growing from the head like two horns, with pleasant symmetry of form, but peculiarly characteristic of this elegant showy bird. These, too, are very prolific layers (as are all the French fowls,) the La Fleche producing tremendous sized eggs, usually — while, for the table, I consider them altogether unexceptionable."

Mr. G. H. Warner, of New York Mills, Oneida Co., who was the winner of the New York State Poultry Society's large gold medal prize, in 1869 for *Houdans*, says of the French fowls, that " were I to keep but two varieties of Domestic Poultry, I would select one of the Asiatic breeds, which we find to be good winter layers, good mothers, and a good table fowl; and my other choice would be the Houdan — in which we find a most excellent layer. They mature early, and, as in each of the other best known varieties, we have an abundance of delicate white meat, in this fowl — which is, also, a non-sitter." To Mr. Warner's fine French stock, of all three varieties, have been awarded the N. Y. Poultry

Society's Gold Medal, and other leading premiums, for their comparatively superior merits.

Mr. Taylor, of Waterloo, N. Y., writes that "this variety are becoming very popular, both as layers and table-fowls. They are of large size, weighing, when fully grown, cock six to seven pounds; hen, five to six pounds. They have proved, with us, the hardiest and therefore the most useful of any of the French fowl, and in our opinion, the farmer cannot select a variety that will pay him better, both in eggs and flesh. They have short legs, a round, well proportioned body, and top-knot falling backward. They are bearded and have five toes on each foot, the same as the Dorking, and are fully equal to that variety as table fowls."

Many fanciers deem these among the choicest varieties yet imported into the country, for their size and in view of their laying qualities. The editor of the *American Agriculturist*, at New York — whose opinions upon poultry is excellent, and whose judgment, too, is more sound than the average of agricultural editors, in this direction — has given all three of the popular French varieties a fair trial, and commends them, very highly. They are certainly an ornamental fowl, and in a late number of the journal referred to, the editors who offered handsome prizes (upon their own account,) at the N. Y. State Poultry Fair in 1870, thus speak of the *Houdans*. "They are a French breed, a little less in size than the other famous French fowls, but not less valuable, being decidedly the hardiest and most prolific. The Houdans combine two valuable qualities — the production of *flesh* and *eggs* — each in a high degree of excellence. . . . They have been thoroughly tried in this country, and prove excellent in every respect. A good cock weighs 7 pounds, a good hen 5 1-2 pounds. The quality of the flesh is fully equal to that of the Dorking." This is strong praise, from one who has tried them.

Another good authority describes the *La Fleche* as bearing " a strong firm body, well on its legs — appearing less than it is, because the feathers are close ; black plumage, having many points of resemblance with the Spanish fowl, from which I believe it to be descended, by crossing with the Crevecœur. It has short-grained, juicy, delicate flesh, and puts on fat easily. As layers, they are superior to any breed except the Spanish ; but for the table, they are not so good as the Dorking." They have a peculiar upright double comb, protruding from the head like two fleshy horns with a slight top-knot at the back of the crown ; and are a stylish fowl, good layers, and the chickens are easy to rear.

Of the three French varieties, the *Crevecœur* is the largest, and the best, says another authority, " while it is better known than the others. It lays a large number of eggs, of good size — like the Black Spanish — and resembles that fine fowl, but for its unique head, crest, and short legs. This variety has the horny style of comb, too. Its legs are black or dark-skinned, its meat excellent, and it is a stately, sober-looking fowl, with a good carriage and fine plumage."

Thus much in favor of these French breeds, the Creve

cœurs, La Fleche, and Houdan fowls, which I have fancied will hardly stand the test of time with us. A friend in Salem, Mass., who paid the sum of eighty dollars for a trio, two years ago, in New York, (of the Crevecœurs,) wrote me not long since, "I have sold them all, and cleaned them out; I have had enough of them. No more French birds for me." Another fancier who has tried them two years, writes me — " I am disappointed with the French fowls, and am tired of them. I very much prefer the Brahmas." And so do *I*, indeed! I know but little of them personally, but I do not fancy them. The coy maiden frankly declared to the distasteful Dr. Fell:

> "I do not like you, Doctor Fell,
> The reason *why*, I cannot tell:
> But this alone I know full well,
> I do not *like* you, Doctor Fell!"

With due deference to other fanciers' opinions, I say —

> I do not like the French Fowls well,
> The reason *why*, I cannot tell;
> But this alone I know full well,
> I do not *like* the French Fowls well.

Other breeders who have tried them thoroughly, are of the exactly opposite opinion, and so, *chacun a son gout;* every one to his taste, as the venerable dame remarked, when she kindly kissed the cheek of her favorite cow.

DARK BRAHMA HEN. WADE'S STOCK, PHIL'A.

CHAPTER XVII.

THE DARK BRAHMAS.

This very popular variety of the race of Brahmas. has within the last few years come to be widely disseminated over England and the United States; and, on several occasions, specimens of these *dark* Brahmas have carried off the prizes, over all competitors, among the Shanghæ tribe, at our Poultry Fairs.

On this branch of the subject matter of our New Poultry Book, namely, *Dark Brahmas*, we submitted to the Editor of the New York Poultry Bulletin, some time since, the following article; which appeared in that excellent journal, in the month of December, 1870.

ED'S. BULLETIN.

Gentlemen: The wide spread interest at present evinced, in this country and in Europe, in favor of the *Asiatic* breed of fowls, induces me to offer you a few lines on the subject of the so-called "Brahmas" of the present day. I know something of this fowl, (or ought to !) and find myself justly accredited by Mr. Tegetmeier, in his exhaustive and superb "Poultry Book," with having introduced into England, from this country, the *first dark* Brahmas ever seen there; which Mr. T. describes, in said "Poultry Book" as the entering of "a *new* variety upon the scene."

"M. Tegetmeier is relied on as *authority* upon the subject of modern poultry history, I believe, and I think very deservedly so. In *this* matter, at all events, he is correct. Until the famous trio of "*dark* Brahmas," which I sent to Mr. Baily of London, in 1853, reached him, there had been *no* Dark Brahmas (or dark "Grey Shanghæs," as I then called them,) ever seen in England. Previously, (in 1852), I had sent to Her Majesty Queen Victoria, a flock of *mature* Light Brahmas, which were hatched early in 1851, of course, for they weighed over 20 lbs. the pair, when shipped from the United States by me. The parent birds these one-year-old fowls came from, were over two years old; and I had bred the stock *two seasons before* I sent out the splendid specimens which I selected to present to the Queen. This would carry us back to 1849 — which was the year I came into possession of my first *grey* Chinese fowls; from which, I solemnly believe all the earlier stock was bred, both in America and England, in connection with the fowls of Mr. Virgil Cornish, and Mr. Hatch ; *which latter turned up to public view in the years* 1850 and 1851.

"But neither of these gentlemen claim, (or ever claimed,) that so early as 1851, they had any but the *light* colored Brahmas; though I observe that Mr. Cornish hints in a late letter that he noticed in his stock a tendency to throw *darker* chickens after a while. And now will you permit me to state what is my firm belief, as to the present color and apparent character of the so-called "Dark Brahmas," of to-day?

"In all the samples I have seen, imported of late years from England, and I think no one here claims to have imported the "Dark" variety from anywhere else, I detect all the characteristics of the dark birds I sent out there, originally — with the single exception of the mottled black breast and lower body feathers in some strains we have received here, from English breeders,—since 1866, for example. "They are very fine fowls. So were the first ones I sent over to England. I don't know that the English breeders have latterly imported from China (or elsewhere) fresh stock, to breed with what they received from me, first; and of which, subsequently to 1852 and '53, I sent hundreds there, of fine samples. But, if they have done so, I have never heard of the fact. And, least of all, has there ever occurred a *second* importation of Brahmas (or any other named fowl) from the port whence is said to have sailed the ship with the first fowls on board, to wit: "*Luckipoor, from up the mouth of 'he Brama Pootra river;*" the name of which ship, or captain, or the sailor who furnished the fowls, cannot be told by anybody.

"But all this is of small consequence, now. Those fowls were *good* ones. They have shown it in the twenty years since they were first bred here. But they were *Chinese* birds—they came from Shanghæ, or Hong Kong as mine did; and they were, and *are* nothing else. I know full well, when and where this "*Brahma*" name originated. I was one of that very "committee" alluded to by Mr. Cornish, who, in consultation, adopted this cognomen — though against my own personal protest, at the time. I *knew*, then, that the "Luckipoor, up the Brahma Pootra river" theory was nonsense. And I claimed that the fowls should be called *what they were* — "Grey Shanghæs;" for they came from Shanghæ, China, and were simply grey, in color. I was over-ruled. It is just as well. But these are *facts*.

"I am firmly of the opinion that this *recently* marked dark-breasted Brahma strain of fowls, which is so greatly admired among some fanciers, and of which several trios have of late come out from England, are skilfully bred in Ireland and England from the dark China hens they have had there since 1853 and 1854, with the dark-plumed Grey Dorking cock; producing *this* variety (so closely resembling the latter in many points,) and upon some of the first of which, raised in England, there not unfrequently appeared the notable fifth toe of the Dorking, now bred off again, by cautious selections. The Light Brahmas hold their own wondrously; the newly-fledged *dark* varieties may continue to do as well, for years, for the blood of both is strong. But I shall not change my opinion in this matter, until I can learn or un-learn more than I *now* know of the "dark Brahma ' strain of the present time." Yours respectfully, G. P. BURNHAM.
Melrose, Sept., 1870.

The comments upon my communication, published by the Bulletin editor, were both fair and good-natured; but do not change the *facts* embodied in my letter. I merely proposed to say that the *first* Dark Brahma fowls ever seen in England (and I sent several cages of fine ones out there, subsequently) were from *my* yards, in Melrose. That they were good ones, that this variety became immensely popular, that I was authoritatively given due credit for these shipments in the proper quarter, that the enterprise paid me well, and that that very stock was bred and distributed all over England, and finally *sent back to the United States, from the very breeders I sold mine to* — are simply matters of history. Having said thus much as to my Dark Brahmas, I have done with discussion upon this point.

Cuts No. 4 and 5 are engraved from the original picture by Harrison Weir (in the London Field) of a pair of the noted trio of Dark Brahmas first sent to England by me, to Mr. John Bailey, Mount Street, London. This pair were exhibited at the Birmingham Poultry Show, took the first prize, and were sold at the close of the exhibition to Mr. E. Taylor, of Shepard's Bush, for one hundred guineas — over $500! Mr. Bailey paid me $100 for this trio, a few months previous to the Birmingham Fair. The Brahmas I now breed are of the same stock, precisely, as well as those of the Light variety, (see cut No. 3,) which I sent the same season from Melrose to HER BRITISH MAJESTY, QUEEN VICTORIA. They have taken many first prizes at the fairs both in England and America, where they have been shown in competition, and have proved first class, uniformly, when bred in their purity.

This stock is pronounced, on both sides of the Atlantic, to be the largest and finest poultry in the known world, and hundreds of breeders and fanciers attest to the fact that, when properly cared for, they are the *best*, either as layers, for the table, or as breeders. I now keep but few fowls, and make a specialty only of raising the great Asiatic fowls — the Brahmas, the Partridge and the Buff Cochins — of which I can supply selected specimens, to order. These fowls are good enough for me — and I have tried all kinds.

The "Dark Brahma" we have in this country at the present time, and which is a very fine fowl — some strains being superior to others, however — has been brought into especial notice only since 1865–6. The editor of the New York American Agriculturist as well as of the Bulletin, have been largely instrumental in bringing the merits of these noble birds to the attention of the lovers of good poultry, and the different importations that have come out from England, from Messrs. Bailey, Tebay, Cooper, Beldon, Boyle, Baker, Taylor, Bates and others, have proved generally very good and satisfactory birds; which have received through the medium of the excellent and widely circulated journals mentioned, deserved encomiums, from time to time, to the great benefit of the importers, and to the poultry-loving community throughout the United States and the Canadas.

But as I hinted in my communication last quoted —

there are unmistakable evidences, in some of these samples of " Dark Brahmas," of what I met with while in England in 1867, and there first noticed — to wit, the palpable presence of the Gray Dorking blood. The black mottled breast, square form, dominique feather, is decidedly Dorking-ish. I saw several specimens of these " Dark Brahmas," so called, upon which I detected the *fifth toe*, which belongs inevitably to that race, as is well known. (See " Gray Dorking," page 220,) I have not seen this peculiarity *here*, yet. That *all* these dark Brahmas are bred with Dorkings, in England, I do not mean to suggest, by any means, and possibly few or none of those that have been imported into this country latterly from Great Britain, have been thus contaminated. But my original " Dark Brahmas " were *not* black-breasted. They were dark mottled gray, and the neck and outer wing feathering was silvery white. In other respects they were like the light Brahmas, in form, etc.

Now *all* these Dark Brahmas, mark, come from England and Ireland — latterly. Has any one in America imported from Shanghæ, or from the Brahma-poutra River, that discharges itself into the Bay of Bengal " (!) or from Cochin China (!!) or from *any* where on earth, else, except Great Britain, during the past five years, any Dark Brahma fowls? Not one! If they have, I have never heard of the fact, and shall gladly stand corrected, upon learning such importer's name. We do *not* get then, in all of these " dark Brahmas," the genuine thing, I apprehend.

We give in cut No. 12, a very fair illustration of these black-breasted Dark Brahmas — the color of which is too dark to suit our own taste; but which strain of blood is certainly very popular among American fanciers.

C. C. Loring of South Boston imported some very good specimens of this variety, which have become well known, and Philander Williams of Taunton, Isaac Van Winkle of Greenville N. J., J. M. Wade of Philadelphia, and other enterprising poulterers and fanciers have imported other samples, of similar stock; the prevailing color of the cocks (as is delineated in illustration No. 12,) being of the very darkly flecked, or quite black breast, thighs, and under feathering — while the neck-hackles, saddles, and upper wing-coverts are silvery white, splashed with pale straw-color.

These male birds all partake in form of the hunchy Dorking fowl, manifestly. The color of the hens, however, is even, and good. But, as *we* have bred the Dark Brahmas, for years past, and as they were first introduced by us, into England, we contend that none of these birds which have latterly come under our observation, are as fine in form, carriage, or color, as were the originals, from which we have for so long a period successfully and satisfactorily bred this variety. And this more strongly confirms us in the opinion that the Dorking has been mixed with these recently imported "Dark Brahmas;" for we can plainly see that the similarity of *form*, as well as deepened color of the Dorking, is strikingly developed in these samples.

It is notoriously known in England that my Brahma stock and that of others sent there from the United States, has been bred to the black-breasted Gray Dorking cock, to produce the coveted "dark mottled body" some of these best specimens show. When, by and bye, the ' fifth toe ' shows itself, here, on our dark Brahmas, then — *nous verrons!*

Meantime, " blood will tell." The strong Chinese characteristics largely predominate in the "dark Brahmas" that I have seen here thus far, and I sincerely hope they will continue to produce their like; for our American fanciers have now expended a deal of money on this variety; and they ought (as I trust they have) to have secured pure-bred birds. This mottled-breasted Gray Dorking is a spendid fowl, and a great favorite, justly, amongst English fanciers. But *I* don't care to breed for a *Brahma* fowl one that has a taint of even the excellent sable-bosomed gray Dorking in it. When I want the latter, I will breed the Dorking, *pure*, if I can procure the stock. But I have yet to be convinced that the crossing of these two breeds improves the heathen Chinee-Brahma, though you may thus get the black breast, for a time. I am looking for it constantly—and I hope yet to see (if my suspicions prove correct) some account of the *progeny* of this new dark Brahma stock, down into the fourth or fifth generation, if possible, *direct;* whereby we may learn whether or not the fifth toe, the long tail, or the smooth leg of the Dorking crops out at last among these chickens!

The Dark Brahmas that have been exhibited within

A PRACTICAL TREATISE ON DOMESTIC FOWLS. 215

the past two or three years at our American Poultry Fairs, have certainly been very fine — except for the reasons I have suggested — that they are a little *too*

PEA-COMB DARK BRAHMAS, AND GAME BANTAMS, AS BRED BY
D. L. STAGE & CO. SCHENECTADY, N. Y.

dark for my taste. But they have given great satisfaction, and, as far as heard from, have bred truly, it is said. Cut No. 5 is a portrait of one of the Dark Brahma hens I sent to Mr. Baily, of London, the premium bird; and the picture is an admirable one — delineating the best contour of this noted fowl.

I was not surprised, a few days since, to receive a letter from a leading breeder of this variety, who has imported several trios of Dark Brahmas, who is a thorough stickler for purity of blood, and who has paid roundly for his specimens imported from England; from which letter I quote the following expressive words — in support of these last suggestions of mine. He says "I have seen enough of Cooper's, Boyle's, and Beldon's fowls, *not* to purchase any more of them. I can beat any of the English Dark Brahmas, infinitely, with my own — and I have now six different English strains of dark Brahmas!" Has my worthy friend begun to discover in the English strains the ' cloven foot,' *alias* the fifth toe, of the black-breasted Grey Dorking, possibly ?

On page 215 may be seen the likeness of another superior male specimen of this noted breed, from imported stock. This represents the stock of Mr. Newton, and those also from the well know establishment of Mr. Wm. H. Pond, Milford, Conn., O. H. Edmonds, Melrose, Mass., and others. These Dark Brahmas are believed to be of perfectly pure China blood, and chickens bred from them come up admirably, thus far. This fowl stock has taken leading premiums at the Fairs in 1869, and 1870, and the progeny promises finely, thus far.

No. II. PAIR OF SILVER SPANGLED HAMBURGS.
From J. Clarence Sidell, Englewood, N. J. 217.

Cut No. 6 represents a third group of superb Dark Brahmas, from the imported stock of D. W. Herstine, of Philadelphia. These, like the others, present the prominent characteristics of the *true* Brahma, in feature, form, and size — and those who have bred from the descendants of these fowls, pronounce the chickens perfect. All this is highly satisfactory. May they continue to do so — is our hearty wish, for the credit of the English breeders, as well as for the benefit of American purchasers; who, as a rule, prefer this strain of fowl without the excellences which may attach to the Gray Dorking, in *its* pure state.

The imported Dark Brahmas of C. C. Loring, of Boston, have attained to very considerable notoriety, and both chickens and eggs from his stock have given great satisfaction. We have yet to see any better samples, however, than those bred last year and this by Mr. Mark Pitman of Salem, and Mr. J. Graves of Reading, Mass.

Mr. E. J. Taylor of Waterloo, N. Y., breeds the Brahmas, light and dark, the Buff and Partridge Cochins, a few of the choicest Games, and one or two French strains, with great care and success. He informs us that he packs eggs for incubation carefully in dry saw-dust, and finds that they hatch a fair percentage. He adds, " I breed only a few varieties, to which I give my attention, and I speak from experience when I say that these few combine all the good qualities, while they are free from many of the faults of other varieties, many of which I have discarded, after testing, at different times, in favor of those I now keep. My breeding stock has been selected with great care, and in accordance with W. B. Tegetmeier's standard, acknowledged the best. I have several breeders, imported from Cooper and Beldon; but I have also my own home-bred stock — equal to the others in size and fine points — while my Games are from celebrated strains, renowned alike for their courage, stamina, and beauty."

DARK BRAHMAS.

Of these Mr. Taylor writes us that "this noble variety are becoming popular very rapidly, and are worthy of all that is said and written in their praise. They are excellent layers, especially in winter, good sitters and mothers, and very good for table use. I have one cock and eight hens of this variety, all of which are elegantly pencilled and free from Vulture hock. The cock, at eight months old, weighed nine pounds two ounces, and is indeed a noble specimen of his class."

Mr. Taylor informs us that he takes especial pride in his yard of light Brahmas, and thinks that no one can produce a finer lot of breeders than he now has in stock of this favorite variety — either for pedigree or exactness in pencilling. Mr. T. purchased of Isaac Van Winkle Esq., his entire stock of the "Duke of York" strain, and a portion of the celebrated "Autocrat" strain — both these being from the splendid imported stock of E. C. Comey, of Quincy, originally. Mr. T's Buff Cochins are said to be very superior, from prize birds, and equal to the best. But this extensive breeder deems the Partridge Cochins altogether unexceptionable. His Buffs are imported directly from the yards of J. C. Cooper, and are pronounced to be among the choicest of this race now in America.

CHAPTER XVIII.

THE ENGLISH GRAY DORKING.

I CALL this superior fowl the *English* Gray Dorking, because, like the Houdan, La Fleche, etc., already described as natives of France, *this* bird is indigenous to Great Britain; and all early English writers set down this really fine variety, par excellence, at the head of the list of domestic poultry. This opinion ruled, however, prior to the introduction of the Queen's Cochin Chinas, or my Brahma fowls, into merrie England; since when, *nous avons change tout cela!* At the head of this chapter we give an authentic portrait copied from an excellent English poultry book, published in 1850; wherein this variety is described minutely.

Englishmen may be permitted best to know the character and value of their own native productions. In regard to the *Dorking* Fowl, the editor of the Farmer's Gazette (in 1859) says of the particular bird above illustrated, that its owner, "Mr. Nolan brought the cock figured above, to our office on the 23d of January, when we had him weighed; the bird was in moult, and his condition much reduced. He weighed, in that state ten and a quarter lbs., and we have no doubt that when in full plumage and condition, he will weigh nearer 14 lbs. than 12. We can also state from our own knowledge, that the common roadside cock, even in the wildest district in Ireland, would weigh alive, from 7 to 9 lbs."

This statement was brought out in reference to the account given of the male Dorking fowls average *weight*, by the Rev. Mr. Dixon, author of "Ornamental and Domestic Poultry;" who therein states that "a fine Dorking cock weighed only about 7 pounds."

The cocks of the GRAY DORKING breed at one to two years old, in good condition, will average from 10 1-2 to 12 lbs. weight, hens of same age, 7 to 8 lbs. They have moderate length of leg, averaging about that of the Shanghæ race, short, plump, roundish bodies, ample tails, square, full dark plumed breast, and their meat is rich, white and juicy. As a table fowl they have no superior; and here we come to the important point already alluded to, as it appears in some recently found "Dark Brahmas," probably crossed with this strongly marked bird. "Their plumage is gray or mottled, the *cocks having black or dark speckled breasts*, and the feet being furnished with the distinctive markings of an additional, or fifth toe. They originated in Surrey county, England, and are described by other early authors, as a very large breed, with five toes, being good layers and sitters.' There can be " no fowl better calculated to enhance the profits of the farm-yard than this, from their goodly size, abundant flesh, and their uniformity in breeding. What we want and expect in this fowl is *size;* and these Gray Dorking birds have it, in perfection."

Columella, who wrote about poultry as far back as sometime in the first century, describes the Gray Dorking of to-day very accurately, and classed it *then* as " the best fowl of his time — speckled *in color*, dark-breasted, of fine plumage, and possessing five toes." Columella also wrote this advice hundreds of years ago about the Dorking: —" Let the *white* ones be avoided, for they are comparatively tender." And Mr. Courtney, who imported the Grays in '43, says " the whites are bred out ; the Gray Dorking variety is now the rage, and are altogether, perhaps, the best barnyard fowls in existence."

It will be seen by the life-like engraving we give (cut No. 8.) that the male Gray (or *true*) Dorking of which we have been speaking, is a very distinctly marked and formed bird. The breast is black, mottled or flecked with white, his comb is either upright or rose, he is short-legged, and square-bodied; most of these characteristics predominating in a greater or less degree, in the new-fashioned "Dark Brahmas;" regarding which latter variety even the ever careful editors of the American Agriculturist remark, in March 1871, that they "have useful characteristics, very clearly resembling the Cochins," but "their plumage bears a striking resemblance to that of the Gray Dorking, in color; having, however, the different fluffy, downy texture of the Chinese fowl." The plumage of the late prize Gray Dorkings at the N. Y, Poultry Show thus referred to in that admirable journal, and illustrated upon the same page, does indeed "bear a striking resemblance" to the plumage of the prize Dark Brahmas. The color and markings upon breast, flanks, wings, saddle and neck — are almost identical!

But the Gray Dorking (see Herstine's fine illustration, cut No. 8) is now preferred in England, by many breeders, over all others, and this chosen variety has had a wondrously steady reputation, there, for centuries. There can be no doubt that this fowl is thus deservedly popular in the Island that produced it, luckily; and the samples which have reached this country have always attracted attention, from their great size and beauty of plumage. But when the excitement began to turn in 1844 '5 towards the Queen's "Cochin Chinas," and subsequently took another surge in favor of the "Brahmas," and then towards the Buff and Partridge Shanghæs, or Cochins, the Gray Dorking was forgotten for the time, even in England, comparatively. But a use was soon found for this temporarily neglected, though ever reliable bird — among fanciers.

Thus it was thought to be a "happy idea" in the individual who first conceived and adopted the plan of utilizing the strong blood of the Gray Dorking, whose speckled plumage somewhat resembled that of the dark colored Brahma, in England, by breeding this Gray Dorking male to grey China pullets. The result was highly satisfactory, in the first generation — for, though the Gray Dorking blood was known to be so well established that it will mark its imprint on *any* race of fowls known — to the surprise and gratification of the breeder, the blood of the China bird proved to be so much the strongest, that this cross produced only an "improved Brahma," instead of the half-anticipated improved Dorking.

But the 'cloven foot' perplexed them. The fifth toe came out upon some of the very best specimens grown in Europe, at the outset. Through breeding these hens back to the grey Shanghæ male, however, this imperfection disappeared; and, persistently followed, the sought-for improved "Dark Brahma" of our later day was in some instances gained. The Gray Shanghæs at Her Majesty's Poultry-house were bred in this way, to the Gray Dorking, for a time, as was admitted by the Queen's poultry-keeper, himself. But this was tried as an experiment, merely — as many other experiments are constantly being tried there. Yet might not some of that very progeny from the royal aviary at Windsor, have found its way into the hands of dealers in London, or elsewhere, readily? The product of the first cross was very fine, and the thus "improved" Gray Shanghæs were really splendid looking specimens of English "Dark Brahmas." In the hands of the uninitiated, or not over-careful sellers of poultry, in England — for there *may* possibly be such dealers in that country — might not the thus Gray Dorking-ized Grey Chinese fowl be rendered a very saleable "Dark Brahma," for the nonce? I think so. But I may be mistaken.

Still, the Gray Dorking, in its purity, will always stand upon its feet alone, as one of the very best varieties of Domestic Fowl in the world. It is a large fowl, too. When well bred, the weight of both cocks and hens average as heavy as the largest. Its meat is unrivalled. They lay good sized eggs, and a goodly number of them, annually. As sitters and as mothers they are faultless. In plumage, they are showy and stately, until they get to be aged — when they 'hunch down,' and become soggy. But, taken all in all, this favorite bird can scarcely be excelled, for most of the qualities that are desirable in a fowl of the very first class, uniformly.

Mr. D. W. Herstine, of Philadelphia, an extensive and spirited breeder, furnishes Cut No. 8, for our pages (among other very good ones) and he writes us that while he "is an advocate of pure breeding, as a rule, yet if a cross is desired for the farmer or large poulterer, none is in his judgment more desirable than the Gray Dorking, upon any variety — for general utility, and satisfactory results to the breeder. But for a prime cross, the great Dorking fowl upon the Brahma or Cochin, is unexceptionable; and will prove the most largely profitable to the producer, both in weight of progeny, at a given period, and in weight of eggs, regularly."

The popular character of this Dorking fowl, which has for centuries been a deserved favorite on the other side of the Atlantic, and superb specimens of which have in late years been imported by several gentlemen into the United States, affords us ample evidence of its genuine merits; and we are well aware that for a cross upon our native or other breeds of fowl-stock — where strictly *pure* blood of any variety is not sought — this fowl has no superior among us.

CHAPTER XIX.

THE GAME FOWL, AND ITS USES.

Epicures insist that no domestic bird known equals the *Game* Fowl, for the spit. Cock-fighting amateurs (in that line of "the fancy,") affirm, with equal emphasis, that this is the only one for the pit. We will take it for granted that both these assumptions are correct. We have eaten this toothsome fowl-meat, frequently, but never raised a game chicken, or fought one; though, in our time, we have been present at more than one contested main, where hundreds of these spunky, beautiful, active belligerents have gone in and won—or lost, the fiercely and hotly-fought battle, *a l' outrance.*

We shall not venture into ecstacies over the pugnacious qualities of this fowl, inasmuch as individually we look upon *this* use of one of God's creatures as equivocal; and the worthy Mr. Bergh has taken the matter of cock-fighting under his care, as a leader in the charity of that benevolent institution known as the "Society for the Prevention of cruelty to Animals," with a view to the extermination of this "sport" in the northern States. When he succeeds in putting a stop to this popular amusement, he will undoubtedly let the public know it!

There be those who raise this fine Fowl in quantities for both pit and spit, and with rare skill, among our poultry fanciers; and our Book would certainly be incomplete without a chapter devoted to this (in many phases) remarkable bird — which is a distinct variety of the race of fowls, and altogether peculiar to itself. Its eagerness for combat, its unyielding courage under fearful punishment, and its plucky, daring, hardy, saucy character, from the shell to its death, are but its natural tendencies.

Those who have never seen these courageous little creatures in a matched battle, can have no idea of the amount of abuse they can endure in the arena. But the sport has now fallen into disuse in our immediate Christian community, though it is practised largely in other parts of America, especially at the South and West, we are informed; and thousands of these Game

Fowls are annually raised, bought and sold, by breeders who have the better strains of fighting-stock, which are sent out in all directions in this country.

The origin of cock-fighting is Grecian, but the Cubans and Spaniards have always largely indulged in what they term this "pastime." At Athens, this amusement was made a political, and at one time partially a religious institution, and was kept up there for a period, for the avowed purpose of "improving the valor and courage of their youth." The Romans fought Quails, as well as Cocks. For the information of our readers, we annex a brief history and description of this Fowl, and the uses to which it is put, written by one who is better acquainted with this particular branch of chicken-raising than we pretend to be.

"It is not known when the 'pitched battle' was first introduced into England. We have no notice of cock-fighting earlier than the reign of Henry II. It is described then, as the sport of school-boys, on Shrove Tuesday; the theatre was the school, and the schoolmaster was controller and director of the sport. The practice was prohibited under Edward III., but became general under Henry VIII., who was personally attached to it, and established a cock-pit at Whitehall, to bring it more into credit. James the First was so fond of cock-fighting, that, according to Monsieur de la Bodenie, ambassador for Henry IV. to the King, he constantly amused himself with it, twice a week. Under 'the good Queen' Elizabeth, this rough sport was not less in vogue, and the learned Roger Ascham then

DERBY GAME COCK AND HEN.

AS BRED BY P. W HUDSON, COL. GEO. MEACHAM, S. J. BESTOR, I. VAN WINKLE, E. I. TAYLOR, AND OTHERS.

favored the world with a treatise on the subject. There was at that time a pit in Drury-lane, Horse-ferry road, and Gray's-Inn-lane, St. James's Park, and another in Jewin-street; but the practice was a second time prohibited, by an act under the Protectorship. The Dublin pits are of a more recent date, where the Meaths and Kildares often proved the powers of their cocks. The fights were managed by men who made a livelihood by it, and were called handlers: they alone were admissible within the "magic circle" of the fighting arena.

"A cock-pit, like a race-course, in a sporting point of view, is for every person; and selection of company is entirely out of the question. The noble lord and the *needy* commoner, were both at home, after they had paid their *tip* for admission, and persons who enter the pit to sport a *crown*, bet a *sovereign*, or to put down their pounds, are too much interested upon the *main*, to consider who they may choose to "*rub* against" for the time being.

"Cock-fighting was kept up with great spirit at Newcastle. At one of their late meetings, the cockers at the above place, in point of extent, exceeded everything of the kind known in Great Britian. Upwards of 200 cocks were fought, and the fighting was generally good. A remarkable circumstance occurred on the Saturday before fighting. A match was made for 20 sovereigns, between Parker and Reed, feeders, and won by the latter after a hard contest. Parker's cock, however, came round so soon after, that his party made a second match, to come, off, on the following Monday, for a like sum, which was again won by Reed, after a severe battle — a circumstance, perhaps, altogether unknown in the annals of cocking. It is also calculated that, at the termination of the races, which finished with cocking, upwards of 1,000 cocks had met their death. Newcastle, therefore, challenged the world for cock-fighting. Cheltenham, Chester, Gloucester, Norwich, Lancaster, Preston, Stamford, &c., &c., were celebrated for their cocks. The patrons were the Earl of Derby, Sir William Wynne, Ralph Benson, Esq., &c., &c.

"The exterior qualifications of a cock are, head thin and long, or, if not, very taper; a large, full eye; beak crooked and stout; neck thick and long (a cock with a long neck has a great advantage in the battle, particularly if his antagonist is one of those cocks that will fight at no other place but the head); his body short and compact, with a round breast (as a sharp-breasted cock carries a great deal of useless weight about him, and never has a fine forehand); his thighs fine and thick, and placed well up to the shoulder (for where a cock's legs hang dangling behind him, he never can maintain a long battle); his legs long and thick, and if they correspond with the color of his beak — blue, gray, or yellow — a perfection; his feet should be broad and thin, with very long claws. With regard to his carriage, he should be upright, but not stiffly so; his walk should be stately, and not plod along, as some cocks do, with their wings upon their backs, like geese; his color rather gray, yellow, or rose, with black breast; his spurs rough, long, and looking inward. As to the color he is of, it is immaterial; there are good cocks of all colors; but he should be thin of feathers, short, and very hard, which is another proof of his being healthy. A cock, with all his stoutness, length, and thickness of leg, rotundity of breast, " fine forehand," firmness of neck, and extent of wing, ought not to weigh more than 4lb. 8 or 10oz.; if he happens to have an ounce or two more in his composition, he is out of the pale of the pit, and is excluded by match-makers, from " fighting within the articles." A bird, to be a bird, " fit for the white bag, the trimmed wing, the mat, and the silver spur," must be light upon the leg, light fleshed, and large boned, but still no more than 4lb. 8 or 10oz.

" A cock-pit was a large, lofty, circular building, with seats rising, as in an amphitheatre; in the middle of it was a round, matted stage, of about 18 or 20 feet in diameter, and rimmed with an edge eight or ten inches in height, to keep the cocks from falling over in their combats; there was a chalk ring in the centre of the matted stage, of a yard diameter; and another chalk mark within it, much smaller, which was intended for the setting-to, when the shattered birds were so enfeebled as to have no power of making hostile advances towards each other. This inner mark admitted of their being placed beak to beak. A large and rude branched candlestick was suspended low down, immediately over the mat, which was used at the night-battles. The birds were weighed and matched, and then marked and numbered; the descriptions were carefully set down in order that the cock should not be changed; the lightest cocks fought first in order. The key of the pens, in which the cocks were set and numbered, was left on the weighing-table; or the opposite party might, if he pleased, put a lock on the door. The utmost care was taken that the *matched* fowls should fight, and that no substitutes should be intruded."

Sometimes the first blow is fatal, at another time the contest is long and doubtful, and the cocks show all the obstinate courage, weariness, distress, and breathlessness which mark the struggle of experienced pugilists. The beak opens; the tongue palpitates; the wing drags on the mat; the legs tremble, and the body topples over upon the breast; the eye grows dim, and even a perspiration breaks out upon the feathers of the back. When the battle lasts long, and the cocks lay helpless near or upon each other, one of the feeders counts ten, and the birds are separated, and set-to at the chalk. If the beaten bird does not fight while forty is counted, and the other pecks or shows signs of battle, the former is declared conquered. And except when one or the other is killed outright, which frequently occurs, this ends the battle between these two — and another matched pair are brought in, to go through this routine, "to death or victory."

The flesh of the Game fowl is white, tender, and delicate; the eggs rather small, mostly inclining to a light buff. Cockers have numerous names for the different colors — such as piles, black-breasted reds, silver-breasted ducks, dark grays, mealy grays, blacks, spangles, cuckoos, gingers, red duns, smoky duns, among all of which good birds may be found : but the following are considered superior to any parti-colored birds—namely: dark reds, dark black-breasted red, dark black-breasted birchin ducks, black-breasted duck-wing grays, clear mealy grays, dark black-breasted grays, and red duns.

The general appearance of the Game hen is quite in character with that of the cock. In one respect, she is a more important personage, as it is an axiom among cock-masters that the produce of an ill-bred hen is worthless, no matter how superior the cock may be;

but that an indifferent cock and superior hen may produce good birds. It is not indispensable that the eggs should be buff-colored: that generally received idea is a popular error.

To enter into further minutiæ of the fighting character of this fowl, would be to furnish little that would interest my readers. Suffice it to say, the cock is confined for a month in a small wooden pen, with but little light; fed at various periods of his incarceration with different kinds of food adapted to bring about the condition of wind and limb required for the battle, and to fit him finally for the cock-pit previous to the setting-to, when they are frequently pruned and trimmed in the shape as seen on next page, and placed in the ring, to be spurred and battered to death.

The rules of the arena for matched game fowls above set down, governed the English and Irish pits. In the American ring the regulations are different, and heavier birds are bred and fought here. The general ideas, however, are followed out, and the amount of this sort of business indulged in at various points in the United States can only be guessed at, from the large sales made every year by those who breed this kind of fowl carefully in various sections. Hundreds and thousands of these birds, male and female, are purchased, however, by gentlemen who never think of entering them in a cock pit; their remarkable laying, sitting and table qualities being first-class, and rendering them very desirable for crossing upon native or other breeds.

One thing is very certain, to wit, that in our exhibition

GAME COCKS TRIMMED FOR BATTLE.

rooms, notwithstanding the attractions that the larger China varieties afford, the visitor's attention is always arrested by the show in the Game pens, and everybody is delighted with the beauty and proud carriage of these martial looking birds. Mr. Hewitt says "among any of the truly bred Game fowls, the superiority of gait, and general contour strikes the eye of parties, even the most indifferent and uninterested; and from this cause I have almost universally noticed that the avenues appropriated to the Games, at our poultry shows, are those most commonly thronged by visitors. And this fully proves how much a good display in these classes tends to the pecuniary success of such exhibitions."

At the present time, a great many American breeders have gone to raising Game fowls, and frequent fresh importations are being made by fanciers in this country, who have turned their attention latterly to this variety, in some instances as a specialty in poultry. From the pugnacious disposition of this fowl, it is not well to breed it contiguously to other varieties, however: and to breed it well, only prime stock should be used, and the utmost care given to the business.

GAME COCK AND HEN.

Those who have tried the game fowls of S. J. Bestor and S. C. Colt, of Hartford, Conn., are unanimous in the declaration that no strains of blood in New England of this variety are bred with greater care, or which excel these in all the attributes that go to make up the best of the race. These fanciers take a becoming pride in importing and producing the choicest kinds of games, and they have uniformly taken first premiums whenever they have competed at the fowl Shows, with their elegant birds of this species. Samples of this stock, bred originally in their walks, have also frequently carried off prizes, when exhibited by purchasers of their fine strains; and they very confidently challenge comparison, for beauty of form, feather, carriage, pluck and reliableness, with the progeny of their superior Game stock. Messrs. Bestor and Colt have in their possession upwards of two hundred premiums which have been awarded them for their exhibited fowls, consisting of medals, plate, monies, diplomas, etc., and it is but just to state that all who have dealt with them have been more than satisfied with what they so carefully send out from their well conducted yards. There are others who breed this beautiful variety, but we know of none who have been so successful, and who take more earnest pains to keep their Game stock up to the fighting standard, so uniformly, as do these gentlemen; and the above spirited engraving — drawn expressly for them, from a Game cock and hen upon their own premises, gives a good idea of the style of their favorite birds.

The spirited illustration to be found in cut No. 9 is a truthful likeness of the ever popular Black Red Games, bred to a nicety. Messrs. Dudley, Brothers, of Augusta, N. Y., write: "we are making the breeding of the Game fowl a specialty, and have added to our previous variety, five kinds during the past year. Though our experience is not so large as some, yet we find there is great satisfaction in the business, and in knowing that we breed pure bloods. It is important that those who undertake this work should have a knowledge of the valuable " points " in such fowls, and then they should select the very best to be had. The Game *hen* should be as large as can be found, so that the chicks should be good sized. The cock should be of the right *color* desired, since the progeny will more generally take their color from the male bird. Early chickens of this breed, like others, are the best, as they then have time to mature, or nearly so, before our cold weather sets in — and such chicks have proved with us to be more hardy, and less liable to disease. We have not been troubled with vermin or sickness in our birds, but always deem it best if we send off fowls, to have them pass through quarantine, before putting them with others; so that if not sound, they may be cured before contaminating their new mates. Precaution of this kind is not troublesome, and ensures greater satisfaction to both seller and buyer. We have satisfied ourselves that careful breeding tells, and we are sure that such a course can be rendered profitable in the end."

Col G. W. Meacham, of North Cambridge, Mass., has expended a good deal of money in importing from the most noted yards of England and Ireland, several choice strains of sturdy Games, which he breeds with cautious nicety and skill; and gentlemen who covet first-rate birds of this variety, can rely upon obtaining genuine bloods of this dealer. Col. Meacham takes pride in having the very *best* that money can procure, from abroad,

No. 12. LATELY IMPORTED DARK BRAHMAS.
Bred by I. Van Winkle, Jos. M. Wade, Philander Williams, J. Graves, G. P. Burnham, C. H. Edmonds, Mark Pitman, etc.

and does not halt at their cost, when he knows he can obtain *the* thing, on either side of the Atlantic, to improve his already well supplied yards at Somerville. He breeds some other fine varieties — among them being the Chinese fowl; but none excel him for reliable and well trained Game birds.

DUCK-WING GAME COCK.

G. W. Felter, of Batavia, Ohio, makes a specialty of Game Fowls, also, and has what is esteemed in the West the leading variety — and the favorite in that section — known as the "Derby White" game; imported in '62, and bred by A. Oskamp, up to '69. They vary in weight from 4 1-2 to 6 lbs., and for style, symmetry and true *game* qualities, these are said to be unsurpassed. Mr. Felter writes me that, in his experience, he has found that "the care of young *chicks* is of the utmost importance, soon after their hatching;" and adds, "I have long been a lover of fine poultry, but until I practiced it, did not appreciate the following mode of benefitting these delicate little creatures — not being for some time aware that *every* chicken taken from the sitting nest, is at first very lousy. I now carefully grease them, the day after hatching, under wings and on the head, and also the mother-hen in the same way and at the same time, using common fresh lard, and repeating the operation in two weeks. The vermin thus destroyed are a source of great trouble and evil to both old and young fowls. I think this has much to do with producing *gapes* in chickens; and this application of the lard, seasonably, will be found an excellent prevention against this troublesome disease." Mr. Felter's plan is an old but good one. A better one, however, is to saturate the nest-box (inside and at bottom,) just before you set your hen, with kerosene oil — and you will find no lice on your newly-hatched chicks.

The following breeders have superb Game birds, all of the best blood and varieties to be had in America. Their stock is imported from England and Ireland, and these dealers are constantly renewing their strains from the best yards in Great Britain. They are experienced in the reproduction of the various styles of popular Game fowl, and inform us that they can supply orders for first-class birds. S. J. Bestor, and S. C. Colt, Hartford Conn., have a splendid stock. Isaac Van Winkle, Greenville, N. J. has paid attention to importing and raising superior bloods, and has recently received from Ireland fresh stock. D. L. Wilbor, of Boonsboro', Iowa, has fine strains, which are well kept up. J. W. P. Hovey, Evanston, Ill's., keeps good stock. C. S. White, Elmira, N. Y., and Geo. Whiston, Buffalo, E. J. Taylor, Waterloo, N. Y. P. W. Hudson, North Manchester, Conn., makes Game-fowl-rearing a specialty. Col. Geo. Meacham, North Cambridge, breeds superior Games, and C. H. Edmonds, Melrose, Mass., will breed the Duck Wing Games this season, and has procured his stock out of prize birds. All these fanciers can supply first-class Game birds; and here we leave them and their favorites to "fight it out, on this line," with the concluding remark upon this bellicose subject, that it it hardly surprising that the Yankee should take to this spunky and beautiful variety of domestic fowl, thus eagerly, since he so naturally inclines to the belief, that, with the right kind of material, fashioned within his own province and supervision, he can "beat all creation," in anything; and it is certain that the Game Fowl has come to be bred to a high state of perfection on this side of the Atlantic, where hundreds of fanciers of this belligerent little tribe announce themselves ready at all times to test their stock against competitors, with any length of gaffle, for amusement, **fame,** or **money.**

Messrs. J. Y. Bicknell & Co., of Westmoreland, N. Y. are extensive breeders of most of the popular varieties now extant among us, and have in late years been the largest contributers to the N. Y. State and other exhibitions, as well as among the leading prize-takers, for good specimens of their valuable and well-bred stock. Messrs. Bicknell & Co. enjoy a deservedly good reputation among a numerous class of patrons, and they have sent out from their capacious establishment large numbers of prime fowls, bred from their imported and other choice strains of bloods, that have given the highest satisfaction to their customers. Of the Asiatic fowls, they have some first class breeding-stock — the light and dark Brahmas, the Buffs, and the Partridge-Cochins — upon which they pride themselves.

CHAPTER XX.

THE BLACK SPANISH, AND GUELDRES.

We pass by the *Malay*, the *Kulm*, the *Bucks* County, and the *Chittagong* Fowls, with a mere reference to the names of these old-style and formerly acknowledged " breeds — " one of these being claimed as the original Java, or gallus giganteus of early authors — because we have few of them around us, at present, and nobody seems to be interested in them; since we can obtain better, finer, and more profitable varieties, among the more modern kinds now to be had, in almost any direction, in the United States and England. Three of the above mentioned varieties were formerly deemed good ones, and we have imported of one kind, and bred that and the other two kinds—to our entire content. They are all illustrated, and dilated on, in the poultry-books of past days; but they are each and every one coarse, bony, ungainly, uneven birds, and could not be had in this country now, if wanted—that we know of, (which they are not,) and so we say no more about them; but pass to the next important and desirable variety, in due course; a celebrity that many breeders and fanciers deem very handsome, and about "*the* thing" for either a gentleman, an amateur, or a farmer; and this is the white faced *Black Spanish* Fowl. See cut No. 7.

A few years ago, as we well remember, this showy, white-cheeked, proud-gaited, coal-black bird was all the rage, for a period. Though from being called Spanish, they are popularly supposed to have come from Spain, yet this fowl is from Holland, and is now well known in England and in this country, and justly estimated, generally. It is a medium sized fowl, but lays a large white egg, and in this respect is a very excellent variety. They are non-sitters, too. Their chickens, are raised without difficulty, but when fledged — like their parents they can "fly like eagles," and it is difficult to keep them in confined quarters by means of any ordinary height of fence surrounding their yards, for they are an active, restless, roaming race — and are thus objectionable to one's neighbors. They are interminable "scratchers," and will tear up a newly-laid-down garden, faster than it can be repaired, if once they get at it, in earnest!

Still, this majestic sprightly fowl has very many admirers; and beautiful specimens — highly bred — may be had of the dealers, almost everywhere now-a-days. An English author thus accurately describes this bird, of which we furnish a very good illustration in Cut No. 7.

" I take the Black Spanish fowl to be a truly distinct variety, and everything experience can acquire of it, adds to its character of originality. A full grown cock weighs about 7 lbs., the hen about 6 lbs.; the cock stands about 22 inches high, and the hen about 19 inches; the plumage is a beautiful glossy black. I have seen some birds showing the appearance of the highest breeding, which have come from Spain; the comb is serrated, and so large as to usually fall at one side, of vivid scarlet; wattles long; ear-lobes white; cheek white, but added to by age; hackles black, tail splendidly plumed; legs blue; flesh and skin beautifully white and juicy; is a first-rate table-fowl; eggs white, large and abundant; chickens grow rapidly, but feather slowly. They are not very pugnacious, if kept together, but if separated, even for a day, they cease to associate quietly with their companions. The hens are not inclined to sit, which is perhaps an Irish cause of their becoming so abundant; they are everlasting layers, and their eggs are usually hatched out by common poultry. They are now to be had in every quarter; indeed they are so splendid a bird, that I consider it a crime against domestic economy, to have a Spanish hen's time taken up with hatching and rearing chickens, when she might be

adding to the stock of her own genus by her egg every day."

I am not an advocate for cross-breeding of any sort, and shall therefore beg to remark that there are many spurious crosses attempted to be made on the Spanish fowl, which should not be encouraged. And among these crosses, Mr. Ch. Jacque, the scientific French author and artist, says in his fine work on poultry, " the *La Fleche* is the tallest of the true French breeds, and has many points of resemblance with the Spanish, from which I believe it to be descended, by crossing with the *Crevecœur*." There is a strong similarity in all three of the French breeds to many peculiarities of the Spanish, though the difference in the shape of combs and top-knots of the others is very apparent.

The chickens of this breed should not be attempted to be raised until late in spring-time, towards the warm weather; for they " come into this breathing world *not* half made up," as to their feathering; and the cold or rough weather, until they get their natural coats on, (for four or five weeks after hatching,) retards, or destroys them. Like the French fowls, the Black Spanish are very superior table poultry.

The *Guelders*, or "Breda" fowls are both clear black, and clear white, in plumage. Mr. Van Winkle of Greenville, N. J., has some very fine samples of this race, which enjoy the peculiar advantage of being entirely combless, and crestless. The Spanish fowls are ' ornamented ' with tremendous combs, on the contrary, both the cock and hens — upon the latter, this appendage drooping quite down upon one side ; and, in winter time, it is difficult to prevent this showy summer encumbrance from getting frozen, in our northern climate. But the Guelders have little or no combs, very small wattles, and the head thus presents quite a gamey appearance. They are said to be small eaters, as prolific and as hardy as the Houdans, and lay eggs nearly as large as the latter. An excellent fowl for family purposes. From all I have seen of these

Guelders, I think they are very like the "Guelderlands" that were formerly so popular and so plentiful in Essex County, though I should say *they* did not average so large a fowl as those of the present time. The "*Sicily*," bred for several years in Cohasset and vicinity, from imported stock, though varying from the Guelders in *color*, were not dissimilar to these, in other particulars— size, fecundity, form, small combs and wattles, hardy, and admirable layers.

The few persons that have latterly tried the Guelder Fowl, deem them superior, and as bred by Mr. Van Winkle, whose other stock we have already alluded to— they are very fine. Mr. Van Winkle furnishes us with the following minute description of this bird, which he thinks "is sure to become, when better known, a highly popular and valuable addition to the best stock in the United States." He says:—

"They are a breed of fowls very little known in England or America. They were first found in Holland and Belgium, and were called Guelderlands, after a province of that name in Holland, lying south of the Zuyder Zee." Mr. Van Winkle of Greenville, N. J., has kept for several years the White, Black, and Cuckoo varieties. He speaks of them as superior to any of the French Fowls, and in some respects prefers them to the Houdan.

He adds, "They are a fowl of medium size, with full prominent breasts, and large flowing tails. Their peculiar characteristics are in the head, which is destitute of either feathers, crest, or comb, which is very peculiar in shape, being hollowed, or depressed, instead of projecting, with two prominent spikes on each side of the back of the comb. To breed them to the standard, they should not have any comb whatever, except the two little spikes projecting. Cheeks and ear lobes red, wattles red, and in the lock very long and pendulous. The beak in the white ones should be of a milk-white color. The thighs well furnished and vulture hocked, and the shanks of the legs feathered to the toes — though not heavily. The plumage is close and compact, like the Game fowl; which makes them appear in size much smaller than they really are, and is of pure white, or of pure black. There is also the Cuckoo colored. This last color has been successfully bred by me through crossing a Black Guelder Cock with a White Guelder Hen. The Guelders are well adapted to our cold and changeful climates. Not even the Asiatics are better able to withstand the Northern climates than are the Guelders. They are very hardy, and less susceptible to sickness than any other class of fowls, are strangers to Catarrhal affections, or Roupe, are small eaters and lay a large, smooth shelled egg, and seldom incline to sit. They will throughout the year lay more eggs than any other class of fowls, in my experience, and especially in cold winter weather; and their flesh is as delicate and as juicy as the Houdan. Mr. Tegetmeier thinks " it would be difficult to say which do better, the Houdan or Guelder chickens." And says " I like the breed so well that I class them next to the Houdans." *I* class them ahead of the Houdans in egg producing and hardiness, and consider them equal to these in flesh."

CHAPTER XXI.

THE DOMINIQUE, LEGHORN, SPANGLED HAMBURGS, ETC.

The fowl that is popularly known as the *Dominique*, is undoubtedly the veritable domestic bird so pointedly described by the machine-rhymester as

> "The old gray hen with the yellow leg,
> That lays her master many an egg;"

though this variety has long been denominated a mere 'barn-yard fowl,' for the reason that it is so commonly known all over the country, either in its purity, or from its admixture with our native farmers' poultry. But we noticed in a Massachusetts agricultural paper, not long ago, an editorial on the merits of this breed, which concluded with these expressive words: " We have tried most known varieties, and we incline to the opinion, from a goodly experience with the feathered race, that one must go a long way to find a better fowl for the farmer's use, than is this same Dominique." There is much of truth in this plain statement.

Dr. J. C. Bennett says of them, in his work on Poultry: "I know of no fowls that have stood the test of mixing, without deteriorating, better than have the Dominique. They are said to have come from the Island of Dominica, but I doubt it, and incline to the opinion that they took their name from being 'tenants at will,' of some feudal sovreignty. Why it is that such *perfect bloods* should have escaped description by poulterers, I am unable to divine. It is true, they are rather small; but that is the worst that can be said of this breed. They were introduced here by the French, and are not a Dutch fowl."

Mr. Pierce of Danvers, Mass., who bred these fowls years and years ago, as we well remember, like many another good breeder in old Essex County — where they were for a long period very plentiful, and as highly esteemed — says, "Taken all in all I believe them to be one of the very best breeds of fowls we have; and I know of none that changes so little by in-and-in breeding. They are first rate layers, and though they do not come to laying so early as do the Spanish, I think them far better sitters and nurses."

The hens are not large, but lay good sized eggs, and a great many of them. As mothers none excel them. Their meat is excellent, and they are very handsomely plumed, where they are purely bred. The color is a mealy, regular gray, inclining to a blueish cast, when in fresh, full feather. Mostly, the cocks have single combs, but some are double combed; and Col. Howland of Chicago breeds them rose-combed. It is said that some have flesh-colored legs, but we have seen hundreds — aye, thousands of them, with the clear bright, yellow leg, alluded to by the poet. They are a remarkably handsome fowl, larger by considerable than the "Bolton Grays," or Dutch "Every-day Layers," and their plumage (though more softly shaded) is not unlike the feathering of that pretty fowl. The barred feather of the Dominique is a peculiar formation, however, which always shows itself in any cross of these fowls upon others. As a race or breed they are distinct, and, with care, thousands may be produced, from the same families, year after year, without change in their appearance. They breed to a "feather" in color.

In England they have the "Cuckoo Fowl," as they term it there, from the fancy some have of the resemblance of their feathers to those on the cuckoo's breast, and these are identical with our Dominique. But they are so hardy, so even, so steady in reproducing their like, so homelike, so motherly, so easily kept, and so generally liked by farmers, that they will always be favorites with those who are content with a medium-sized, good layer, and a bird that they can always count on — if kept by themselves — "as a sure thing," in the poultry line.

Cut No. 10 gives an admirable representation of this popular fowl, and the engraving is beautifully executed, too; showing a pair of *Dominiques* illustrating this splendid stock. We agree with the editor whom we briefly quoted a page or two back. "One must go a long way to find better fowls generally for the farmer, of its size, than the pure-bred Dominique."

The *Silver-Spangled Hamburg* (see Cut No. 11,) is a very elegant bird to look at. It is sometimes called

"Silver-penciled Dutch" too. It comes from Holland, originally. There is the *golden* spangled Hamburg, also; a sub-variety of this Hamburg Fowl; and both are very beautifully formed and plumed birds. They are comparatively small, however, though like all minor-sized poultry, they are excellent, steady (sometimes called everlasting) layers.

They are busy creatures, when abroad, the little spunky cocks crowing frequently, and the hens cackling riotously, upon laying an egg, for instance. But they are easily kept, small feeders, hardy, and healthy — though the chickens, which are for the most part raised under other breeds of hens, (for the Hamburgs seldom incline to sit) are tender, and must be bred with some care to bring to maturity.

The pullets lay early, and keep right on, all winter, if they have good warm shelter. The cocks weigh 4 to 5 pounds, the hens 3 1-2 to 4. They have the rose-comb, also. Their heads are smallish, and the female is a gamey looking bird. They are not pugnacious, however. As layers, they are first rate, though the egg is small. But they keep at it wondrously, all through the season, and can be kept, if they have good summer range, about as easily and as cheaply as so many pigeons. The "Silver Spangled Hamburgs," as they are bred by J. C. Sidell, of Englewood, N. J., portrayed so beautifully in Cut No. 11, are as fine as any we ever saw, and we have seen and handled vast numbers of these tasteful little creatures, in our time. We call this strain of Sidell's very perfect, and do not doubt that his stock is choice.

The *Golden* Spangled Hamburg is another variety of this breed, the color of the feathering being brilliant yellow and black, instead of silvery white and black, as in the first named. The Cock of this breed is beautiful, and his plumage is remarkably fine. This is sometimes called the Golden Pheasant, from its markings being similar to the wild cock-pheasant. These are rose-combed, too, and the carriage of this proud little fowl is very aristocratic, as he struts about with his pretty hens, in his rich coat of shining golden feathers, tipped and shelled and barred with their uniform lustrous spangles and mottling of black. The hackles are of a reddish coppery hue, as are the breasts and back, usually. Altogether, they are a magnificently plumed fowl, and their general characteristics are similar to those of the Silver-spangled, already noted.

Several breeders of the Golden and Silver Spangled Hamburgs sent us communications for this chapter, which did not come to hand in time, however, for this edition.

We were favored by one or two gentlemen who breed this fowl with small illustrations of their birds, but the cuts came to hand too late to be used, as we intended. The engraving on page 255, and the large cut of Mr. Sidell's Hamburgs will give the reader a clear idea of the plumage and character of these pretty fowls. They differ from the two varieties of Spangled *Polands* only in being devoid of crest or top-knot ; their size, form, and colors being very similar.

Mr. E. J. Taylor, of Waterloo, N. Y., sends us some

fine drawings of the different varieties of fowls he breeds, which will be found in the appropriate places. The Golden Hamburgs are fully described in this chapter, by J. C. Sidell, in detail, but in regard to the above birds, Mr. Taylor, says " my Golden Spangled Hamburghs took first premium at the exhibition held in New York city, December, 1870. For beauty, and as egg producers, they cannot be surpassed by any other variety of fowl. They are called by some the Dutch everlasting layers, and, according to my experience with them, are worthy the name. They are strictly non-sitters, small eaters, and excellent table fowl, although not very large."

The *Bolton Grays* — a still smaller fowl, but entirely distinct variety — we will close this chapter with a brief description of. These came originally from Holland, also, and their plumage is white body-feathers, minutely speckled and splashed with clear black. It is the original " pencilled " style of plumage, of which so much is heard, of late.

These are nearest like the Silver Spangled, as already mentioned, in general contour. But they are a smaller, and an entirely distinct race of fowl, well known both in England and the United States, as marvellously abundant layers of smallish eggs, and non-setters. They are pretty pets, the male weighing about 4 to 4 1-2 lbs., and the hen about 3 1-2 lbs. These four varieties — the Dominique, the Golden and Silver Hamburg, and the Bolton Grays, each have many admirers; and the breeder who produces the stock clean and pure, can always find a sale for these, at fair rates.

Of the beautiful Spangled Hamburgs as represented by cut No. 11, Mr. J. C. Sidell, of Englewood, N. J., says: " This truly valuable breed commends itself to favorable consideration by possessing the important characteristics of beauty and utility. Its origin is obscure but they have been bred in the North of England a long time under the name of Gold and Silver "Pheasant fowls," Gold and Silver "Mooneys," and "Red Caps." They are *not* entitled to the name of Hamburgs, it having been given to them at Birmingham, Eng., from their resemblance to the "Pencilled Dutch," and they formerly bore the name of "Dutch every-day-layers." The Lancashire Silver Mooneys have a silvery-white ground-color, with large, round greenish black spangles or moons, on the tips of the feathers. The true Mooney cock, generally has a hen-feathered tail, and small deaf ears, not pure white, but streaked with red or pink. The hackle is silvery white, and free from yellow tinge; some of the cocks have full feathered tails, but they are seldom pure white, being either black, or white streaked with black. The hens should have pure white body-feathers, tipped with large round black spangles; the hackle white, striped with black; the tail silver on the outside and darker on the inside, tipped with black round spangles; the deaf ears are of a leaden color, or what is termed "opaque-white."

The Yorkshire "Silver Pheasants," have smaller spangles, somewhat crescent shaped; the hackle of the cock is white, frequently has a yellow tinge, and is tipped with black; the tail is white, tipped with black spangles in both cocks and hens; the cock's breast is deficient in the spangling which is exhibited by the Mooney, being much darker; deaf ears white, and in the hens generally brighter than in the Mooney hens.

The Golden Mooneys are of a rich golden-bay color, each of the body-feathers having a large, round greenish black spangle on the end. The hackle is striped with black; the tail is black in both sexes; the upper part of the breast of the cock, is generally greenish black, and on the lower part, spangled with large, round moons; the deaf ears small, not pendant, and not always pure white.

The Yorkshire Pheasants are differently marked from the Mooneys; the spangles being crescent shaped, somewhat of the character of acing; their deaf ears are generally pure white, and their combs are .arger and looser. The bay-ground color is frequently mossed; tail black in both sexes. In the cock, the spangles on the breast run up the edges of the feathers, resembling a lacing, and cause the breast to have a streaky appearance.

In England it is usual to exhibit Mooney hens, with cocks bred between Mooney and Pheasant fowls; this is because the Mooney cock is small, seldom has a pure white deaf ear, and generally has a dark breast. The deaf-ear is a special point in Hamburgs, and no bird with red ones would stand any chance of winning at an English Show, no matter how perfectly he might be marked.

All Hamburgs should have rose combs, with a "peak" behind, and be rather square in front; it should be full of small "spikes," and without a hollow or depression; this describes a perfect comb; but it is frequently the case that many of the chickens of a brood (especially the cocks) will have combs not entirely answering the description; sometimes there will be no depression in the centre, but no peak behind: these are termed "nub combs;" again, the hollow will be a glaring one, but the peak will be a model. A comb falling over so as to obstruct the sight, is a disqualifying defect. The legs should be blue, and any other color is not admissable.

There is a variety of golden spangled Hamburg called Red-caps, which differs materially from the Mooney and Pheasant Fowls, being larger and not possessing such beauty and regularity of spangling. The cock's breast is dark, and the most striking feature of the breed is the remarkable development of comb, the cocks showing them sometimes three inches wide in front, and between four and five to the extremity of the peak. The hens have combs as large in proportion, which are rarely erect as is the case generally with the Mooneys and Pheasants. They lay larger eggs than any of the Hamburgs and as many of them, and are more hardy, standing the cold of our winters as well as Brahmas.

It will be seen that no breed taxes the skill of the fancier to produce what are called "Exhibition birds" more than Hamburgs. Birds may frequently be seen with exquisitely perfect markings, perfect comb, and a blood-red deaf-ear; others with black breasts, but all other points in perfection; others, with almost every point, but much below the average size, and again, single-combed birds, generally beautifully marked, are met with; they may be bred from birds in which no possible evidence of a single comb is apparent, but it is rarely the case that many chicks of a brood will show other than rose-combs. There is probably no breed which will lay a greater number of eggs in a year than this. Each hen will produce about 225 per annum, which, although they are small, the aggregate weight will perhaps be found to exceed that of some of the larger breeds. If Hamburgs were bred merely for their beauty, as Pheasants are, they would still find plenty of admirers; but when their extraordinary egg-producing qualities are taken into consideration, the question of profit comes into view, and with many persons the economic merits of a fowl are the ones to which the most value is attached. Hamburgs are excellent table fowls, the flesh being tender and of fine flavor; but as *all* the essentials have never yet been combined in one breed, they cannot be expected to compete with their larger and clumsier rivals as candidates for the spit, the stew-pan, or the gridiron.

In breeding 'hem they should not be hatched before the weather in the spring is settled, as they are *not* so easy to rear as Brahmas or Cochins. All chickens thrive better for being kept free from dampness, and Hamburgs are no exception. The eggs should be put under other hens, as this is classed among the non-sitting breeds, although occasionally a hen will show an inclination to sit and sometimes will hatch and rear a brood with commendable care. They are impatient of restraint, and should have a wide range. If it is inconvenient to let them be unconfined, the fence of the yard should be at least twelve feet high and not more than two thirds as many fowls kept in the same space that could be devoted to Brahmas or Cochins."

The illustration given herewith and thus fully described by him, represents specimens bred by Mr. J. Clarence Sidell, of Englewood, N. J., who probably breeds this variety of fowls to a greater perfection than any other fancier in this country.

The Crested fowls — such as the *Polands* — are out of date with us, latterly. The White *Leghorns*, and White *Dorkings* are bred and fancied by many. Both of the latter are excellent layers, and most large dealers can supply them. (See cut No. 12.)

The Rev. Henry Ward Beecher is a lover of White Leghorns, and in a gushing spring article in a late issue of the *N. Y. Ledger*, entitled, "Oh for the country," thus discourses upon chickenology. "The day is bright, the sky has sunken back to the uttermost, and the arch seems wonderfully deep above your head. Little cloud-ships go sailing about in the heavens, as busily as if they carried freight to long expectant owners. It is a day for the country. The city palls on the jaded nerve. I long to hear the hens cackle. There are lively times now in barn and barnyard, I'll warrant you. If I were lying on the east verandah of a cottage that I wot of, I should see the white *Leghorns,* wind blown, shining in the sunlight, searching for a morsel in and out of the shrubbery, the cocks crowing and the hens crooning. The Leghorn, of true blood, leads the race of fowls for continuous eggs, in season and out of season; eggs large enough, of fine quality and sprung from hens that never think of chickens. For a true Leghorn seldom wants to set. They believe in division of labor. They *provide* eggs, others must *hatch* them. Other fowls may surpass them on the spit, or gridiron, but as egg-layers, they easily take the lead. They are hardy, handsome, and immensely productive. As it is just as easy to keep good fowls as poor ones, thrifty housekeepers should secure a good laying breed. Not *every* pure white fowl is a Leghorn. There are many White Spanish sold as Leghorns. They may be known by their gray or pearl-colored legs. The pure Leghorn has a yellow leg, a single comb, quite long, and usually lapping down. This breed is well known about New York, but no description of it can be found in English Poultry books. Indeed, we are informed that Tegetmeier, the standard authority, but recently knew anything about them, and then from a coop sent from New York.

WHITE LEGHORN, or "WHITE SPANISH FOWLS.
Bred by George A. Deitz, and others.

"The *Brahmas* and *Cochins* have good qualities. They are large, even huge. They are peaceable, and the Cochins do not scratch — an important fact to all who have a garden, and who desire to let their poultry run at large. They are good layers, admirable mothers, yield a fine carcass for the table, but the meat is not fine, though fairly good. But a more ungainly thing than buff Cochins the eye never saw. A flock of Leghorns is a delight to the eye. One is never tired of watching them. Their forms are symmetrical and every motion is graceful. But the huge poddy Cochins waddle before you like over fat buffoons. They are grotesque, good-natured, clumsy, useful creatures, good layers, but with a great love of setting. Every Cochin hen would like to bring out two broods in a season; while the white Leghorns fill their nests with eggs, and then think their whole duty done. We keep Cochin hens to set on Leghorn eggs. Better mothers cannot be.

"I hear my hens cackle! These bright spring days are passing, and the concert of the barnyard is in full play, but I am tied up to the pen. Patience! I shall be green enough in a few weeks. The city shall not always prevail. In due season, I shall go to grass. Already I smell it. The odor of new grass can be perceived but only for a few days in spring. It should be noticed then, for it is unlike any other perfume, and will be perceived no more until another year. How happy are they that dwell among open fields! Or how happy they might be, if they but knew their privileges!"

No. 13. TRIO OF GOLDEN SEBRIGHT BANTAMS.

GOLDEN SEBRIGHT BANTAMS.

CHAPTER XXII.

THE GOLDEN SEBRIGHT, AND OTHER BANTAMS.

"Proud of his plumage and his spurs,
The feathered coxcomb struts, gallant and blithe
As any beardless cornet of dragoons!"

This exquisite diminutive representative of a distinct breed of the domesticated feathered tribe, takes acknowledged precedence over all the small fowl, denominated *Bantams*. The Sebrights are said to have had their origin in India — Sir John Sebright, the M. P. for Herts England, having, it is stated, brought this beautiful variety out with him from that country, some years ago. Among the sales that were made at auction at an early Poultry Show in London, it is recorded that Sir John run the price of one of these small hens of his up to 29£. sterling ($145) and bought her in at that figure, rather than part with her! And the London News announces, in February 1847, that two hens and a cock of this petite variety sold for 50£. 1s. or rising $250! These, and similar prices, were paid in England — not by Yankees, however.

Specimens were introduced into this country from Great Britian twenty-odd years since, and they came at once to be a great favorite. Formerly we had the little yellow Nankin, the red Game, the pure white Pantelet, or falcon-hocked, and the mottled Bantams. But all were much larger than the Sebright, and far more irregular in color. Subsequently we had the ' Black Spanish ' Bantam, see page 245, very small and beautiful, with white cheek and high thin comb. Then we had the *Silver* Sebright, (just like the Golden, in markings) but the finest of all this diminutive race, ever seen in this country. They have been bred but rarely here — for they have been found very delicate, while chickens, and troublesome to bring to maturity. Still, there are some breeders who take pains with them, and succeed in producing beautiful specimens of these gallant, proud, important pigmies of the feathered race.

The Bantams should have no tuft, and some of the Sebrights have single combs, which is a blemish, the highest bred birds requiring the full rose-comb; *hen*-tailed — that is, devoid of the long sickle-feathers of the old-style — wings well down in the flanks, and drooping, with perfectly clean delicate dark-skinned legs. Both the flesh and flavor of their meat is fine, but they

A PRACTICAL TREATISE ON DOMESTIC FOWLS. 267

are so small that this furnishes but a tit-bit, in that particular : and they are bred only for fancy, as a rule. They are abundant layers of small white eggs. The black-breasted red, if trimmed of his comb and wattles, is a perfect miniature representative of the Game cock, and in his way, quite as spunky.

RED GAME-BANTAM.

This is the nearest approach to the *Bankiva* Cock, or wild cock of Java; and so like it, in some individuals, as to be difficult to distinguish them. The black variety, called " Black Spanish " Bantam in this country, from its perfect resemblance to that fowl, has all the pugnacity of its congeners. The whole of the clean-legged tribe are recommended as good mothers. The Naukins are those in use at the great aviary of the Earl of Derby, for hatching out the various sorts of Quail, Partridge, and Pheasants, to which Mr. Thomson has added Cantelo's Incubator; and few in Great Britain, can boast of so much success or experience, as that experienced ornithologist. The white are precisely the same as the others, only different in color. James Walters, of Windsor, gives a rather unflattering account of their destroying their eggs; others have kept them, and never discovered this fault.

The Booted, Pantelet, or Feather-legged Bantam, should not escape notice. They are of all colors; those with the greatest quantity of feathers on the legs, are usually spotted, red, black, and white. Some have feathers three inches long on their legs, so as to impede their walking. These are becoming scarce, and even promise to become extinct; the objection, of the fanciers, is, that their leg feathers getting damp, is apt to addle the eggs put under them for incubation. They, however, have their advantages, as they seldom do an injury by scratching, and are frequently kept as ornamental pets about a garden, which is all that any of these pigmy birds are good for, of any variety.

The " SEBRIGHTS " have deservedly taken the lead among this tribe, altogether. Some fancy the Silver, but most American breeders raise only the Golden Sebrights, see cut No. 13. G. H. Warner of N. Y. Mills, has this variety in great perfection. Edwin N. Rice, Clinton, Mass., has produced some fine Game, and Sebright Bantams. Geo. Smith, Holliston, Mass., also, of the latter — very handsome birds. Ezra Dibble, New Haven, Ct., breeds the White Bantams, said to be very perfect, and among the *smallest* in the world. E. J. Taylor Bros., of Waterloo, N. Y. breed the Sebrights, finely. Thos. Gould, Aurora, N. Y., and E. P. Howlett, Syracuse, also supply these of both varieties. The Sebright portraits which head this chapter, are truthful likenesses of prize birds, which took the first premium at the New York State Show, in 1869 and '70. G. W. Felter, Batavia, Ohio, breeds the Golden Sebright, as does also J. E. French, Abington, Mass, and some others, whose address has not reached us.

As we remarked above, the *Bankiva* fowl (the wild Cock of India) so closely resembles what we call the common black-breasted Red Bantam, that it is believed by ornithologists that this bird is the original progenitor of the Bantam race — if not of most of our domestic fowl. The eyes and throat of the Bankiva are bare of plumage; the comb large, of irregular shape; two wattles hang from the lower mandible; the head, back, and sides of the neck, surrounding the bare skin upon the throat and the rump, are covered with long, rounded feathers, of a clear and brilliant golden orange. Below the hackles, the upper part of the back is bluish-black, and the centre of a rich, deep chestnut. The greater coverts are steel-blue, with a broad margin of chestnut; the quills brownish black, edged with reddish yellow. The hen is of a dusky gray, and resembles our common poultry more than any other wild variety; they inhabit the forests of India, and from them it is thought that the common barnyard varieties, so generally disseminated all over the western world, came direct, originally; as they frequently even now mix with and cross the tame birds on the borders, though they are never themselves domesticated.

The Sebrights will always remain a favorite pet fowl, from their rare beauty of plumage, and uniformity in breeding, when properly cared for. They command good prices everywhere, at this time, and a clutch of these exquisite little birds is certainly ornamental, together. But the males should not be allowed to run loosely among other breeds of fowl, if the fancier wishes to keep his breeding stock pure. They will readily cross any other fowl — large or small.

CHAPTER XXIII.

MANY MEN HAVE MANY MINDS.

Fortunately for the furtherance of the general objects of poultry breeders, as well as for the purposes of the Societies fostered through their good intentions, the many men engaged in this and other countries in fowl-raising, have many different minds as to the intrinsic merits and value of the varieties of domestic birds now current among us; and, while the mass of American breeders are inclined to favor some strain or color of the great Asiatic fowl, others make a speciality of raising the diminutive Bantams only, and will have no other upon their grounds — while there are not a few enthusiastic admirers of fancy *pigeons*, simply; a portrait of one exquisite variety of which, from the " White Calcutta Fan-tail " stock of Messrs. Bestor and Colt, of Hartford, Conn., heads this chapter, and a most extraordinary fine specimen it is, too.

Then there be those whose favorites are the White Dorkings, White Leghorns, and White Aylesburys, for ducks. Dr. Eben Wight, of Dedham, Mass, an old and experienced poulterer, was an ardent fancier of this white plumed style of birds, and bred them many years, to a great degree of perfection. The beautiful aristocratic Black Spanish are deemed by thousands of amateurs, and gentlemen of nice taste, to be the only domestic fowl fit for a genteel estate. They are interminable layers, and are deservedly a favorite in many quarters. The Dominiques are considered by hundreds of farmers and country breeders as the only right thing for their use.

Within the past few years, the showy but moderate-sized French fowls — the Houdans, Crevecœurs and La Fleche — have come into very considerable notoriety among us, and these birds are now being bred in various parts of this country with zeal and admiration by those who favor novelty in poultry raising. The majority of those who have carefully experimented with this class, pronounce favorably upon their good traits, very decidedly; inasmuch as they have proved great layers, non-sitters, and easy keepers, while for the table, their meat is certainly unexceptionable. All these promising qualities are in their favor, and it is not surprising that these should have their friends, largely, among those who breed for the general improvement of poultry around us.

Then we have a number of fanciers who import and breed with cautious nicety the sprightly and beautiful Game fowl — of which there are numerous varieties —

as the Shawl-Game, the Grays, the Black-breasted Reds, the White Georgians, the Earl of Derby strains, the magnificent silver and golden Duck-wings, the Red and smoky-duns, the Spangled, the Piles, the Mealy-Grays, the Ginger-reds, etc., which are favorites not merely for their good fighting quality, but that the hens are the best of mothers and the steadiest of sitters — and their meat is unrivalled, at almost any age, young or old.

Referring to the French fowls once more, briefly, having expressed our own personal opinion in regard to that tribe, we very willingly state that some of the leading New York, Philadelphia, and Western fanciers who have given them a fair trial, speak very decidedly in their favor — for some reasons — and write us earnestly regarding their good character. Mr. Van Winkle, of Greenville, N. Y., who has bred all three of the varieties, informs me that his Crevecœurs are large birds, and since he has had them he has carefully studied their characteristics and tested their performances. He finds them excellent layers of large sized eggs, and a goodly number of them. They lay in the fall months, he adds, when other fowls are moulting. Their meat is as fine as that of a capon, and he deems them a superior bird — from their strong blood — to cross upon other fowl, for general use. In Mr. Van W.'s opinion, the Houdan is one of the choicest breeds of foreign fowl that has been brought into America for many years, on account of its extraordinary fertility, its early maturing, and the general hardiness, in his experience with them, of both the adults and young birds. These, he says, "are compact in form, their meat is rich and white, they are admirable layers, and are the most valuable fowl we have, in my experience."

But among the great multitude of buyers, at this time, the Chinese fowl — as either the Brahma, the Buff, or Partridge Cochin, and the Red, White or Black Cochin — are far in excess in general demand, over all other varieties, taken together. The uniformity of great size attained by this race; the truthfulness with which they breed year after year; the greater *weight* of eggs they yield in a season; the quiet disposition of these birds; the ease with which they are kept and managed, either at large or in confinement; their thorough hardiness, even amidst our coldest winters; their fine plumage and stately appearance, when in good trim and well provided for; their unchanging characteristics from generation to generation; and their general uniform good qualities both as layers and breeders, render them beyond comparison the most desirable and the most salable domestic fowl we have ever had in America. And they are to-day more popular, more largely sought after, more extensively bred, and more deserving for either the fancier or farmer's use, in view of all their striking qualities of excellence — than any variety we ever *shall* have, (in our judgment,) in the United States. This may seem over-partial; but it is our confirmed opinion.

Another gentleman in Massachusetts, who has tried the French strains, commends them to us highly. He writes: "I have had all three of the varieties, and have bred them two years now, with fair success and good satisfaction. They are unique in form and plumage, handsome birds upon the green, the best of layers, but do not care to sit often, and they are fair in size: not a large fowl, but averaging like the Black Spanish. I have found the French fowls very good layers, I must say, and I am much pleased with them, so far."

A friend in Rhode Island informs me, per contra, that he bought a few of them, and gave them a trial. "I was so greatly taken with their pretty odd appearance, when I saw them in New York," he writes, "that I purchased a few, and took them home. You know how I breed my fowls. I gave them a good chance, and hoped to do nicely with them. But I did not succeed. In my experience with them, the chicks are tender, and do not come up well. The hens are fair layers, certainly, and the cocks are stately proud fellows; but I would not give a trio of good Light Brahmas for three trios of the French-men. I have seen worse fowls, but I have seen many better ones." We have received several other letters upon this same subject, for which we cannot find space, however. The amount of comment to hand we think is decidedly in favor of this fowl, however; yet we incline to the opinion that breeders do not know sufficient of the French birds as yet, in this country, to give an opinion as to what they may prove here, by and bye. They unquestionably possess some rare good qualities, and we wait to see how they may turn out, hereafter.

The Gueldres or "Breda" fowl described by Mr.

Van Winkle, of Greenville, N. J., is a superior variety. The Silver and Gold-spangled Hamburgs, accurately delineated by cut No. 11, and so well depicted by J. Clarence Sidell, in Chapter XXI, are another favorite race with many fowl-fanciers, and not without good reasons, too. In their showy and parti-colored plumage, the Spangled Hamburg rivals the pheasant, and is called in England, oftentimes, the Hamburg, or Pheasant fowl. The same colored fowls, with the heavy crest and muff, (of the "Poland" variety,) were largely bred in America some years since, and, with the exception of their tufts, were almost exactly like this superb Hamburg variety. Fine samples came here years ago, from the yards of Prince Albert, as a present to Hon. Daniel Webster, among the first received in America, if I remember rightly. A portion of these fowls were afterwards sent by Mr. Webster to Col. Jaques, of Tenhills Farm, Medford, to breed; and the Colonel turned out, for a few years, the finest birds of this then taking variety that ever were produced in Massachusetts. These crested fowls — the Black, the Golden, and the Silver-laced are all good layers. Boswell states that "the whole crested breed are much esteemed by the curious, and reared with care." And Buffon says, "There can be little doubt that all the fowls with crests have originated from intercrossing with the Paduan or Polish." It was from the crested variety of fowls that Mowbray stated he "obtained from five hens in eleven months, five hundred and three eggs; weighing, on an average, one ounce and five drachms, exclusive of the shells."

A PRACTICAL TREATISE ON DOMESTIC FOWLS. 277

DR. BENNETT'S "INDIAN GAMES."

The above are likenesses of a pair of Dr. J. C. Bennett's so denominated "Wild Indian Game" birds; a fowl he produced several years ago, from a cross of the Irish game cock with a very gamey hen he procured, I think, from Calcutta. The progeny were very unique and remarkable birds, and proved quite popular for a time, among the fanciers of this species of fowl. I have heard nothing of them of late years, and take it for granted that this so-called " breed " did not hold out.

We here reproduce the original drawing of the *first* " Bramapooters " exhibited and thus named by Dr.

278   BURNHAM'S NEW POULTRY-BOOK;

PORTRAITS OF DR. BENNETT'S THREE ORIGINAL "BRAMAPOOTERS."

Bennett in 1851, at the Boston Fowl Show. The slight top-knots we have alluded to, will be found at the back of the heads of these birds; and the portraits are faithful, though drawn on a small scale. In other respects it will be observed that the figures very nearly resemble the light Brahmas of to-day. But this trio were bred (as we know) precisely as has already been stated in the pages of this work.

There are still a few other named varieties, that here and there find a casual admirer; but beyond those enumerated in these pages, there are none that are now bred to any extent. The "Silky" fowl, the "Rumpless," the "Creeper," the "Frizzled," and a few others, are little known and less cared for among fanciers generally, at the present time. Of the varieties we have noted, a good selection can be made of large or small domestic birds. And these may be had in almost any county in the United States, now-a-days, of those whose taste and inclination prompt them to raise one or another of these various breeds.

There are certain technical *terms* applied to fowls, not universally understood, which we will here briefly explain. The "neck-hackles" are the pendant feathers around the neck. "Saddle-feathers," or "back-hackles" are those upon the back, falling down over the flanks. "Wing-coverts" are the feathers upon the upper and middle parts of the wings. "Flight-feathers," the long end plumes of wings. "Sickle-feathers" are the longest drooping sickle-shaped plumes in the cock's tail. "Broody" is the inclination to sit. "Crest" is the same as "top-knot," or "head-tuft." "Fluff," or "fluffy plumage," is the term for the soft cushiony feathering on the sides and stern of the Cochins. "Moult" is the annual shedding of the feathers. "Rose-comb" is a full wide oblong comb, peculiar to the best bred Sebright Bantams, the Dominique, Hamburg, or White Leghorn fowl. "Pea-comb" is a small compact *triple* comb, seen on the Malay, and contended for by most breeders now as requisite to perfection in the hens of the dark or light Brahma. It is a central comb, with a smaller one on each side, upright. "Serrated comb" is the straight thin upright comb, with the rising projections like notches or the teeth of a coarse saw. "Vulture-hock" is applied to the form of feathers that droop and grow backward on the thigh, below the hock joints of fowl — as on the Pantalet-bantams, the Ptarmigans, etc. "Carunculated" represents the uneven warty exterior flesh upon a cock-turkey's head and neck, and that upon the Muscovy drake's, also.

We have said little on the subject of fowl-*diseases*, for the reason that in our own practice we have constantly aimed at prevention, rather than attempted to cure a sick bird. The latter course is attended, ordinarily, with more trouble than the fowl is worth; but it is easier to prevent sickness occurring, to any great extent, among poultry — and I have in this volume advised such measures as to their food, care, shelter, and general management, as will usually keep fowls in high health. Still, they will sometimes get ill, and it not infrequently occurs that a favorite bird may be saved from death, through doctoring.

Gapes among fowls will spread, astonishingly, and *roup* will be readily communicated from one to another, more especially when your poultry is kept in confinement, or in limited quarters. *Swelled crop* is another troublesome complaint to which fowls are subject, occasionally. *Colds* are very common, too. A cure for gapes, if adopted when first discovered, is a teaspoonful dose of common sweet oil, given two or three days in succession; the oil destroys and removes the little gape-worms from the gullet. Another good remedy is to place ordinary whole grains of wheat in a phial, and pour upon them sufficient kerosene to cover them in the bottle. The grain will in twenty-four hours absorb the oil. Give one of these wheat-grains daily, three days, (at night and morning) to your gapey chickens, and it will kill the worms in their throats. In cases of roup, castor oil and alum is very good, for internal affection, and the latter, in solution for washing the head and nostrils of such affected bird. *Cholera* (as it has been called) in fowls has been very destructive in Pennsylvania, the past year. Mr. G. A. Deitz, of Chambersburgh, says, " this fearful disease among fowls has swept some yards of every fowl in many parts of the State, and I have heard of none, as yet, or found as good a remedy as castor oil and alum. One or two doses of castor oil, say a tablespoonful at a time, will generally cure the fowl; and, at the same time, place alum water where the fowl can drink it. With it I have cured the worst cases of cholera, and found it also a good remedy for cold, or light cases of roup; as this mild remedy seems to put the whole system of the fowl in a healthful condition."

An excellent preventive to disease, is placing of a bit of common assafœdita at the bottom of the water-vessels, for poultry. *Colds* contracted from long exposure to bad weather, will break down many a good bird. But *vermin* permitted in your fowl houses, is worse than all else. Never suffer a drooping or sick bird to remain with the well ones an hour, after you discover the fact. Remove it; nurse it, (if you are inclined for any reason,) and save, or restore it, if possible.

But I accept a "short shrift" with such subjects, as I have already stated. If they don't come round quickly, my rule is to relieve them from their troubles, and give them decent burial. And this kind of 'happy despatch' does not occur often, on my premises.

Every housewife thinks she knows how to *cook* eggs appropriately. If any one has not tried the following plan, we can commend it as a very good one. Have your eggs for cooking, fresh, though these require a little more time to boil. To render them soft, delicate, and highly palateable, drop them into the water *not* until it boils. Leave them from three to four minutes, boiling vigorously, and eat from the shell, with an egg-spoon. If you wish them for salad, boil them as above, ten minutes. Then immerse them in *cold* water, and roll them gently upon a table or board, and the shells can be quickly and easily removed.

As to fancy pigeons, we have no space in this volume to devote to this interesting class of beautiful birds, which are so widely bred and so greatly admired, in certain quarters. We have placed at the commencement of this rather desultory chapter, however, a remarkably effective drawing of perhaps the most unique and most generally esteemed variety of this tribe, the White Calcutta Fan-Tail — as bred by S. J. Bestor, of Hartford, Conn. and which particular strain of this favorite blood is pronounced by judges to be par excellence, the most perfect as well as the finest that has ever been seen in this country. Their purity of plumage, extraordinary carriage, elegance of shape, and unusual size commend them very markedly; and those who have seen them have aptly described these Fan-Tails to be more like miniature swans, in their graceful and proud movements, than like anything of the pigeon species.

We have made but brief allusion to the Ptarmigan the Paduan, the Jungle, the Russian, the Javas, and one or two other wild varieties of fowl, about which we know so little that is of general interest — because we do not deem it essential in this work to repeat the speculations of ornithologists who have studied the early history and genealogy of these birds — but no two of whom agree in their accounts of these fowls; a matter at this day of very little consequence, however.

MALE WILD TURKEY.

CHAPTER XXIV.

THE AMERICAN WILD TURKEY.

THE *Turkey* is an American 'institution,' as everybody knows, and the enormous number of these birds that are annually devoured in the United States is almost incredible. We devote a couple of chapters to this splendid representative of the feathered race, gathering our accounts and directions as to its history, feeding, hatching, rearing, etc., from the best authorities extant, having had little personal experience with this fowl, except in the way of eating it; at which performance, we have in our time been blessed with the opportunities to do our share, perhaps, first and last.

This bird is a native of the wilds of North America, and for excellence, in its domesticated state, stands at the top round of the roost, as head representative of the farm yard feathered tribe. The *wild* turkey is found all over this country, north, west and south—in greater or less profusion. Its plumage is close, brilliant, and of a **metallic** lustrous hue of bronze — formed of glossy chestnut, green, black and brown. The feathering of the male is the most showily brilliant; that of the female being dull, comparatively, and monotonous.

All authorities aver that the wild cock-turkey averages larger than the domestic bird — some specimens having been found to reach fifty pounds' weight, when secured in their native forests; and " its great size and beauty," says Audubon, " and its value as a delicate and justly-prized article of food, render it the most interesting of the birds indigenous to the United States of America. The flesh is even more delicate than that of the domestic Turkey, and the Indians so value it that they call it " the white man's dish."

Other authorities describe the wild male when fully grown to be " nearly four feet in length, and more than five in extent of wings. The bill is short and robust. The head, which is small in proportion to the body, and half the neck, are covered by a naked bluish corrugated skin, on which are a number of red, wart-like elevations on the superior portions, and whitish ones on the inferi or; interspersed with a few scattered bristly hairs, and small feathers which are still less numerous on the neck. The naked skin extends farther downwards on the surface of the neck, where it is flaccid and membranous, forming an undulating appendage, on the lower part of which are cavernous elevations, or wattles; a wrinkled, fleshy, extensible carbuncle, hairy and pencellated at tip, arises from the bill at its junction with the forehead. When the bird is quiescent, this process is not much more than an inch and a half long. But when excited by love or rage, it becomes lengthened, so as to cover the bill, and fall over it. The body is thick, somewhat long, truncated feathers, dusky beneath, but to this dusky portion succeeds a broad, effulgent, metallic band, changing now to copper-color or bronze gold, then to violet or purple, according to the incidence of light. The lower portion of the back, and the upper part of the rump, are much darker, with less brilliant gold reflections. The upper tail coverts are of a bright bay color, with numerous narrow bands of shining greenish. The under tail coverts are blackish, glossed with coppery towards the tip, and at the tip are bright bay.

"The wings are concave and rounded, hardly passing the origin of the tail. The smaller and middling wing coverts are colored like the feathers of the body. The spurious wing is plain blackish, banded with white. The secondaries have the white portion so large that they may be described as white banded with blackish, and are, moreover, tinged with yellow. The tail measures more than a foot and a quarter; is rounded and composed of eighteen wide feathers. It is capable of being elevated so as to resemble a fan, when the bird parades, struts, or wheels.

"The wild turkeys do not confine themselves to any particular kind of food. They eat maize, all sorts of berries, fruit, grasses, beetles, and even tadpoles, young frogs, etc., their more general predilection is for the acorn, on which they rapidly fatten. The males, usually termed *gobblers*, associate in parties, numbering from ten to a hundred, and seek their food apart from the females; whilst the latter either move about, singly or with their young till nearly two thirds grown, sometimes consisting of 70 or 80, all intent on avoiding the old males, who, whenever opportunity offers, attack and destroy the young, by blows on their skulls.

"Early in March they pair, and in April the female makes her nest in the ground, of dry leaves and twigs, and into this receptacle the eggs are deposited, sometimes to the number of twenty, but more usually from nine to fifteen. They are whitish, spotted with reddish-brown, like those of the domestic bird. Their manner of building, number of eggs, period of incubation, etc., appear to correspond throughout the Union.

"The wild hen-turkey is not easily driven from her nest by the approach of apparent danger. But if an enemy appears, she crouches low and suffers it to pass. A circumstance related by Mr. Audubon, will show how much intelligence they display on such occasions. Having discovered a sitting hen, he remarked that by assuming a careless air, or talking to himself, he was per-

THE FEMALE WILD TURKEY.

mitted to pass within six feet of her; but if he advanced cautiously, she would not suffer him to come within twenty paces, but ran off thirty yards, with her tail expanded, when she paused, on every step, occasionally uttering a chuck. They seldom abandon their nests, on account of being discovered by man; but should a snake, or other animal suck one of the eggs, the parent leaves them altogether. If the eggs be removed, she again seeks the male, and recommences laying. The mother will not forsake her eggs when near hatching, while life remains. She will suffer an enclosure to be made around, and imprison her, rather than abandon her charge. Mr. Audubon witnessed the hatching of a brood, while thus endeavoring to secure the young and mother.

" In proportion to the abundance or scarcity of food,

No. 14, THE MAMMOTH BRONZE TURKEY.
Bred by G. H. Warner, Wm. Simpson, Jr., Jos. M. Wade, G. W. Felter, E. J. Taylor, and others. 289.

and its good or bad quality, they are small or large, meagre or fat, and of an excellent or indifferent flavor; in general, however, their flesh is more delicate and better tasted than that of the *tame* turkey. They are in the best order late in autumn, or in the beginning of winter. A gentleman residing in Westchester County, New York, a few years since procured a young female wild turkey, in order to make the experiment of crossing the breed; but, owing to some circumstances, it did not succeed, and in the ensuing spring, this female disappeared; in the following autumn she returned, followed by a large brood; these were quite shy, but were secured in a coop, and the mother allowed her liberty; she remained on the farm until the succeeding spring, when she again disappeared, and returned in the autumn, with another brood. This course she has repeated for several successive years."

The *domesticated* turkey's habits and needs are of more consequence, in our treatise, however, and the above accounts are given because they possess extraordinary interest, from reliable authority, as to this bird in its wild state.

CHAPTER XXV.

REARING THE DOMESTIC TURKEY.

Six or eight hens are sufficient to assign to one male turkey, though twice that number are bred to a male, often. The hens lay, ordinarily, a couple dozen of eggs, before they incline to sit — which they evince by stealing away from the rest, and seeking a nest out of sight, in the nearest woods, if there be any, or in any out of the way secluded place.

When ready to sit, she will cover twelve to fifteen eggs, advantageously ; but she needs to be watched, lest she lay these eggs beforehand, secretly, abroad. She sits persistently, after she commences, and from twenty-nine to thirty-one days. She should be undisturbed, for the domesticated turkey is shy and timid. The male should be removed from her, as he inclines to break up the nest, and destroy the eggs, if he is permitted to be about. When the chicks are hatched, the hen turkey proves a good careful attentive mother, but delights in wandering away with her new brood, at the earliest opportunity, when permitted to do so.

Take the young chicks from the nest, give them no food for six or eight hours, then feed them on hard boiled eggs, chopped fine, and bread crumbs, at first. It is best to house both mother and young for a few weeks, unless the weather is dry and fine. Their second food may be mush, cooked, of barley or oatmeal; and feed often, four or five times a day, daily. Finely cut up liver, or meat soups is good to mix with their second feeding. They should be kept clean, while in confinement, and a layer of fine, dry gravel, or sand, left for them, with a fresh tuft of short, sweet grass. When the chicks are three or four weeks old, coop the hen abroad for a couple of hours, daily, in fine weather, with a moderate sun. When six weeks old, coop out of doors, daily, for a fortnight, that the chicks may obtain strength before the hen is set at large. When half grown, and well feathered, they become sufficiently hardy, and, in a good range, will provide themselves throughout the day, requiring only to be fed at their out-letting in the morning, and on their return at evening. If confined to the poultry-yard, their food and treatment are similar to the common cock and hen. Turkeys would prefer roosting abroad, upon high trees, in the summer season, could it be permitted.

Breeders complain of the difficulty of rearing turkeys. That can be obviated, by *keeping the chicks dry;* they will not bear to be draggled through the ditches and wet grass, or subject to the rain; and after shooting what is called the *red*, (which, at a certain age, becomes the color of the head,) they become hardy, and evince a desire to perch in the open air — which should not be allowed, till they are two or three months old.

Open sheds are consequently best suited to them, with roosting-bars, fixed as high as convenient from the ground.

If you can take the chicks from any one of your hens, and add them to another clutch, the hen from which you take them will speedily begin to lay, and have a second clutch about July. They evince their wild propensity, if in the neighborhood of a wood; they will stray away and procure their food, at all seasons of the year. A turkey loses a third of its weight when ready for the spit. Live weight, 21 lbs; dead weight, 14 lbs. Turkeys are said to be difficult to rear, but with due care and attention, which, rightly considered, in *all* things, give the least trouble, they may be produced and multiplied with no loss; and the same may be averred, with all truth, of the rest of our domestic fowl; the losses and vexations annually deplored, arising almost entirely from ignorance and carelessness. Turkeys, under a judicious system, may be rendered an object of a certain degree of consequence to the farmer.

In Rhode Island and Connecticut, large numbers of domestic turkeys are kept, and annually raised for market, as well as in the north and at the eastward. In the cold season, particularly, they come into market plentifully; though, as an article of food, they are continually in use, in all our cities and large towns, throughout the year, both at the hotels and eating-houses, as well as for private family use. The turkey does not come to its full size until the fifth or sixth year, or not perfect plumage until the seventh. It has been ascertained beyond a doubt, that a single service of the cock is sufficient for the whole season, but there may be cases in which it has been unsuccessful.

The male turkey (see cut No. 14) should be of the largest size procurable, for breeding purposes. He does not attain his vigorous growth until the third or fourth year of his age, and a cock two or three years old is much better than a yearling, for your breeding hens. It is best to *change* your male bird every season, by which means stronger chicks are had, and your two year old hens (and upwards) will be found best also. Keep them up well, with good feeding during the winter. Not to fatten them, but to have them in finer breeding order in the spring. If set early (in April) the young ones have more time to grow, prior to Thanksgiving and Christmas, when the demand and price obtained for good poultry is greatest.

They love freedom, and will roost on the fences, rails, or in the trees, in preference to any sheltered place, even in the cold seasons. In very hard weather, in winter, they may be advantageously protected. But they are fond of out-of-door life, and suffer little from exposure, apparently.

The hen is a good sitter, and she will usually hatch out all, or most of the eggs under her. Her nest may be given her in a sheltered place, where she will not be likely to be disturbed by other birds, or night vermin. If they have a neighboring wood to range in, when the chicks are old enough to be trusted with the mother abroad, they will do nicely, with little daily feeding, otherwise. In the fall, feed them twice a day, with dry corn, and boiled roots and potatoes — with cooked Indian meal, which is excellent for their growth and enlargement.

In most places where turkeys are raised, the farm is large, and they have ample " scope and verge enough " to roam, at will. In confinement, from the outset, turkies could not be raised, at all satisfactorily; and it would cost far more than they would ever come to. The farmers, however, who make a business of this, in the interior, are satisfied with their returns, it is to be presumed, inasmuch as they continue to follow up the business, year after year; and the demand for this unrivalled kind of domestic poultry increases annually. Very good prices have ruled of late years, in the principal markets, and the raising of turkeys probably pays.

The broody hen-turkey shows her desire to sit by clucking somewhat like the common hen, and remains in her nest until her breast-feathers come out freely. When she has hatched her eggs and the chicks have been taken care of, as they must be for five or six weeks, at first, heed should then be taken that, for at least as long again, the young are kept both *dry*, and out of the hot sun, too. Either wet exposure or undue heat will injure or destroy them. In their wild state they are reared in the forests, mainly, where it isn't wet, and where the hot sun does not reach them. And a hilly farm, with woods for ranging grounds, is the best location for the purpose of raising turkies upon.

The Frenchman loves his wine, and all classes, down

to the poorest peasant, use it as a beverage. They think the turkey loves it, therefore; and so *they* advise mixing the food of the young chicks with wine. Bread soaked in wine they advise, at first. Our people haven't this article so handy, and so substitute sour milk with the young chicks' food. Indian meal should never be given them without cooking, and not at all until they are some weeks old. Shallow vessels, with but little depth of water, should be kept where they can have plenty of it, and *fresh*, without wetting their feathers. Dampness, wet, rain, and exposure to the hot sun, kill more than any other causes, after the turkey chicks begin to be able to wander about, as they so quickly incline to do.

House the young birds, invariably, until the night dews are off the grass, too. When you come to the fattening — in the fall — when they are five to six months old, feed them with any substance that will fatten other poultry, and give them all they will eat up clean. They put on flesh rapidly, then, and soon become fit for roasters. If you so manage as never to allow them to be low in flesh, it is much the best way, since you can then dispose of them advantageously at any size or age after four or five months old.

Some turkey-raisers recommend to " wash the young chicks in a strong decoction of tobacco, if they droop." This is said by others to be an excellent way to *kill* them, as quickly as the veriest executioner could desire! An old up-country farmer, who has raised thousands of turkeys, in New Hampshire — and good ones, too — for the Boston market, writes me thus:

"I never meddle with the young turkey-chicks at hatching, for half a day after all are safely out. Then we put them in a dry place (which is indispensable) and afterwards feed them frequently, a little at a time, half a dozen times a day, till they are a fortnight old. The hen is cooped, and not till the young ones are five or six weeks old, do we let her out; and then not till after ten o'clock in the morning. Keep them clean, vary their food, always avoid letting them out in rainy days, till they get strong and well formed, and there is no trouble in bringing up, to good account, your broods of turkeys — in the country, where they can have range, (woods, or good pasture grounds,) at the proper age. After they "shoot the red" safely — which is a tender season with them, we do not lose one in twenty birds. And we simply look after them systematically, and feed regularly. At harvesting, they pretty much take care of themselves, in the fields. We fatten quickly, and kill off from the middle of November to December 20th, as you know."

Avoid giving anything that is over-salt to the young birds. Mix their food with skim-milk, curd, &c. Give the hen pure fresh water, as well as good food. She will take good care of the little ones, ordinarily, but all the better for being kept in good condition. In the spring, obtain a fresh male, by exchange, or otherwise; let him be over two years old. Breed your old hens, which are far the best, and go on again. And you will not find it difficult to raise good turkeys.

Among the prominent raisers of fine *breeding* stock

of Domestic Turkeys, we may mention the Brothers Murdock, of Meridan, Conn., T. B. Smith & Co., Plantsville, Conn., E. J. Taylor & Bro'., Waterloo, N. Y., Wm. Simpson Jr., of West Farms, N. Y., (very fine,) D. W. Herstine, Philadelphia, A. Failor, Newton, Iowa, and C. N. Palmer & Sons, Gallipolis, Ohio; of either of whom Turkey-breeders may always readily procure prime specimens of this race, to replenish their poultry-yards with — and the *male* bird of which tribe should be used only during a single season, on the same farm — to procure the best results.

Several fanciers have sent us the announcement that amongst their stock they are now giving a share of their attention to breeding the mammoth *Bronze* Turkey — a cross of the wild cock, with selected domestic hen-turkies; thus producing the largest fowl we have ever had in this country, beyond comparison. Enormous sizes have been reached with the male birds of this cross, within the past few years; one firm informing us that pairs of these turkies have attained the extraordinary weight of *sixty* pounds, at fifteen months old! They are large, very showy, and handsome — hardy, and as easily reared as the twenty-five pounds per pair turkies. The plumage is of a glossy black, shaded with glittering bay and brown, giving the general hue of a rich bronze. The hen's plumage is similar, except that the tinge is not so brilliant as in the male. In some sections, this colossal bird is being brought to great perfection, through careful manipulation among those experienced in rearing them, and the fine portrait from life, which we give in cut No. 14, will give the reader an idea of the proportions of a stalwart representative of this grand favorite among the domestic feathered race.

Messrs. C. N. Palmer & Sons, of Gallipolis, Ohio, are this year breeding a goodly variety of fowls, from the best strains of imported stock procurable, and amateurs in the western states can obtain of these gentlemen good birds of most of the leading varieties. In addition to the Brahmas, Cochins, Houdan, and Black Spanish, they have the monster Bronze Turkies, of which they raise fine samples, and also the large white Bremen Geese, Crested (or Cuban) Ducks, and some other varieties. They have selected their fine breeding stock with great care, and give their attention to reproducing all their poultry in its purity.

In the Poultry Bulletin for May, "Topknot" gives the following concise recommendations regarding his method of raising turkies, and thus states his experience with the mammoth Bronze turkey, which is now being bred with great success by that gentleman and others; in different parts of the country. He states that " the Bronze turkey is a great improvement over the common variety. The cocks weigh at maturity 40 lbs. and hens 22 lbs. Hens in their second year are the best for breeding. I prefer using a young tom, as old ones are so heavy they are apt to skin the backs of the hens. When the turkeys are about to lay, place a few old barrels on their sides, and make nests in them ; put in a few nest eggs, and partly cover the entrance with brush to make it private. I remove the eggs every evening, and when the hen wishes to sit, fix a good nest by putting some ashes and fresh hay on it, and give her about 17 eggs. The young ones will require no food the first day after they are hatched. The best food for them is curd with young onion tops chopped fine and mixed with it. I generally give them hard boiled eggs the first few days. They require feeding little and often, every two hours, if possible ; after they are a week old they can have some cracked corn, and oat and wheat grits. In fact, this mode of feeding is just right for all kinds of young poultry. Do not fail to give fresh cool water three times a day ; milk is good for an occasional drink. If they have any lice on them, rub on some dry flour of sulphur, and they will soon be free from them. When the turkeys are hatched, I put them in a coop and have a yard around it, which is made by nailing four boards together. This makes a little fence to keep the young turkeys from straying ; it should be about fifteen inches high ; it is moved around every few days, on short grass. The old and young are shut up in the coop at night, in storms, and when the grass is wet ; at all other times they have their freedom of the little yard. The old one will not go off and leave the young, and does better for not being confined. As soon as the young are able to fly out, they may be allowed to roam and scratch for grasshoppers, and it is surprising how many they will devour, and how they thrive on them. I generally set the first clutch of eggs under hens, seven to nine each ; the turkey will then lay her second clutch in the course of a few weeks, if not allowed to sit, and they are not too late to make fine birds. Last season, I tried a third clutch, but they were too late to be profitable. I weighed my first brood of last season's turkeys, with the following result; they were just eight months old. Eight gobblers weighed from 23 1-2 lbs. to 29 1-2 lbs. each, and averaged 25 1-2 lb. Six hens from 13 1-2 to 15 lb. each. average a little over 14 lb. The Common turkeys of the country will hardly average these weights; so your readers can form their own opinion as to the merits of the Bronze Turkey."

CHAPTER XXVI.

WILD, BREMEN, TOULOUSE, AND MONGREL GEESE.

The 'Canada goose,' is the American Wild Goose; every where known upon this Continent, as well as in Europe. It is a very handsome water-fowl, (see cut No. 15) with its black head and neck, and its sable tail and rump, and dark brown back — while the rest of the feathering is a dingy but decided gray.

The regular migrations of this widely known fowl are noted as the forerunner of coming Spring and Winter, as they sail north or south — from season to season. Wilson, the celebrated ornithologist writes that " except in calm weather, the flocks of American wild geese rarely sleep on the water, generally preferring to roost all night in the marshes When the shallow bays are frozen, they seek the mouths of inlets near the sea, occasionally visiting the air or breathing-holes in the ice ; but these bays are seldom so completely frozen as to prevent their feeding on the bars at the entrance."

Breeding the Wild Goose with the Common Goose of our poultry-farms, produces only mules, that will not breed again ; but there is no difficulty in crossing this bird with the others, if a male wild goose can be had, which is difficult except in case where one is wounded, and secured alive. Colonel Thayer, of Braintree, Mass., informed the American Agriculturist, some years ago, that he was thus successful, and bred a fine gander on his premises. He says — " A few years since, a neighbor of mine shot at a flock of wild geese, while they were passing to the south, wounded one in the wing, took it alive, and very soon domesticated him. He became very tame, and went with the other geese. I bought him, and kept him three years, and then mated him with an old native goose. They had several broods of young ones, and the old goose became feeble, so much so that she could not sit long enough to hatch out her eggs. I accordingly put them under another goose, where they did very well. In the fall of the year I gave her away, and mated the wild gander with another. In the spring following, about six months after, I heard that the old goose had got better, and was in good health. She was brought home and put into my poultry-yard. The wild gander and his new mate were at a distance of about eighty rods, in another pasture. As soon as the old goose was put into the yard she made a loud noise, which the wild gander heard. He immediately left his new mate and came down to the yard, recognized his old mate, entered into close conversation, and appeared extremely happy in seeing her again."

"In their spring and autumn migrations, wild geese are well known to the inhabitants of the interior as well as the coast and great lakes of America, from our lowest latitudes, and have been seen as far north as has yet been approached by our most intrepid navigators, and then pursuing their journey northward. The English at Hudson's Bay depend greatly on geese; and in favorable years, kill three or four thousand, and barrel them up for use. In a good day, a single Indian will kill two hundred. The feathers are an article of commerce, and are sent to England. Their food is tender aquatic herbage, and a marine plant called sea-cabbage, together with grain and berries. Their flight is heavy and laborious, generally in a straight line, or in two lines approximating to a point thus, > : in both cases the van is led by an old gander, who, every now and then, pipes his well known *honk*, as if to ask how they come on, and the *honk* of "All's well" is generally returned by some of the party. When bewildered in foggy weather, they appear sometimes to be in great distress, flying about in an irregular manner, over the same quarter, making a great clamor, during which the inhabitants deal death and destruction amongst them. The wounded birds are easily domesticated, and readily pair with the tame gray goose, and their offspring are found to be larger than either; but the markings of the wild goose predominate."

The *Bremen*, or Embden, Goose (Cut No. 16,) was

originally introduced into America in 1821, I think, by Colonel Samuel Jaques, of Tenhill's Farm, Medford, Mass., and was bred by him for many years, with great success, on his fine estate near the mouth of the Mystic River. The name Embden is that of a town in Holland, where they first came from — but Col. Jaques was never inclined to multiply names, unnecessarily; and as he got his original stock of these monster white birds from Bremen direct, he called them Bremen Geese.

They are in all particulars like the common geese, except that they are very large — year-old ganders frequently weighing 28 to 35 pounds each, alive. The quality of the flesh is superior, and they are so ponderous and heavy that they move about but sluggishly, and thus put on fat very readily. Mr. Sisson, of Warren, R. I., five years after Col. Jaques imported his Bremens, had three direct from the same port. He says, in the N. E. Farmer, "their properties are peculiar. They lay in February, sit and hatch with more certainty than the common goose, will weigh nearly, and in some instances quite twice their weight, have double the quantity of feathers, never fly, and are all of a beautiful snowy whiteness." Dr. John C. Bennett furnished the author with half a dozen of these monstrous geese in 1851, that averaged 51 1-2 lbs. per pair. And in 1852, I received through a German friend a pair direct from Bremen, that weighed on shipboard 55 3-4 pounds, alive. I sent these two geese to Felix Ducayet, Esq., of New Orleans, with four others, for which he paid me fifty dollars the pair. They are a beautiful fowl, and resemble the white swan upon the water, at a short distance. The *Bremens* are now bred in their purity, I believe, by C. N. Palmer & Sons, Gallipolis, Ohio, D. W. Herstine, Philadelphia, T. B. Smith, Plantsville, Conn., and a few other gentlemen, but they are not now so commonly bred in Massachusetts, as formerly.

The *Toulouse* Goose, (see cut No. 16,) as its name implies, is from France, and is known from the ordinary dark gray goose of this country by being much larger, and its color darker, as well as uniform, in the different samples imported and bred here. Its abdominal part is very large, and hangs down prominently behind, sometimes almost touching the ground, as they clumsily waddle about.

Dixon, in his Poultry Book, says "this variety of goose, which has been so much extolled and sold at such high prices, is only the common domestic, enlarged by early hatching, very liberal feeding during youth, fine climate, and perhaps *by age*. I am in possession of geese, hatched at a season when it was difficult to supply them with abundance of nourishing green food, that are as much undersized as the Toulouse goose is oversized; they are all domestic geese, nevertheless." But, although I have seen hundreds of good samples of the Toulouse Goose, and thousands upon thousands of our natives, *I* never saw one of the latter that approached the enormous size of the French goose — and I doubt very much if there be not an error in this statement.

I have seen specimens of the Toulouse Geese that

would draw 42 pounds to the pair; and, in the yard of Col. Jaques, a few years ago, that gentleman showed me pairs that were heavier than this, even, by a pound or two, I was informed. It is of some importance to the farmer, who has the facilities for keeping waterfowl, that he have the best breed of geese attainable — even if he cross them (in the first instance) upon the common goose; for the increased weight and size — at an early age — produced through this process, *tells*, in the fall, when he comes to Christmas-ize his ' yearlings,' or the goslings of the same year's raising. We have no doubt that the Toulouse is a distinct variety, and we are certain it is a very fine one. The breeders of the *Bremen*, whom we have named in this chapter, furnish the Toulouse, also, we learn; and we can safely commend this splendid bird to all who go for size, easy keeping, hardiness, and truthfulness to their like, if bred together, in the raising of first-class geese.

The great African Goose, (Cut No. 16,) is another of the large birds of the genus *anser* — said by some authors to be *the* largest of all we have had in this country, from abroad. It has been called the "Knobbed Goose," from the peculiarity of possessing a hard knob on its head — a sort of brown fleshy substance, formed from the base of the bill, backward. It has a large dew-lap, also, under the throat, down the neck. It is called the " Swan Goose," from its size — the " Hong Kong," the " Brown China," etc. Its color is not unlike that of the Toulouse, but darker brownish. The ganders of this variety are enormous fellows. Thirty pounds' weight is not unusual, for a three-year old. We have seen none of this once famous and popular bird for some years. They were formerly bred in Weymouth, Braintree, and Randolph, Mass., finely, but the race has disappeared from among us, in this neighborhood.

"It is somewhat larger," says Brisson, "than the tame goose; the head and the top of the neck are brown, deeper on the upper side than on the under; . . . . on the origin of the bill there rises a round and fleshy tubercle; . . . . under the throat also there hangs a sort of fleshy membrane." Klien regards this goose as a variety of the Siberian, which is the same with the Guinea goose. "I saw," says he, " a variety of the Siberian goose, its throat larger, its bill and legs black, with a black depressed tubercle."

By whatever name it should be known, it is a remarkable bird, and we have been surprised that it has been suffered to " run out " around us, when we are informed by the breeders of this variety to whom we have alluded (in Massachusetts) that it was "no more trouble to raise this, than the common goose; while its weight at same age was double, and its meat really better than the mongrel."

The other varieties of Geese — such as the " White Chinese," " the Barnacle," the Egyptian," etc., are little known, and less used among Poulterers, and we make no farther reference to them. These three varieties we have described can be chosen from for breeders to advantage, and we will conclude this chapter with a description of the habits and needs of the Common well known native Goose of the country — the 'Mongrel —' that is bred everywhere so largely in the northern states of America.

A noted old English breeder of Geese, suggests the following directions, the result of long experience, which we deem both practical and applicable to the raising of these favorite water-fowl in our own country; where so many thousand of these birds are reared for disposal in the city markets of America, annually. He says of the Toulouse Goose, that the abdominal pouch peculiar to this variety (of which we have spoken) "which, in other geese, is an indication of old age, exist, in those from the shell. Their flesh is tender and well-flavored. It is quite certain that their cross on our domestic goose, would be found a most valuable acquisition." He then adds that "there are two prevailing colors amongst our *Domestic* (or Mongrel) Geese — white and gray." This applies with us also, uniformly. He says, farther, " we have a large, white variety, usually termed Embden (or Bremen) geese, which are very superior, from their extra size, and additional value of the feathers. If you wish a gray goose, by all means cross with the Toulouse, than which nothing can be finer. One gander is sufficient for five or six geese ; the goose lays from ten to twenty eggs at one laying; but by removing the eggs as fast as they are laid, and feeding her well, you may increase her laying to fifty eggs. If well cared for, you may have three clutches in the year. The care necessary, *is good housing and feeding*. "You will readily perceive when a goose is about to lay; she carries straw to make a nest; when that is observed, she should be confined, lest she lay out. If you induce her, by confinement, to lay her first egg in any particular place, she will be sure to deposit the remainder of her clutch in the same nest. Her inclination to hatch is indicated by her remaining in the nest longer than usual after laying. The nest may be of straw, with a finer lining, dry hay, or moss; and be sure it is sufficiently deep to prevent the eggs rolling out. About fifteen eggs is thought a sufficient clutch. The less the goose and her eggs are tampered with, the better; she sits from twenty-seven to thirty days. The gander never molests her on the nest, but acts as a sentinel to repel intruders."

It will be necessary to see that the goose be fed while hatching, as, if she find a difficulty in providing food, she may be kept too long off her nest, and perhaps at length desert it. The goslings will not require food for twelve hours after leaving the shell; their food may be bread, soaked in milk, porridge, curds, boiled greens, or bran, mixed with boiled potatoes, given warm, but not hot. Do not allow them to be subject to rain, or cold wind; keep them for at least forty-eight hours after hatching, *from* the water, which would be likely to bring on cramps. Although so fond of water, if you wish to keep your geese well, you will have to house and bed them at night, dry and comfortably. Grass is essential to the well-keeping of geese, their favorite being the long, coarse, rank grass, rejected by cattle, and therefore, through the goose, is turned to profit

The goose is easily kept, but if intended for market, they require, in addition to green food, some boiled potatoes, mixed with bran, given warm, but not hot. To fatten goslings for market, give potatoes or turnips, bruised with barley or oatmeal, at least twice a day.

Mr. Cobbet says, the refuse of a market garden, would maintain a great many geese, at a very small cost; but, in addition to the green food, they would require boiled or steamed potatoes, given warm; or oatmeal, peas, or maize, beat up with boiled potatoes, carrots, or turnips. An objection has been made to allowing geese to run over a pasture, their excrement being acrid and unwholesome. But common geese in this country are raised upon premises usually of no great value, otherwise; and the traveller upon the railways going into New York city, for example, for the last ten leagues, will remember the myriads of geese that dot the cheap places upon either side of the track, which are annually raised there by the poorer classes, for the neighboring market; to which fact, as a single instance, the reader is pointed in proof of the ease with which this bird is multiplied among us, if one has the fancy. It is *not* a difficult thing — with almost any kind of accommodations — to raise geese.

CHAPTER XXVII.

THE AYLESBURY, ROUEN, AND COMMON DUCK.

The Aylesbury (see next page) is the largest and most beautiful variety of pure white Duck we have in this country, and the most valuable, at this time. It was imported from Europe many years ago, in limited numbers, and has been very considerably bred, in different parts of this country. It is a great favorite with fanciers of ornamental water-fowl, and justly so, and may now be had of most of the leading dealers, in the Eastern and Middle States.

Those who have bred this splendid variety say, that no Duck is more easily raised that this, and from its large size, it is useful as well as ornamental. They are productive of beautiful white soft feathers, the meat is white, delicate, and savory, and the Aylesburys always command a ready sale, in market, for their acknowledged superiority of size and quality.

TRIO OF AYLESBURY DUCKS.

No. 15. 'CANADA" OR AMERICAN WILD GOOSE. 313.

When judiciously fed, they will weigh at maturity seven to eight pounds each — and will average (male and female) about twelve pounds the pair. They are very profitable layers, while they are easy keepers, not being usually so voracious as the common Duck. They are not so noisy either, and come up to their weight rapidly, at a less age than the others. It is quite a distinct variety. Mr. John Giles, formerly of Rhode Island, bred the Aylesbury among the earliest in this country. He describes those he brought out with him from England, as being " pure white; with white bills; their flesh is of a beautiful white; their weight eight to ten pounds per pair, when fully grown." Mr. Mowbray wrote many years since, that "the great white Aylesbury ducks are a beautiful and ornamental stock. They are early layers and breeders, and are in great demand. Many families derive a comfortable living from breeding and rearing ducks; the greater part of which — the early ones at all events—are actually reared by hand by cottagers."

All authorities agree that this bird is the finest duck we ever had in America. A New York agricultural journal pronounces them " the only variety which really rivals the Rouen as a useful and economical bird. These are a pure English variety, good feeders, and by some decidedly perferred to the Rouen."

The *Rouen* Duck (see cut opposite) takes its name from the city of Rouen, in France, where it is bred largely. Epicures pronounce its meat first class, and like the Aylesbury, it is a prolific layer of large eggs

314   BURNHAM'S NEW POULTRY-BOOK;

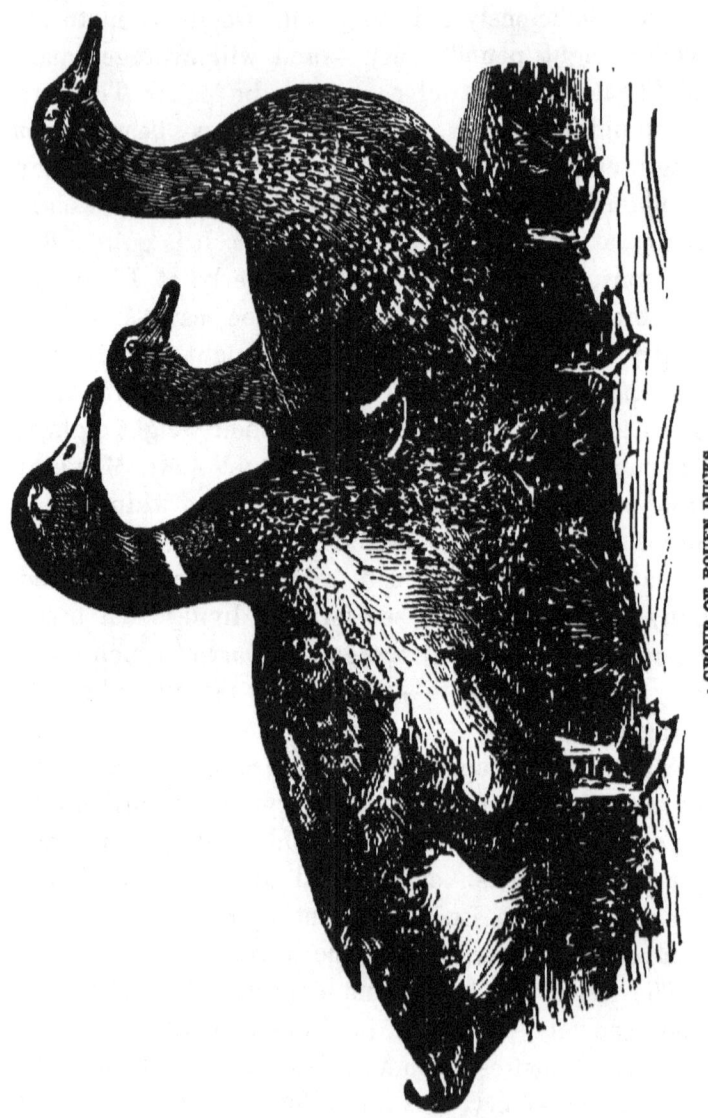

GROUP OF ROUEN DUCKS.

Its color is much like the wild duck, and the drake's, especially, is very showy and beautiful. The female is of a splashed dark brown and black, even and regular in form of the feathering. The drake's head and neck is a beautiful green, with a white ring around it at the base. The breast is a rich brown, and the rest of the body plumage similar to the plumage of the wild mallard.

It is a heavy, waddling, sleepy kind of fowl, and puts on flesh and fat quickly. They are very hardy, however, and the Common Duck of the country everywhere shows the markings of this fowl, with which it has been extensively crossed, for years, among us. They lay steadily from the beginning, sometimes dropping fifty to seventy eggs without missing a single day — then laying every other day, perhaps, for months longer. They are good sitters, but hens are better to set their eggs under, they are so heavy and clumsy.

The "Cayuga Black" Duck is another large variety which breeders in New York State reproduce, most largely. The late Dr. Eben Wight of Dedham, Mass., formerly raised upon his place good specimens of all three of these varieties—though, (as he fancied the white Dorkings) he preferred the white Aylesbury to all other varieties of duck. The Cayuga was first known, we believe, upon the shores of Cayuga Lake, in Central New York — whence its name — and it is now bred there in considerable numbers, very successfully. Its size will average fully that of the Rouen, and it is a clear black duck, for the most part, in its purity.

The Summer, or Wood duck, is the most beautiful in

plumage of all the race we have here. It is much smaller than the others, and is a wild bird. I have never known it to be domesticated, though Col. Jaques of Medford, some years since showed me a flock he had, (whose wings he had jointed to keep them from flying away,) which he attempted to tame and breed; with what success I never learned.

Wilson describes this as the most beautiful of all our Ducks, which has no superior for its richness and variety of color. It is called the wood duck, from the circumstance of its breeding in hollow trees; and the summer duck, from remaining with us chiefly during the summer. It rarely visits the sea shore, or salt marshes, its favorite haunts being the solitary, muddy creeks, ponds, and mill-dams of the interior.

The summer duck flies in flocks of not more than three or four together, and most commonly in pairs, or singly. Their flesh is inferior to that of the blue-winged teal. They are frequent in the markets of Philadelphia. Among other gaudy feathers with which the Indians ornament the calumet or pipe of peace, the skin of the head and neck of this duck is frequently seen covering the stem.

We have also the Canvas-back, Red-head, the Blue-winged Teal, the Muscovy, etc., but the mass of ducks furnished for our markets are the native *Domestic Duck*; which is too well known to need a description, and too varied in color to be described in detail. They run from white to black — speckled, spotted, gray, and Rouen colored. These can readily be traced to the wild originals, and are easily multiplied. The Domestic Duck will find its own food, for the greater part of the year, if it have sufficient scope of water to furnish it with aquatic plants; or, if permitted to ramble, the beechmast and acorns furnish it with nutrition, meadows and pasture grounds afford it insectivorous matter, and if an occasional feed of boiled potatoes, with a little grain be given, it will flourish. One drake is sufficient for five or six ducks. They begin to lay in February, when they require additional food. They usually lay either at night, or early in the morning — a circumstance that should be attended to, as, if permitted to ramble away, when about to lay, they frequently drop their eggs in the water; but, if confined a few times, they incline to lay in the same place. The time of incubation is thirty days; after which the young follow the parent, and should be kept *from* the water for a couple of days. Soft food agrees with them; barley-meal and water, mixed thin, or chopped egg and oat-meal, is a favorite food.

The illustrations we give of the Ducks are from Messrs. D. L. Stage & Co. of Schenectady, who breed the finer varieties, purely, and whose birds have taken prizes at the American Poultry shows, frequently, we learn. Both the Aylesbury and Rouen Duck are largely bred by others — Mr. Warner, of New York Mills, Messrs. Murdock of Meriden, Conn., T. B. Smith & Co. of Plantsville, Conn., Isaac Van Winkle, Greenville, N. J., D. W. Herstine, and J. M. Wade, of Philadelphia, etc., being among the principal poulterers who give attention to these fine water-fowl.

CHAPTER XXVIII.

WHAT I KNOW ABOUT POULTRY, AND FOWL-SHOWS.

In the final chapters of my "New Poultry Book," I have thought it pertinent — at the risk of its being deemed somewhat egotistical, perhaps — to state something of what I know about Poultry, in a general way, and what I have learned, in my long experience, as amateur, importer, and breeder of Domestic Fowls.

I learned, at an early date in that experience, that it is not profitable to place too much reliance upon the unsettled opinions, or loose statements — often made in entire good faith, nevertheless, of a great many people who deal in poultry, and particularly of some who make this occupation a specific business.

I have since learned that the ideas and notions of

certain persons of this class are inclined to be bigoted, and that their judgment is warped, through selfishness frequently; but oftener through positive ignorance of the business in which they engage — for their own personal aggrandizement, alone — heedless of what may be the interests of others, in the same line of trade, who may be abundantly able to compete with them.

I have ascertained that few men engaged in the fowl-trade are disposed to enlarge their usefulness by disseminating their choice stock, at reasonably moderate prices, so that the farmer, the poor man, and the multitude can avail themselves of the benefits of the "improvement" they nominally propose to undertake in the character of the poultry-stock of this or other countries, through the introduction of new varieties, and fresh blood, from abroad.

I have found that the breeder or fancier in Europe or America, is yet to be discovered, who will take three pounds sterling for his birds, so long as he can obtain five; or accept ten dollars, while he can get fifteen, or twenty! And I do not hesitate to admit that like the others, I was long troubled with this same affection; for the reason, I suppose, that this predilection is inherent in the chicken-raiser, in all nations, alike.

I have become satisfied that it does not pay to give one's time to breeding specimen fowls for the exhibition room, alone; more especially, if the breeder happens to be a moderately modest, honest 'outsider;' who — though he *may* be able to contribute a cage or two of the best samples shown, does not luckily chance to belong to "our set," or "our ring." And there be many earnest striving amateurs who have had the opportunity to share with me in acquiring this item of information, to their cost, during the past score of years in this country.

I have found out that Poultry Societies are most excellent institutions, in their way, when well managed, and fairly conducted towards all their members, indiscriminately — and that Fowl Exhibitions have proved both beneficial and profitable, where they have been regulated justly and generously, in the interests of the whole, rather than for the aggrandizement of a few of their more fortunate, and so influential members.

I have made it certain, in my own mind, that the "judges" at Poultry exhibitions in the United States — though usually honest and fair meaning men — are not selected so much for their experience in these matters, and their competency to pronounce upon the genuine merits of the fowls placed in competition for their decisions, as they might be; and that we have in America, to-day, but few men who will undertake this duty, and decide a case for themselves, individually, upon any nice point, without being affected by " outside pressure," or the opinions of co-laborers on the Committees.

I have proved the fact, to my entire satisfaction, that the poulterer who permits fowls of different varieties to run promiscuously together in the fall and winter, and only separates them in the spring, a month before breeding them, can never afterwards restore his pullets to *pure* breeders, again. Hens thus jeopardized, are contaminated, for life; and no known natural law will effect a recovery from the injury, communicated through this careless process, altogether too common among fanciers and amateurs who subscribe to the doctrine that the presence of any desired male with the female, *for a few days*, or weeks, only, (prior to setting her eggs) is sufficient to insure *pure*-bred chickens from such fowls!

I have observed that the dealers generally have found from experience that eggs sent from their establishments for hatching, to any great distance, cannot safely be warranted, however cautiously they may contrive to pack them; and honorable men admit now-a-days, that there is a risk in such transportation, owing to the rough treatment they must almost invariably encounter en route. This being the exact truth, buyers must "take their chances," and be satisfied, as a rule, that though eggs so forwarded may be in perfect condition, when shipped, the receivers cannot count confidently upon getting the same number of chickens from them as there are eggs in the boxes.

I have become convinced that poultry dealers, as a class, are prone to deem the particular variety or strain of blood *they* possess to be better than that owned by others; and I have not been obliged to travel out of my way to meet with more than one gentleman who really believed in this theory, and was honest in his declarations; yet who did not think there were any *pure* Cochins in America, until he imported a few, recently, from England!

I have learned that in the details of this business, as

in many other affairs of life, it is a very easy thing to be mistaken, in our estimation both of a rival breeder's stock and his real intentions. And that the more we cry down the character of a competitor's poultry, be it good or indifferent — the more business we make for him, and the less for ourselves, as we go. The harder you rub a rusty copper, the brighter the old coin will shine.

I have become convinced that this goodly world of ours is large enough for us all, and that there is sufficient room in it for us to get on, comfortably, without elbowing or jostling our neighbors; and, at the same time, I have found from experience, that while a deal of money may be made by attending courteously to our own affairs — a deal more can be made by decorously leaving the concerns of other people alone — even in the chicken trade.

Well tried experiments have taught me that "prize birds," either from the English or American show-rooms, are not generally to be relied on as the best fowls *to breed from*. Enterprising fanciers, who contrive to put into the exhibition-hall their superior pair or trio of imported or high-bred specimens, are obliged to cram these birds, ordinarily, to bring them to perfection in size, plumage, and condition, for competition. Oftentimes these fowls are aged, fat, and dropsical, and the eggs of such forced samples don't throw chickens that come up to their parents in fine quality, by any means; and, oftener than otherwise, these immense, showy hens will be found to lay no eggs at all, after being thus forced and stuffed, on two or three occasions.

It is within my own experience that show-birds thus purchased — at enormous figures — have in the last named particular disappointed the buyer, altogether, having never given him an egg, after he placed them triumphantly in his fine fowl-house! And so lately as in the year 1870, at one of our leading shows, the owner of the first premium fowls, in a certain class, was offered twenty-five dollars for a dozen eggs from the two prize-hens; but, up to May 1871, neither of them had laid one. Yet this same trio, placed again in competition in any show-room in the United States, would again bear away the highest honors; for, to look at, they were, in all respects, certainly extraordinary fine fowls.

In this connection, experience has exemplified, to *my* thorough satisfaction, that the Brahma or the Cochin fowl need not always be the largest, the highest upon its legs, or the weightiest, to be the most desirable to breed from. Points tell. Fine chickens may be, and are raised, from medium-sized cocks and hens, if they are judiciously fed, and wisely cared for. But an observant writer in a late number of the Rural New Yorker, says that he discovered in a recent coop of prize-birds there, that " the adipose tissue of these fowls was alarmingly in excess, and he thought that apoplexy would soon follow," in their case, from the *stuffing* process to which they had evidently been subjected, before they left England, where they had been forced up to great weight, and from whence they had recently been imported, for this very occasion.

I have seen the plan so many times and oft-repeated at exhibitions, where the successful fancier has borne away the palm by showing such fowls, and I have myself so frequently been the victim of misplaced confidence, in this respect, at heavy cost, that I feel I am doing but a simple act of justice to others, when I state that *I* have learned not to pay the high prices such birds readily command, with a view ever to be able to breed from them such progeny as will give either me or my patrons satisfaction. And I am certain that other zealous breeders have, within a few years, through *their* experience, arrived at this self-same conclusion.

I am no longer in doubt as to the fact that there are now in this country plenty of men who can, and do, breed first-class poultry, as well as you or I can do it — reader; and if you chance to be one of those who do not agree with me, in this opinion, I trust you may quickly and hopefully be brought to see the error of your way — as I was — several years since.

I have *not* yet learned the address of the sailor who "brought into New York the first Brahma fowls, in a ship that came direct from up the Brama-poutra River — " 'which, I wish to remark, and my language is plain' — " is a stream that discharges its waters into the Bay of Bengal." And, as an inquirer after truth, I shall take it kindly in any brother-poulterer who will give me this information — if *he* ever learns it — though

I really don't think he will. 'Which is why I remark that this statement is dark; which the same I am free to maintain.'

I have concluded, from what I have had to do with poultry — of all descriptions — imported, home-bred, and crossed — that the most valuable fowl for all the purposes of the fancier or the farmer, in America, is the *Chinese* strain, whether it be adopted from among the Brahmas, the Cochins, or the Shanghæs. And notwithstanding the decisions and Reports of Poultry-Show Judges that "there are more profitable breeds than this," I still think that time will show this assumption of Committees to be erroneous.

I have learned that this matter of the 'decision of judges' is a very important one, and that it ought to be so contrived that disinterested, competent, willing, unprejudiced, intelligent men only should be placed upon such Committees; and that unfortunately we find precious few such persons in the poultry societies of this country, while in England, even, they are quite as rarely to be met with, so far as I can gather.

I have informed myself that the "Cochin China" and the Shanghæ fowl are *not* precisely the same bird, and I have long since been of the opinion that calling a breed of fowls by any outlandish or new-fangled name, simply, does not change the character and merits or demerits of the bird so afflicted — while it answers no useful purpose, either to the breeder, or the fowl, first or last; and only serves to aid in bringing the business of poultry-raising into disrepute, and ridicule, both at home and abroad.

I have ascertained that with the right sort of management of good stock, the finest fowls in this world can be raised in these goodly United States of ours; and that repeated experiments have proved that birds of the choicest kinds to be had in England, sent over to this country and bred here as fowls ought to be bred, have been returned to that country so improved (in all essential particulars) *not* by crossing — but by legitimate breeding — that the same stock has scarcely been recognisable there. This is one thing the Yankee can accomplish, *sure*.

I have determined that in my judgment we can — and so we ought to — breed poultry in America that will beat the world, in all the desirable qualities that go to make up a first-class fowl, for the spit, the pit, or the gentleman's lawn ; and it is in no spirit of boasting that I make this statement, since the fact is well known, and acknowledged, on both sides of the Atlantic, by those who are the best able to judge of the truthfulness of this assertion — one candid English writer in the London "Field" using the frank expression that "since Brother Jonathan made the Brahmas, I wish he would make us something more."

I have found out many other things of kindred character, in relation to the handling, exhibiting and breeding of poultry, which I will not trouble the reader with, for the present — for chicken-raisers will sooner or later learn all these matters from their own individual experience and observation, as I have acquired the information here submitted.

CHAPTER XXIX.

TWENTY-FIVE GOOD RULES FOR FOWL-BREEDERS.

In conclusion, I set down the following five and twenty rules and hints, in brief, for the benefit of those who may not be familiar with all these matters; which I deem highly important, however, to be observed by those who would breed fowls well and successfully.

I. — WHO TO PURCHASE FROM.

In selecting poultry or eggs for incubation, apply for for what you seek only to a known reliable breeder, who will faithfully send what you order, and pay him for. There are plenty of such dealers to be found now-a-days, in this country.

II. — ABOUT TRANSPORTING EGGS.

Never send to a distance for eggs for hatching, when you can procure them near home; as the danger of injuring by transportation is imminent, in conveying this delicately formed article over our railways and rough roads.

III. — HOW BEST TO SET A HEN.

When you get your eggs, set them at once, and don't handle them more than is absolutely necessary, until you can place them under your hens. Then let them alone for three weeks, and "take your chances."

IV. — LET THE YOUNG ONES ALONE!

When your young ones are hatched, don't meddle with them, for four and twenty hours, in your impatience to see them eat. As a rule, they will eat enough to satisfy your most ardent desires in this direction, afterwards.

V. — TO CURE EGG-EATING FOWLS.

To prevent fowls eating their eggs, blow half a dozen, and fill the shells with a mixture of yolks and cayenne pepper, or kerosene. Close them up, and place *these* eggs where the offenders can try this decoction. A single taste will content them!

VI. — GIVE FOWLS AMPLE RANGE.

Release your old fowls early in the day, if you have a range or yard, for them; and the larger the better, if you keep them in quantity. Ample runs, or walks, for poultry, seven or eight months in the year, are almost indispensable.

VII. — ADOPT A REGULAR SYSTEM.

However you feed, do it in a cleanly manner, upon system, and whatever else you do, be sure they have *clean* fresh water, and plenty of it, at all times. This is a pre-requisite to assure their health and prosperity.

VIII. — WHAT TO DO TO HAVE EGGS.

Supply them with plenty of gravel, ground bones, pounded oyster-shells, ashes and powdered sulphur to roll in, and both green and animal food — when confined — if you expect them to lay eggs, or keep in ordinary health, meantime.

IX. — DON'T WET A SITTING HEN'S EGGS.

Never adopt the stupid whim of the ignorant, about *wetting your eggs*, in the hen's nest for ten days after she sits. Who " wets eggs " for the hen that steals her nest? or that sits and hatches in the wild state?

X. — SET THE FRESHEST EGGS, ALWAYS.

Procure your eggs for setting from the freshest you can find; and never buy, until your hen is ready to cover them. By following this rule, you will get more chicks, and meet with less disappointment, always.

XI. — YOU MUST CARE FOR YOUR FOWLS.

Adopt a regular *system* in breeding poultry, and remember that any kind of live stock, to be made to pay, must have its due share of care and attention. In proportion to the cost, no stock pays so well as this.

XII. — HOW TO AVOID VERMIN.

To prevent the presence of vermin, give fowls raw onions, chopped fine, occasionally; and dampen your roosts and nest-bottoms weekly, with kerosene, or spirits of turpentine. Your fowls will thus never be troubled with lice.

XIII. — HOW TO CURE A SICK FOWL.

If a bird gets sick, remove it directly from the rest. If it doesn't recover quickly, knock it on the head, and bury it. This is the easiest, surest, and cheapest way it can be 'cured,' and save the others, perhaps.

XIV. — LIGHT, WARMTH, AND AIR.

Give your poultry light, in the fowl-house, warmth and protection in winter. In summer let them have all the out-door enjoyment they can get. They do not love *heat*, but crave protection from cold winds and storms.

XV. — SAVE AND SELL THE MANURE.

Place a board flooring directly under your roosts, to catch the droppings of the fowls during the night. Remove this excrement, daily, and save it. The leather-dressers will pay you six dollars a barrel for it.

XVI. — TO BREED POULTRY PURELY.

If you aim to breed fowls *purely*, never permit a male of another variety to reach your pullets, from the start. Thus, *only*, can you prevent the female from being contaminated, for all time, to a greater or less degree.

XVII. — HOW TO BREAK UP A BROODY HEN.

Never adopt the brutal mode of putting a broody hen into cold water, ' to break her up.' Place her in an open slatted coop, with nothing but a roost inside — feed her from the outside — and she will quickly forget her ' fever.'

XVIII. — LOOK OUT FOR SNOW-WATER!

Avoid giving *snow*-water to poultry; it is poison to them. A lump of oil-cake scraps, (to be had at the pork-houses,) is excellent, placed in the fowl-houses, where they can peck it at their pleasure.

XIX. — CHICKENS ALWAYS READY TO KILL.

Keep your fowls in good condition, from the shell, by judicious feeding. They will eat no more than they want; and thus you will be able, with a few day's extra fare, at *any* time, to put those to be slaughtered in the best shape for marketing.

XX. — THE BEST SITTING HEN'S NEST.

In setting your hens, make it a rule to place at the bottom of the nest-box, a thick fresh sod; upon which place the straw or hay for the eggs. The moisture from the earthy sod will be found a valuable aid to the more successful hatching.

XXI. — DON'T THINK YOUR FOWLS "THE BEST."

If you raise fowls for exhibitions, don't imagine that yours "are the *best* ones" shewn, until the Judges decide this little matter (perhaps *against* you!) The adage is true — though musty — that "you can't tell who is Governor, till after election."

XXII. — PROPER AGE TO BREED FROM.

Breed from two-year old fowls, for increased size, of any variety, as well as to insure chicks that will earliest mature. Year-old pullets are very well, but the others are best; and a two-year-old cock is always preferable, if you have one.

XXIII. — THE *FOWLS*, NOT THE CAGES, WIN!

Never expend money foolishly on ornamental *coops*, for the show-room, but remember that the *contents*, (not the expensive cage) will give you the award, if deserving — provided the Judges are competent, honest, and fair men, in their decisions.

XXIV. — ' FIRST CLASS WHITEWASH.

Whitewash your hen-house three or four times in a season. For the *inside*, mix half a pail full of lime and water, make a starch of half a pound of flour, and pour this in, while *hot;* or, a little glue, will answer. For outside work, add a handful of salt and boiled rice to the above, and when dry, see if you can *rub it off*.

XXV. — HOW TO PRESERVE EGGS IN WINTER.

To preserve your family supply of eggs, for winter use, lay them down in the fall, or summer, in a liquid composed as follows: one pint of lime, and one pint of common salt, dissolved in four gallons of boiling water. When *cold*, put your eggs into this liquid, *in a stone jar* — and they will keep for months. I have tried this, for years, without failure.

These rules are a part of what I have learned in my experience; and I have succeeded in raising pretty good fowls, and a great many of them, in my time. If my reader will follow out these hints, he can not go far out of the right way; and I can venture to assure him that he will be able, thus, to succeed to his satisfaction, in " Selecting, Housing, and Breeding Domestic Fowls— " as I have done.

CHAPTER XXX.

RAISING FOWLS IN QUANTITIES, TO PROFIT.

Whatever business pursuit is worth undertaking to do *at all*, is worth doing *well*. The stock-raiser who attempts to breed good cattle, horses, sheep or swine, is obliged to devote capital, time, study and care to his enterprise, to assure success, even in a comparative view. And there be many who have distinguished themselves, thus, who have found that their animals should be the best to be procured of their class, and that unless the breeder continually devotes himself to their necessities and well-being, competitors in the same line will excel him in production, and win the palm, as a natural sequence to their more faithful or superior management.

In the multiplying of poultry, both breeders and farmers in the United States have notably been remiss in carrying out the principle that *this* pursuit, like any other, should be skillfully and attentively conducted, if success is aimed at; and it is too frequently the case that the farmer's poultry is deemed of such minor consequence, that it is left to take care of itself. But when the fact is presented that in this present year (1871) the *market* value of the domestic poultry and eggs in the United States approximates the colossal sum of nearly twenty millions of dollars, it will be admitted that this is no mean item to be considered, as a single branch of the live stock interest in this country; and it ought assuredly to be looked at as one of the leading sources that contribute to the grand aggregate of our national rural wealth.

If the farmer who raises his dozen or score or two of chickens, annually, which he indifferently obliges to roost in the barn-cellar or among his trees, at night, and to forage about the farm by day, for sustenance — who never cares to house his fowls in winter, and gives them no heed in summer, except to gather what eggs he can pick up about the hay-mow, or in the cattle-mangers — would give a tithe of the attention to his poultry that he bestows upon his pigs or sheep, he would realize the difference in the returns that would be forthcoming from his too often neglected fowls.

A good deal has been effected through the persistent efforts of societies and a few poulterers in the Eastern and Middle States, of late years, towards influencing the farmers in the right direction, in this business; and, in many quarters, we hear of the waking up of the country people to their own interests in this matter. With a little extra care in selecting, breeding, and properly providing accommodations for fowls, every husbandman in our land — in addition to a generous supply of eggs for his own family use — could have upon his table, at a nominal cost, a brace of good chickens twice or thrice a week, if he desired; or these same six or eight chickens weekly, could be slaughtered and sent to the nearest market, to find a ready cash sale, at a figure that would pay the raiser doubly the sum that he can, at similar cost and with greater labor, obtain for the same number of pounds of pork, mutton, or beef. This being the fact, it is surprising that poultry is not better cared for on the farm, than it has thus far been in America.

There is always a call for good chickens in any city market, at remunerative prices; and eggs will always command cash, at similar figures at any season. There never yet has been a surfeit of either. The demand is unceasing, too, and year by year the statistics show that this demand increases. There is no danger of overdoing this thing. Good clean, bright, fat poultry will always find ready purchasers, in our cities and large towns in any quantity; and thus it behooves the farmers of the country to look at this subject of fowl-raising with an eye to their own pecuniary benefit; since it can be accomplished with such small effort.

Numerous experiments have been tried among the class of men of whom we are writing, the results of which, when the accounts have been accurately kept, have shown that an ordinary clutch of fowls upon the farm has paid a profit of fifty to seventy per cent. of the cost, feed and care. What kind of live stock or gardening, or farming, will return any thing like such percentage as this?

And this is not theoretical, remember. In a town in California, contiguous to market, there now lives a poulterer and farmer who has kept several thousand fowls, for some years past, and who is making a reasonable fortune in that country, through this means. The climate is in his favor, of course; but he makes a business of it upon system, for marketing purposes, and can raise more pounds of poultry and eggs, he avers, at the same cost, than he can of pork or beef; and his chickens and eggs bring him twice or thrice the price, per pound, that he can realize from the best sheep, swine or cattle he can raise even in that favored country.

Mr. Lewis, in his lately issued 'Practical Poultry Book,' gives an account of a South American poultry farm, carried on by Don San Fuentes, who now keeps some six thousand fowls upon his large estate, and who proposes to double or quadruple this number the coming season. He commenced operations with only two hundred birds, a few years ago. But he colonizes his immense stock, and they have unlimited range over a ranche of thousands of acres. He keeps some fifty hens and a few cocks, only, in the same colony, however, and scatters these families of fifty or sixty each over the broad extent of his generous sized farm, so that they are kept precisely as we recommend — to wit, in separate *small* collections. Thus only can numbers be kept, at all. His houses are of the cheapest kind, for the accommodation of this vast congregation of the feathered tribe, and five or six hands are employed to look after the stock, constantly, as Mr. Leland and

No 16. AFRICAN, TOULOUSE, AND BREMEN GOOSE. 337.

other extensive poulterers find it necessary to do. This South American breeder collects two hundred dozen eggs a day, and states that his profits upon this product, and the sale of killed poultry, last year, reached eleven thousand dollars.

If poultry-keeping on a large scale can be carried on in one place to a profit, there is no good reason why it cannot be accomplished in another section. The farmer who has hitherto raised only his score or two of fowls, may raise a hundred or two, in the course of a season, about as easily. Instead of having twenty or thirty dozens of eggs in a twelvemonth, he may have as many hundreds — with but trifling additional labor, and but slightly increased attention to his poultry.

Since then it *can* be done, why not do it? Every agriculturist, every fancier, every amateur fowl-breeder can contribute his mite to this desirable project, if he has the inclination. And since no other kind of live stock *pays* so well, it really seems to our view that it is but a duty the farmer owes to the community, that he gives more and better attention to the multiplying of good poultry and eggs, for general consumption.

If the nominal intention of breeders and poultry societies to "improve" the condition of this branch of rural trade means anything, we hope to see *their* efforts directed to the advancement of the chief means whence this market supply properly originates — to wit, towards the interests of the *farmers* of the country.

Quoting once more from the N. Y. Poultry Bulletin, we observe that its talented editor lately insists that the majority of farmers have always considered their poultry of little or no consequence, and they have allowed them to run wild and take care of themselves, and degenerate from year to year. They generally let them roost in their pig-pen, on their wagons, or wherever they can find a place. They seldom, if ever feed them, except it be a little in winter, and allow them to make their nests on the hay, under the barns, and all over the premises. But they very rarely coop them and keep them out of the wet grass, or feed them regularly; in consequence of which, full seventy per cent. die. This has resulted in reducing the size of poultry and eggs to an alarming degree, so that the farmers' chickens and ducks average from 2 to 4 lbs., turkeys and geese from 6 to 8 lbs. and eggs 10 to the pound, etc. And these plainly stated facts account, in a great measure, for the almost universal opinion current among American farmers that "poultry keeping don't pay." It never will pay, conducted in this reckless way, and it ought *not* to pay, so managed; since if it is not worth the little trouble requisite to keep it in good condition, it is not worth keeping at all.

Mr. Leland's poultry establishments, previously alluded to, are the most extensive, if not *the* largest in the Northern States. He has over four thousand Brahma fowls in stock, three hundred ducks of different kinds; four to five hundred turkies, and one hundred and fifty breeding geese. He kills from one to two hundred head weekly, for his great hotel in New York; and the business pays him handsomely, since he has a quick market through this channel for his poultry, all of which has hitherto been raised for the " Metropolitan ; " from the refuse dry offal of which immense establishment, Mr. L. has the advantage of being able to furnish his fowls with a great variety of acceptable food, at small cost, of course. He states that he turns out about three thousand chickens every spring.

Thus it has been demonstrated, in late years, that poultry *can* be kept to profit, in quantities, if the right management, care and location is accorded the fowls. Formerly it was found that the attempt to keep and breed this kind of farm stock to any great extent, upon one estate, failed of success ; and it is only a few years since, that Hon. Lewis F. Allen, in response to a correspondent who asked his advice as to " how a chicken-house should be constructed, to accommodate about a thousand fowls," replied as follows: " If my poor opinion is worth anything, you will not build it at all. Fowls, in any large numbers together, will not thrive. I have seen it tried, but I never knew a large collection of several hundred fowls succeed *in a confined place*. I have known sundry of these enterprises tried ; but I never knew one *permanently* successful. They were all in turn abandoned."

Thirty years ago, to wit, in 1839 to 1841, I planned an extensive range of fowl-houses in Roxbury, Mass., having leased " Williams' Garden," at the foot of Mt. Pleasant, for the purpose of trying to raise poultry on a large scale. I had a fine establishment, good location, what I supposed was ample space, and I erected twenty fowl-houses, in a circle — connected together *under one*

general shed roof, with small yards attached to each
house. I had glass houses, too, a pond on the premises,
and every apparent convenience was at hand that seemed to be needed. But the enterprise did not succeed.
Five hundred fowls were massed *upon one spot*; and
they soon failed, retrograded, sickened and died. In
winter time they could not be kept in good health, within the limits of the house-confinement; and after three
years' trial, I gave it up. But the error committed
in *that* instance was in huddling too many fowls together
under one roof. Only by colonizing them, a few in a
place, scattered about over your farm or estate, in numbers of not over forty to fifty together, can you breed
poultry to advantage, or keep them in health.

And to effect this — time, labor, and attention must
be given to the object. The thriving merchant rises
early, goes to his store, and remains there attending
to his business till evening, and thus obtains a good
living, or makes money. The mechanic who succeeds
in life, begins his work with the sun's rising, and labors
assiduously to its setting — to get on comfortably in the
world, and lay up something for a rainy day. The
artisan devotes ten or twelve hours, daily, to his labors
and studies, or he runs behind his more enterprising
rivals. The lawyer and the doctor are necessarily
obliged to give their days (and nights often,) to their
duties, constantly; and very few in these professions get
rich, through either! The farmer toils from dawn to
evening, over his live stock, his crops, or his fields —
and obtains comfort and subsistence only by attending
to his work industriously and steadily.

And so every business pursuit in life must needs be followed with zeal, care, skill, and determination — to prove more or less successful. If any one desires to raise poultry to profit, in an ordinary way, *he must attend to it*, precisely as he would to any other business, or profession; or there is nothing in it, for *him*. Domestic Fowls will not take care of themselves, advantageously. They must have shelter, in bad weather; they must be kept from crowding each other, in limited quarters; they must be fed and cared for, *upon system;* and they need constant looking after, during the day, precisely as any other live stock does. And this undertaking should be attempted (on a scale to any great extent,) only as any business, pursuit, calling, or profession is followed —— if the party interested expects to make the occupation remunerative.

The same number of hours daily, regularly, and *faithfully*, that the shop-keeper, the mechanic, the artisan, the lawyer, the laborer, the farmer, or other stock-raiser gives to his duties, profession, or business, devoted to the care of two or three thousand fowls, upon a suitable location, within reach of market, will yield very much better returns, in proportion to the outlay of capital, cost of keeping, etc., than will the multiplying of *any* live stock grown. There is little of mystery, little of difficulty to be encountered, in this employment, and no hard labor. But to succeed in producing *good* fowls, or in multiplying this kind of stock, *in numbers* — your poultry must be systematically attended to, and never be left to shift for themselves. And, in this respect, the business of raising fowls is, in no particular, different from any other calling. It is a good business, a paying enterprize, a healthful occupation, a pleasant employment, and will be attended with satisfactory results—*if well followed.* Attempted otherwise—it will only be coupled with failure; precisely as *any* business pursuit is certain to fail, if inefficiently, or recklessly left to manage itself.

Thus, in plain phrase, I have endeavored to set forth in this New Poultry Book such general rules and advice as I deem useful, pertinent, and practically feasible, for the successful keeping and rearing of chickens and fowls, and the production of eggs either in fancy breeding, or the more useful and desirable pursuit of poultry-raising for household and marketing purposes.

By reference to our previous pages, the reader may find the names of many of the principal good breeders and dealers in this country who raise the finest stock, and who are prepared to supply orders, honorably and promptly, I believe. And we are happy in being able to conclude our present pleasant task with the knowledge that a new impulse has of late been given to the subject, among us, which I make no doubt will be followed with largely beneficial results to the poultry interest in the United States, in the future.

Very likely I leave many things yet to be learned, concerning the matters treated of herein. But, if the recommendations I have submitted are followed, poultry-keepers will not be disappointed in the results attainable through an observance of the suggestions contained in this work, which has now reached

THE END.

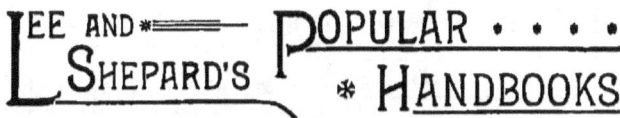
LEE AND SHEPARD'S POPULAR HANDBOOKS

Price, each, in cloth, 50 cents, except when other price is given.

Forgotten Meanings; or an Hour with a Dictionary. By ALFRED WAITES, author of Historical Student's Manual.

Handbook of Blunders. Designed to prevent 1,000 common blunders in writing and speaking. By HARLAN H. BALLARD, A.M., Principal of Lenox Academy, Lenox, Mass.

Beginnings with the Microscope. A working handbook containing simple instructions in the art and method of using the microscope, and preparing articles for examination. By WALTER P. MANTON.

Field Botany. A Handbook for the Collector. Containing instructions for gathering and preserving Plants, and the formation of an Herbarium. Also complete instructions in Leaf Photography, Plant Printing, and the Skeletonizing of Leaves. By WALTER P. MANTON.

Taxidermy without a Teacher. Comprising a complete manual of instructions for Preparing and Preserving Birds, Animals, and Fishes, with a chapter on Hunting and Hygiene; together with instructions for Preserving Eggs, and Making Skeletons, and a number of valuable recipes. By WALTER P. MANTON.

Insects. How to Catch and how to Prepare them for the Cabinet. A Manual of Instruction for the Field-Naturalist. By W. P. MANTON.

What is to be Done? A Handbook for the Nursery, with Useful Hints for Children and Adults. By ROBERT B. DIXON, M.D.

Whirlwinds, Cyclones, and Tornadoes. By WILLIAM MORRIS DAVIS, Instructor in Harvard College. Illustrated.

Warrington's Manual. A Manual for the Information of Officers and Members of Legislatures, Conventions, Societies, etc., in the practical governing and membership of all such bodies, according to the Parliamentary Law and Practice in the United States. By W. S. ROBINSON (*Warrington*).

Universal Phonography; or, Shorthand by the "Allen Method." A self-instructor. By G. G. ALLEN.

Hints and Helps for those who Write, Print, or Read. By B. DREW, proof-reader.

Lessons on Manners. By EDITH E. WIGGIN.

Water Analysis. A Handbook for Water-Drinkers. By G. L. AUSTIN, M.D.

Exercises for the Improvement of the Senses. For Young Children. By HORACE GRANT, author of "Arithmetic for Young Children." Edited by WILLARD SMALL.

Hints on Language in connection with Sight-Reading and Writing in Primary and Intermediate Schools. By S. ARTHUR BENT, A.M., Superintendent of Public Schools, Clinton, Mass.

Sold by all booksellers, and sent by mail, postpaid, on receipt of price.

LEE AND SHEPARD Publishers Boston

LEE AND SHEPARD'S POPULAR HANDBOOKS

Price, each, in cloth, 50 cents, except when other price is given.

Exercises for the Improvement of the Senses. For Young Children. By HORACE GRANT, author of "Arithmetic for Young Children." Edited by WILLARD SMALL.

Hints on Language in connection with Sight-Reading and Writing in Primary and Intermediate Schools. By S. ARTHUR BENT, A.M., Superintendent of Public Schools, Clinton, Mass.

The Hunter's Handbook. Containing lists of provisions and camp paraphernalia, and hints on the fire, cooking utensils, etc.; with approved receipts for camp-cookery. By "AN OLD HUNTER."

Universal Phonography; or, Shorthand by the "Allen Method." A self-instructor. By G. G. ALLEN.

Pronouncing Handbook of Three Thousand Words often Mispronounced. By R. SOULE and L. J. CAMPBELL.

Short Studies of American Authors. By THOMAS WENTWORTH HIGGINSON.

The Stars and the Earth; or, Thoughts upon Space, Time, and Eternity. With an introduction by THOMAS HILL, D.D., LL.D.

Handbook of the Earth. Natural Methods in Geography. By LOUISA PARSONS HOPKINS, teacher of Normal Methods in the Swain Free School, New Bedford.

Natural-History Plays. Dialogues and Recitations for School Exhibitions. By LOUISA P. HOPKINS.

The Telephone. An account of the phenomena of Electricity, Magnetism, and Sound, with directions for making a speaking-telephone. By Professor A. E. DOLBEAR.

Lessons on Manners. By EDITH E. WIGGIN.

Water Analysis. A Handbook for Water-Drinkers. By G. L. AUSTIN, M.D.

Handbook of Light Gymnastics. By LUCY B. HUNT, instructor in gymnastics at Smith (female) College, Northampton, Mass.

The Parlor Gardener. A Treatise on the House-Culture of Ornamental Plants. By CORNELIA J. RANDOLPH. With illustrations.

Sold by all booksellers, and sent by mail, postpaid, on receipt of price.

LEE AND SHEPARD Publishers Boston

READINGS FOR HOME HALL AND SCHOOL

Prepared by Professor LEWIS B. MONROE
Founder of the Boston School of Oratory

HUMOROUS READINGS In prose and verse For the use of schools reading-clubs public and parlor entertainments $1.50
"The book is readable from the first page to the last, and every article contained in it is worth more than the price of the volume." — *Providence Herald.*

MISCELLANEOUS READINGS In prose and verse $1.50
"We trust this book may find its way into many schools, not to be used as a book for daily drill, but as affording the pupil occasionally an opportunity of leaving the old beaten track." — *Rhode-Island Schoolmaster.*

DIALOGUES AND DRAMAS For the use of dramatic and reading clubs and for public social and school entertainments $1.50
"If the acting of dramas such as are contained in this book, could be introduced into private circles, there would be an inducement for the young to spend their evenings at home, instead of resorting to questionable public places." — *Nashua Gazette.*

YOUNG FOLKS' READINGS For social and public entertainment $1.50
"Professor Monroe is one of the most successful teachers of elocution, as well as a very popular public reader. In this volume he has given an unusually fine selection for home and social reading, as well as for public entertainments." — *Boston Home Journal.*

DIALOGUES FROM DICKENS Arranged for schools and home amusement By W. ELIOT FETTE A.M. First series $1.00

DIALOGUES AND DRAMAS FROM DICKENS Second series Arranged by W. ELIOT FETTE Illustrated $1.00
The dialogues in the above books are selected from the best points of the stories, and can be extended by taking several scenes together.

THE GRAND DICKENS COSMORAMA Comprising several unique entertainments capable of being used separately for school home or hall By G. B. BARTLETT Paper 25 cents

THE READINGS OF DICKENS as condensed by himself for his own use $1.00

LITTLE PIECES FOR LITTLE SPEAKERS The primary-school teacher's assistant By a practical teacher 16mo. Illustrated Cloth 75 cents Also in boards 50 cents

THE MODEL SUNDAY-SCHOOL SPEAKER Containing selections in prose and verse from the most popular pieces and dialogues for Sunday-school exhibitions Illustrated Cloth 75 cents Boards 50 cents
"A book very much needed."

Sold by all booksellers or sent by mail postpaid on receipt of price

LEE AND SHEPARD Publishers Boston

NARRATIVES OF NOTED TRAVELLERS

GERMANY SEEN WITHOUT SPECTACLES; or, Random Sketches of Various Subjects, Penned from Different Standpoints in the Empire
By HENRY RUGGLES, late United States Consul at the Island of Malta, and at Barcelona, Spain. $1.50.
"Mr. Ruggles writes briskly: he chats and gossips, slashing right and left with stout American prejudices, and has made withal a most entertaining book." — *New-York Tribune.*

TRAVELS AND OBSERVATIONS IN THE ORIENT, with a Hasty Flight in the Countries of Europe
By WALTER HARRIMAN (ex-Governor of New Hampshire). $1.50.
"The author, in his graphic description of these sacred localities, refers with great aptness to scenes and personages which history has made famous. It is a chatty narrative of travel." — *Concord Monitor.*

FORE AND AFT
A Story of Actual Sea-Life. By ROBERT B. DIXON, M.D. $1.25.
Travels in Mexico, with vivid descriptions of manners and customs, form a large part of this striking narrative of a fourteen-months' voyage.

VOYAGE OF THE PAPER CANOE
A Geographical Journey of Twenty-five Hundred Miles from Quebec to the Gulf of Mexico. By NATHANIEL H. BISHOP. With numerous illustrations and maps specially prepared for this work. Crown 8vo. $1.50.
"Mr. Bishop did a very bold thing, and has described it with a happy mixture of spirit, keen observation, and *bonhomie*." — *London Graphic.*

FOUR MONTHS IN A SNEAK-BOX
A Boat Voyage of Twenty-six Hundred Miles down the Ohio and Mississippi Rivers, and along the Gulf of Mexico. By NATHANIEL H. BISHOP. With numerous maps and illustrations. $1.50.
"His glowing pen-pictures of 'shanty-boat' life on the great rivers are true to life. His descriptions of persons and places are graphic." — *Zion's Herald.*

A THOUSAND MILES' WALK ACROSS SOUTH AMERICA, Over the Pampas and the Andes
By NATHANIEL H. BISHOP. Crown 8vo. New edition. Illustrated. $1.50.
"Mr. Bishop made this journey when a boy of sixteen, has never forgotten it, and tells it in such a way that the reader will always remember it, and wish there had been more."

CAMPS IN THE CARIBBEES
Being the Adventures of a Naturalist Bird-hunting in the West-India Islands. By FRED A. OBER. New edition. With maps and illustrations. $1.50.
"During two years he visited mountains, forests, and people, that few, if any, tourists had ever reached before. He carried his camera with him, and photographed from nature the scenes by which the book is illustrated." — *Louisville Courier-Journal.*

ENGLAND FROM A BACK WINDOW; With Views of Scotland and Ireland
By J. M. BAILEY, the "'Danbury News' Man." 12mo. $1.00.
"The peculiar humor of this writer is well known. The British Isles have never before been looked at in just the same way, — at least, not by any one who has notified us of the fact. Mr. Bailey's travels possess, accordingly, a value of their own for the reader, no matter how many previous records of journeys in the mother country he may have read." — *Rochester Express.*

Sold by all booksellers, and sent by mail, postpaid, on receipt of price

LEE AND SHEPARD Publishers Boston

YOUNG FOLKS' BOOKS OF TRAVEL

DRIFTING ROUND THE WORLD; A Boy's Adventures by Sea and Land

By CAPT. CHARLES W. HALL, author of "Adrift in the Ice-Fields," "The Great Bonanza," etc. With numerous full-page and letter-press illustrations. Royal 8vo. Handsome cover. $1.75. Cloth, gilt, $2.50.

"Out of the beaten track" in its course of travel, record of adventures, and descriptions of life in Greenland, Labrador, Ireland, Scotland, England, France, Holland, Russia, Asia, Siberia, and Alaska. Its hero is young, bold, and adventurous; and the book is in every way interesting and attractive.

EDWARD GREEY'S JAPANESE SERIES

YOUNG AMERICANS IN JAPAN; or, The Adventures of the Jewett Family and their Friend Oto Nambo

With 170 full-page and letter-press illustrations. Royal 8vo, 7 x 9½ inches. Handsomely illuminated cover. $1.75. Cloth, black and gold, $2.50.

This story, though essentially a work of fiction, is filled with interesting and truthful descriptions of the curious ways of living of the good people of the land of the rising sun.

THE WONDERFUL CITY OF TOKIO; or, The Further Adventures of the Jewett Family and their Friend Oto Nambo

With 169 illustrations. Royal 8vo, 7 x 9½ inches. With cover in gold and colors, designed by the author. $1.75. Cloth, black and gold, $2.50.

"A book full of delightful information. The author has the happy gift of permitting the reader to view things as he saw them. The illustrations are mostly drawn by a Japanese artist, and are very unique." —*Chicago Herald.*

THE BEAR WORSHIPPERS OF YEZO AND THE ISLAND OF KARAFUTO; being the further Adventures of the Jewett Family and their Friend Oto Nambo

180 illustrations. Boards, $1.75. Cloth, $2.50.

Graphic pen and pencil pictures of the remarkable bearded people who live in the north of Japan. The illustrations are by native Japanese artists, and give queer pictures of a queer people, who have been seldom visited.

HARRY W. FRENCH'S BOOKS

OUR BOYS IN INDIA

The wanderings of two young Americans in Hindustan, with their exciting adventures on the sacred rivers and wild mountains. With 145 illustrations. Royal 8vo, 7 x 9½ inches. Bound in emblematic covers of Oriental design, $1.75. Cloth, black and gold, $2.50.

While it has all the exciting interest of a romance, it is remarkably vivid in its pictures of manners and customs in the land of the Hindu. The illustrations are many and excellent.

OUR BOYS IN CHINA

The Adventures of two young Americans, wrecked in the China Sea on their return from India, with their strange wanderings through the Chinese Empire. 188 illustrations. Boards, ornamental covers in colors and gold, $1.75. Cloth, $2.50.

This gives the further adventures of "Our Boys" of India fame in the land of Tea and Queues.

Sold by all booksellers, and sent by mail, postpaid, on receipt of price

LEE AND SHEPARD Publishers Boston

Bright and Breezy Books of Travel
---- BY SIX BRIGHT WOMEN ----

A WINTER IN CENTRAL AMERICA AND MEXICO
By HELEN J. SANBORN. Cloth, $1.50.
"A bright, attractive narrative by a wide-awake Boston girl."

A SUMMER IN THE AZORES, with a Glimpse of Madeira
By Miss C. ALICE BAKER. Little Classic style. Cloth, gilt edges, $1.25.
"Miss Baker gives us a breezy, entertaining description of these picturesque islands. She is an observing traveller, and makes a graphic picture of the quaint people and customs." — *Chicago Advance.*

LIFE AT PUGET SOUND
With sketches of travel in Washington Territory, British Columbia, Oregon, and California. By CAROLINE C. LEIGHTON. 16mo, cloth, $1.50.
"Your chapters on Puget Sound have charmed me. Full of life, deeply interesting, and with just that class of facts, and suggestions of truth, that cannot fail to help the Indian and the Chinese." — WENDELL PHILLIPS.

EUROPEAN BREEZES
By MARGERY DEANE. Cloth, gilt top, $1.50. Being chapters of travel through Germany, Austria, Hungary, and Switzerland, covering places not usually visited by Americans in making "the Grand Tour of the Continent," by the accomplished writer of "Newport Breezes."
"A very bright, fresh and amusing account, which tells us about a host of things we never heard of before, and is worth two ordinary books of European travel." —*Woman's Journal.*

BEATEN PATHS; or, A Woman's Vacation in Europe
By ELLA W. THOMPSON. 16mo, cloth. $1.50.
A lively and chatty book of travel, with pen-pictures humorous and graphic, that are decidedly out of the "beaten paths" of description.

AN AMERICAN GIRL ABROAD
By Miss ADELINE TRAFTON, author of "His Inheritance," "Katherine Earle," etc. 16mo. Illustrated. $1.50.
"A sparkling account of a European trip by a wide-awake, intelligent, and irrepressible American girl. Pictured with a freshness and vivacity that is delightful." — *Utica Observer.*

CURTIS GUILD'S TRAVELS

BRITONS AND MUSCOVITES; or, Traits of Two Empires
Cloth, $2.00.

OVER THE OCEAN; or, Sights and Scenes in Foreign Lands
By CURTIS GUILD, editor of "The Boston Commercial Bulletin." Crown 8vo. Cloth, $2.50.
"The utmost that any European tourist can hope to do is to tell the old story in a somewhat fresh way, and Mr. Guild has succeeded in every part of his book in doing this." — *Philadelphia Bulletin.*

ABROAD AGAIN; or, Fresh Forays in Foreign Fields
Uniform with "Over the Ocean." By the same author. Crown 8vo. Cloth, $2.50.
"He has given us a life-picture. Europe is done in a style that must serve as an invaluable guide to those who go 'over the ocean,' as well as an interesting companion." — *Halifax Citizen.*

Sold by all booksellers, and sent by mail, postpaid, on receipt of price

LEE AND SHEPARD Publishers Boston

BOOKS FOR YOUNG LADIES BY POPULAR AUTHORS

SEVEN DAUGHTERS.
By Miss A. M. DOUGLAS, Author of "In Trust," "Stephen Dane," "Claudia," "Sydnie Adriance," "Home Nook," "Nelly Kennard's Kingdom." 12mo, cloth, illustrated. $1.50.

"A charming romance of Girlhood," full of incident and humor. The "Seven Daughters" are characters which reappear in some of Miss Douglas' later books. In this book they form a delightful group, hovering on the verge of Womanhood, with all the little perplexities of home life and love dreams as incidentals, making a fresh and attractive story.

OUR HELEN.
By SOPHIE MAY. 12mo, cloth, illustrated. $1.50.

"The story is a very attractive one, as free from the sensational and impossible as could be desired, and at the same time full of interest, and pervaded by the same bright, cheery sunshine that we find in the author's earlier books. She is to be congratulated on the success of her essay in a new field of literature, to which she will be warmly welcomed by those who know and admire her ' Prudy Books.'" — *Graphic.*

THE ASBURY TWINS.
By SOPHIE MAY, Author of "The Doctor's Daughter," "Our Helen," &c. 12mo, cloth, illustrated. $1.50.

"Has the ring of genuine genius, and the sparkle of a gem of the first water. We read it one cloudy winter day, and it was as good as a Turkish bath, or a three hours' soak in the sunshine."— *Cooperstown Republican.*

THAT QUEER GIRL.
By Miss VIRGINIA F. TOWNSEND, Author of "Only Girls," &c. 12mo, cloth, illustrated. $1.50.

Queer only in being unconventional, brave and frank, an "old-fashioned girl," and very sweet and charming. As indicated in the title, is a little out of the common track, and the wooing and the winning are as queer as the heroine. The *New Haven Register* says: "Decidedly the best work which has appeared from the pen of Miss Townsend."

RUNNING TO WASTE.
The Story of a Tomboy. By GEORGE M. BAKER. 16mo, cloth, illustrated. $1.50.

"This book is one of the most entertaining we have read for a long time. It is well written, full of humor, and good humor, and it has not a dull or uninteresting page. It is lively and natural, and overflowing with the best New England character and traits. There is also a touch of pathos, which always accompanies humor, in the life and death of the tomboy's mother."—*Newburyport Herald.*

DAISY TRAVERS;
Or the Girls of Hive Hall. By ADELAIDE F. SAMUELS, Author of "Dick and Daisy Stories," "Dick Travers Abroad," &c. 16mo, cloth, illustrated. $1.50.

The story of Hive Hall is full of life and action, and told in the same happy style which made the earlier life of its heroine so attractive, and caused the Dick and Daisy books to become great favorites with the young. What was said of the younger books can, with equal truth, be said of Daisy grown up.

The above six books are furnished in a handsome box for $9.00, or sold separate, by all booksellers, and sent by mail, postpaid, on receipt of price.

LEE AND SHEPARD Publishers Boston

Irene E. Jerome's
.... Art Books

SUN-PRINTS IN SKY TINTS. Over Thirty Illustrations engraved on wood, accompanied by appropriate selections in Poetry and Prose. Elegant cover design. Size, 7½ x 11¼ inches. Price, $3.00.

FROM AN OLD LOVE LETTER. Designed and Illuminated by IRENE E. JEROME. Antique covers, tied with silk, boxed, $1.00. Each page beautifully decorated and containing some selection from the New Testament on the subject suggested by the title.

ONE YEAR'S SKETCH BOOK. An Original Series of Illustrations from Nature, comprising forty-six full-page Pictures (9½ x 14 inches) of great power and beauty, engraved on wood by George T. Andrew, in the best manner. The volume is bound in gold cloth, full gilt, gilt edges, $6.00; Turkey Morocco, $15.00; tree calf, $15.00; English seal style, $10.00. The same bound in four books, sold separately, Spring, Summer, Autumn, Winter; Each book bound in a unique style of boards, with decorated dies, boxed, $1.50 each.

NATURE'S HALLELUJAH. Presented in a series of nearly fifty full-page original Illustrations (9½ x 14 inches), engraved on wood by George T. Andrew. Elegantly bound in gold cloth, full gilt, gilt edges, $6.00; Turkey morocco, $15.00; tree calf, $15.00; English seal style, $10.00.

IN A FAIR COUNTRY. With fifty-five full-page Illustrations, engraved by Andrew. Nearly 100 pages of Text by Thomas Wentworth Higginson. Gold cloth, full-gilt $6.00; Turkey morocco, $15.00; tree calf, $15.00; English seal style, $10.00.

A BUNCH OF VIOLETS. Original Illustrations, engraved on wood, and printed under the direction of George T. Andrew. 4to, cloth, $3.75; Turkey morocco, $9.00; tree calf, $9.00; English seal style, $7.00.

THE MESSAGE OF THE BLUEBIRD, Told to Me to Tell to Others. Original Illustrations engraved on wood by Andrew. Cloth and gold, $2.00; palatine boards, ribbon ornaments, $1.00.

"The daintiest combinations of song and illustration ever published, exhibiting in a marked degree the fine poetic taste and wonderfully artistic touch which render this author's works so popular. The pictures are exquisite, and the verses exceedingly graceful, appealing to the highest sensibilities. The volumes rank among the choicest of holiday souvenirs, and are beautiful and pleasing." — *Boston Transcript.*

"Every thick, creamy page is embellished by some gems of art. Sometimes it is but a dash and a few trembling strokes; at others an impressive landscape, but in all and through all runs the master touch. Miss Jerome has the genius of an Angelo, and the execution of a Guido. The beauty of the sketches will be apparent to all, having been taken from our unrivalled New England scenery." — *Washington Chronicle.*

Sold by all booksellers, and sent by mail, postpaid, on receipt of price.

LEE AND SHEPARD PUBLISHERS BOSTON

www.ingramcontent.com/pod-product-compliance
Lightning Source LLC
Chambersburg PA
CBHW030350230426
43664CB00007BB/593